IBM PC BASIC

Peter Rob
Professor of Information Systems
Middle Tennessee State University

Wadsworth Publishing Company/Belmont, California/A Division of Wadsworth, Inc.

To Anne

Computer Science Editor: Frank Ruggirello
Editorial Assistant: Serina Beauparlant
Production: Mary Forkner, Publication Alternatives
Designer: Christy Butterfield
Copy Editor: Patricia Cain
Technical Illustrator: Carol Johnston
Cartoonist: Rand Renfroe (Used with permission of Tiger Eye Graphics)
Cover Photo: Mason Morfit
Cover: Michael Rogondino & Associates
Print Buyer: Ruth Cole
Signing Representative: Mark Francisco

Printed in the United States of America

2 3 4 5 6 7 8 9 10—90 89 88 87

ISBN 0-534-06456-6

Library of Congress Cataloging-in-Publication Data

Rob, Peter.
IBM PC BASIC.

Includes index.
1. IBM Personal Computer—Programming. 2. BASIC
(Computer program language) I. Title.
QA76.8.I2594R623 1986 005.265 85-29570
ISBN 0-534-06456-6

H. Stopping the scrolling of program output

1. Press and release the [Ctrl] and [Num Lock] keys simultaneously.

Press and release any letter key or the space bar to continue.

I. Interrupting a program

1. Press and release the [Ctrl] and [Scroll Lock] keys simultaneously. (The Scroll Lock key is also the Break key!)

Type RUN and press/release the ENTER key to run the program again.

J. Clearing the screen

Type CLS and press/release the ENTER key.

K. Showing programs and files currently located on the diskette

1. Type FILES and press/release the ENTER key.

2. If the diskette is located in drive B and drive A is the default drive, type FILES "B:" and press/release the ENTER key.

L. Renumbering program lines

Type RENUM, followed by the new starting line number, the old starting line number, and the increment. Example: Renumber a program that now begins with line 50 to one that begins with line 500, using an increment of 10:

```
RENUM 500,50,10
```

M. Merging programs

A program in memory may be merged with a program on a diskette by using MERGE, followed by the name of the program on the diskette. The program on the diskette must have been saved in ASCII format. Use the RENUM feature to renumber program lines, if necessary. Example: Merge a program in memory (SAMPLE1.BAS) with a program on the diskette (SAMPLE2.BAS) to create a program named SAMPLE3.BAS. Save the merged program back to the diskette.

```
LOAD "SAMPLE1.BAS"
MERGE "SAMPLE2.BAS"
SAVE "SAMPLE3.BAS",A
```

II. GENERAL SEQUENTIAL FILE PROCEDURES

File name "CONTRIBS.DTA", buffer number 1, field names N$,C

A. General preparations: Name the file

```
100 F$ = "CONTRIBS.DTA"
```

B. Opening the file

1. To put data into the file:

```
120 OPEN "O",1,F$
```

2. To read data from the file:

```
120 OPEN "I",1,F$
```

C. Working with the file contents

1. Entering the data into the file: Five records. (Note that the file is closed in line 220.)

```
100 F$ = "CONTRIBS.DTA"
120 OPEN "O",1,F$
140 FOR I = 1 TO 5
160     INPUT "ENTER NAME, CONTRIBUTION";N$,C
180     WRITE #1,N$,C
200 NEXT I
220 CLOSE 1
```

Wadsworth Series in Computer Information Systems

Ageloff and Mojena, Applied Structured BASIC
Ageloff and Mojena, Essentials of Structured BASIC
Amsbury, Data Structures: From Arrays to Priority Queues
Athappilly, Programming and Problem Solving with VAX-11 BASIC
Brown, From Pascal to C: An Introduction to the C Programming Language
Clarke and Prins, Contemporary Systems Analysis and Design
Duffy, Four Software Tools
Rob, Big Blue BASIC: Programming the IBM PC and Compatibles
Rob, IBM PC BASIC
Rob, Introduction to Microcomputer Programming
Rob, Programming with dBASE II and BASE III
Senn, Information Systems in Management, 2nd edition
Texel, Introductory Ada: Packages for Programming
Vasta, Understanding Data Base Management Systems

CONTENTS

A033951

Chapter 1 Some Programming Basics 3

Chapter 2 Writing More Complex Programs: Comparisons and Loops 39

Chapter 3 Conversations with the Micro 61

PREFACE

Until IBM ("Big Blue") entered the microcomputer marketplace, BASIC textbook authors were faced with two unhappy choices, given the existence of many different BASIC dialects. Either the authors used a "minimal" BASIC, or they showed several different versions of each program. Using minimal BASIC meant the selection of the simplest code that could be expected to run without modification on the more common microcomputers. The minimal BASIC approach tended to yield bland, unstructured programs that could not be expected to do anything useful. Showing different program versions using the various BASIC dialects usually meant that the more useful programming features could not be addressed, given the need to control the book's size. (Thousand-page textbooks do not tend to sell well.) In addition, showing different versions tends to confuse students when the programs become, well, more interesting.

The IBM PC's introduction, its rapid acceptance, and its subsequent dominance created a *de facto* standard based on Microsoft BASIC. IBM compatibility has become the mark of market acceptance. Programs created on IBM-formatted diskettes will run on the Zenith 150, Sperry, Compaq, Leading Edge, Columbia Data Products, and many other IBM-compatible microcomputers. Diskettes containing programs written on these microcomputers will run on the IBM PC. Perhaps even more important is the fact that IBM created an aura of respectability. Many potential microcomputer users simply did not believe that a computer was a "real" computer unless its label spelled I-B-M, known affectionately as Big Blue. Not surprisingly, this book assumes the use of an IBM PC or a fully IBM-compatible PC. Therefore, only a single BASIC version is used and the more interesting programming applications potential can be addressed.

Once the decision to teach BASIC programming has been made, a crucial question remains. What should be the expected level of programming proficiency when the student emerges from the course? Most students take only a single BASIC programming course. Given such limited exposure, a tendency may exist to deal only with the trivial aspects of programming in order to "keep things simple." I believe that such an approach serves neither the student nor the educational institution.

An introductory programming course is worthwhile when sufficient programming skill is developed to enable the student to write simple applications. The text used in such a course should be easy to read. Its organization, its choice of programming techniques and principles, and its examples should be aimed at building proficiency.

Because I could not find a text with the desired characteristics, I was persuaded to write a programming book that would be easy to read and yet would develop a relatively high programming skill level. So, after much agonizing and even more work, I completed a book named *Big Blue Basic*. The book turned out to be big as well as successful. However, market response indicated that a smaller, more compact text could find an important niche in the BASIC programming curriculum. Such a text could also be used as a supplement to a more general programming course. In addition, experience with *Big Blue Basic* led me to appreciate the need for even tighter programming structure. Thus was born the text named *IBM PC BASIC.*

IBM PC BASIC retains its parent's strengths, and it adds some important new ingredients of its own. As you examine this book, you will notice some very important features. Each of these features is designed to help guide the student toward greater programming skill without posing an unacceptable degree of difficulty.

1. System features integrated into the text
2. Structured programming techniques
3. Techniques designed to emphasize the applications potential
4. Extensive coverage of sequential and random access files
5. Common errors sections
6. Chapter summaries
7. Extensive problem sets requiring the use of practical programming techniques
8. Summaries of commonly used system and BASIC commands and functions on the book's inside covers

System Features Integrated into the Text

Learning to program is a sufficient challenge without having to decipher cryptic messages in computer manuals and appendixes. Therefore, *IBM PC BASIC* helps students get started by showing how to turn the computer on, how to use the master disk, what to expect on the screen, how to respond to the screen prompts (What on earth does A⟩ mean?), and how to prepare the computer to accept the first program lines. When the first program is written, the text shows—just when the commands are needed—how to LIST, SAVE, and RUN the program. Later (and again when necessary) the text shows how to LOAD a program, how to make a COPY, how to EDIT program lines, how to renumber program lines, how to merge programs, and so on.

IBM PC BASIC does not duplicate all the features of the DOS manual, but students are shown how to get started. After they have programmed for a while, they will not be as likely to be intimidated by the computer's DOS manual. Covering the necessary system features as they are needed and integrating them into the text smooths the learning process significantly.

Structured Programming Techniques

As a programming language, BASIC lacks the tight structure of such languages as PASCAL. Unfortunately, many BASIC programmers have interpreted BASIC's properties as a license to practice what may be charitably called "loose" programming. Such "loose" programs tend to be especially numerous in BASIC textbooks. Programs may consist of incredible collections of GOTO statements criss-crossing the program lines; headers may be found in computation sections, and the use of subroutines may be completely ignored.

Lack of program structure is not an obvious shortcoming when programs are very simple. If the program yields errors, they are found easily enough. But when students attempt to write more useful and (inevitably) more complex programs, the unstructured program often becomes an efficient error generator, not yielding the intended output. Logical errors are especially hard to spot in an unstructured program. So, while BASIC itself may lack tight internal structure, it is very important that the programming techniques be structured carefully.

IBM PC BASIC introduces structure to BASIC programming, without making structure an end in itself. A structured program is ultimately easier to write; it is easier to read; and it makes it easier to correct errors if they do occur. Consequently, while GOTO is recognized as a legitimate command, its use is minimized. Instead, FOR/NEXT and WHILE/WEND are emphasized. As greater programming expertise is gained, modular programming techniques are introduced, based on the use of subroutines. In fact, Chapter 7 is devoted to subroutines and the reasons for their use.

Useful Techniques

Computer programming should emphasize that programs are most useful when they are written and produced so that they may be used easily by others who may have only minimal exposure to microcomputers. Consequently, *IBM PC BASIC* shows you how to write a very short but powerful screen/printer option, how to develop menu-driven systems, and so on.

Extensive Coverage of Sequential and Random Access Files

Information storage and retrieval are among the computer's most important functions. Therefore, sequential and random (direct) access files are covered extensively in Chapters 8 and 9. Whereas many other programming texts cover only the most fundamental aspects of file construction, *IBM PC BASIC* demonstrates all file options ranging from their creation to record retrieval, correction, addition, and deletion. Because all file options are shown completely for both sequential and random access files, a simple file system can be made merely by merging the various file options to create subroutines and adding a menu that will access those subroutines. The format is flexible enough to serve as a model for almost any sequential or random access file application.

Common Errors

At the end of each chapter is a Common Errors section. This section alerts the reader to likely programming errors and shows the necessary corrections in the adjacent column.

Extensive Problem Sets

IBM PC BASIC contains nine exercise sets. Each set has a sufficient number of problems to enable students realistically to evaluate their newfound programming skills. Problem sets are carefully developed so that students are gradually challenged to use techniques that can lend themselves to the development of practical applications.

Many of the problems may be used as "add-ons." That is, as greater programming skills are acquired in later chapters, more features can be added to the original input and output. Programming techniques, too, are expected to reflect a higher skill level. For instance, initially two numbers may be added by a program's user and the result is compared to the computer's answer. Next, a scoring option is added to create a self-scoring quiz. Finally, the program is modified to store the quiz results in a file. A program that initially creates an output heading within the body of the program is later modified to produce the heading with the aid of a subroutine. A program that initially uses data lines is later modified to use the data in a random access file, and so on.

Summaries

The inside covers contain a very handy summary of DOS and BASIC commands, functions, and procedures. The DOS summary includes how to format a diskette, how to copy a disk, how to copy a program, and so on. The BASIC summary shows how to name, save, list, or delete a program; how to renumber program lines; how to open sequential and random access files; and many other reminders.

Acknowledgements

IBM PC BASIC exists because Frank Ruggirello, Wadsworth Senior Editor, prodded and cajoled me to condense and restructure *Big Blue BASIC.* After Frank achieved the desired response—I started writing—*IBM PC BASIC* became a labor of love.

To find out which parts of *Big Blue BASIC* could be eliminated without doing damage to continuity, logic, and programming proficiency, Frank enlisted the help of some truly outstanding reviewers. William Baker, Brigham Young University, and Kevan Croteau, University of Dubuque, will find that much of their advice was heeded. Many thanks for their efforts.

Dr. William J. Grasty, who chairs the Department of Accounting and Information Systems at Middle Tennessee State University, has helped push for the development of microcomputer courses and the use of microcomputers in other courses. My teaching in such an operations environment made writing this book that much easier. I thank Bill especially for his willingness to embrace new technology and teaching techniques.

When one pares down an existing text and updates its remaining features, a grand opportunity exists to create chaos. Serina Beauparlant, assistant to Frank Ruggirello when this text was written, typed inserts and made sure that the pieces somehow fit into the manuscript. Her willingness to go the extra proverbial mile and her enduring sense of humor in the midst of writer-induced paper blizzards are much appreciated.

The herculean task of producing a textbook out of the incredible collection of program inserts, deletions, and last-minute updates was given to Mary Forkner, owner of Publication Alternatives. These pages clearly illustrate her technical expertise and her "can do" approach to all the challenges that came her way during the production of this book. Mary's magic production touch and that of her assistant, Claudia Willrodt, has made *IBM PC BASIC* one of my favorite books. Many thanks for your unfailing professionalism.

A programming text, no matter how carefully written and produced, can easily cause a case of reader mego (My Eyes Glaze Over). I am, therefore, grateful to Rand Renfroe, whose artistic talent and wit help prevent the mego problem by creating the bug cartoons you see on *IBM PC BASIC*'s pages.

Finally, I owe much to Anne, my best friend and wife for these past 24 years. She gracefully accepted my preoccupation with teaching and my writing on weeknights, during weekends, and during vacations. Her willingness to serve as a sounding board, proofreader, critic, and dispenser of coffee and quiet conversation during too-infrequent breaks are hereby gratefully acknowledged. Her presence and support provide the catalyst for all my endeavors. Therefore, I have dedicated all my work to her. This book, too, is dedicated to Anne.

Peter Rob

IBM
PC
BASIC

1

Objectives

- To start the IBM microcomputer and to format a diskette.
- To distinguish between strings and numeric values.
- To define and name variables.
- To use the PRINT command.
- To space output on a CRT or printer by using a semicolon or a comma.
- To write a simple BASIC program.
- To learn the use of the BASIC commands LIST, RUN, SAVE, DELETE, LOAD, and FILES.

SOME PROGRAMMING BASICS

In Chapter 1 we learn how to turn on the IBM PC and how to format a diskette so that we can both write and save BASIC programs. Chapter 1 also introduces some rules and terminology of BASIC: how to define and name variables, how to use line numbers, how to write your first complete program, and how to print the results. The chapter ends by combining these techniques, definitions, and concepts into a complete BASIC program.

1.1 Preparations for Programming

Before You Turn on the Microcomputer

To perform its numerous functions the microcomputer requires the use of a 5¼-inch flexible plastic diskette that contains the disk operating system (DOS). The DOS diskette is also known as the master diskette.

You will also need several blank diskettes to make a back-up copy of the master diskette and to save the programs that you will write. Programs are carefully written sets of instructions that cause the computer to perform the tasks you require. The programs in this book are written in a language known as BASIC (Beginner's All-purpose Symbolic Instruction Code).

Before you attempt to follow the instructions in the next few sections of this chapter make sure that you carefully examine Figures 1.1 and 1.2. You should be familiar with the microcomputer's and diskette's components.

Turning on the Microcomputer

Before writing your first program, you must know how to turn on (**boot**) the microcomputer so that it will be ready to receive the program's instructions. The booting process causes the computer's I/O devices to be set up and the operating system to be loaded. The following sequence will soon become second nature to you. The computer's DOS manual gives many additional options and procedures, and as you gain more experience with the IBM microcomputer, you will want to explore these suggestions and procedural discussions. However, the following steps will get you started properly. Assuming you are the first person to use the computer:

1. Make sure that the computer, CRT, and printer (if available) are turned OFF.

figure 1.1
A COMPLETE MICROCOMPUTER SYSTEM

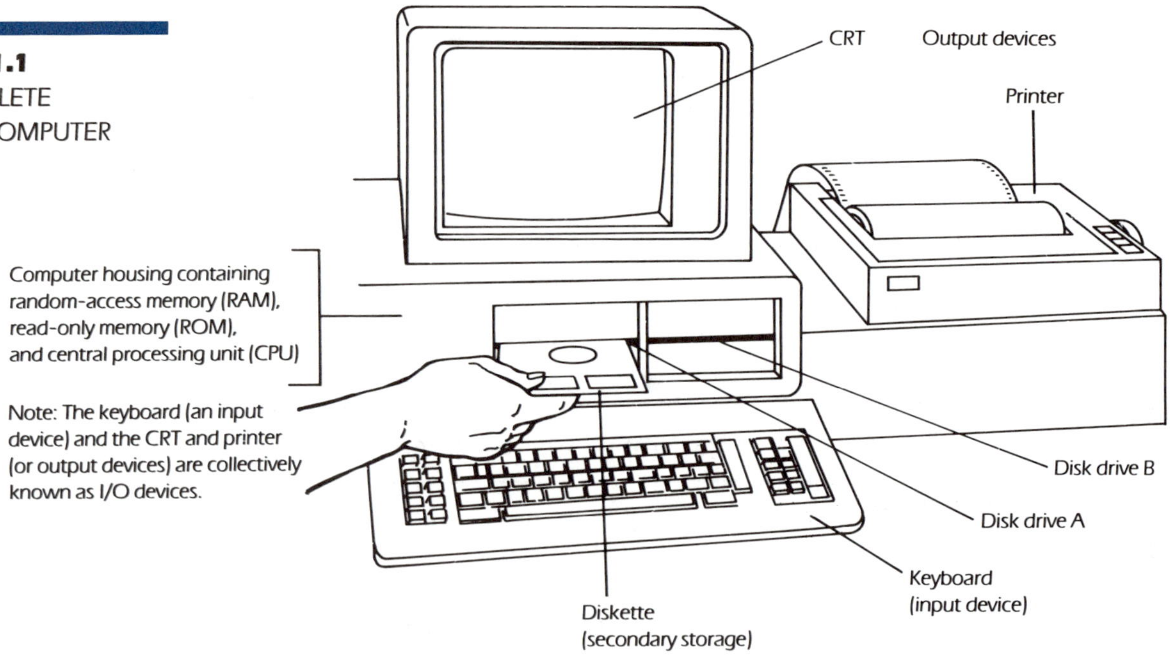

figure 1.2
DISKETTE COMPONENTS

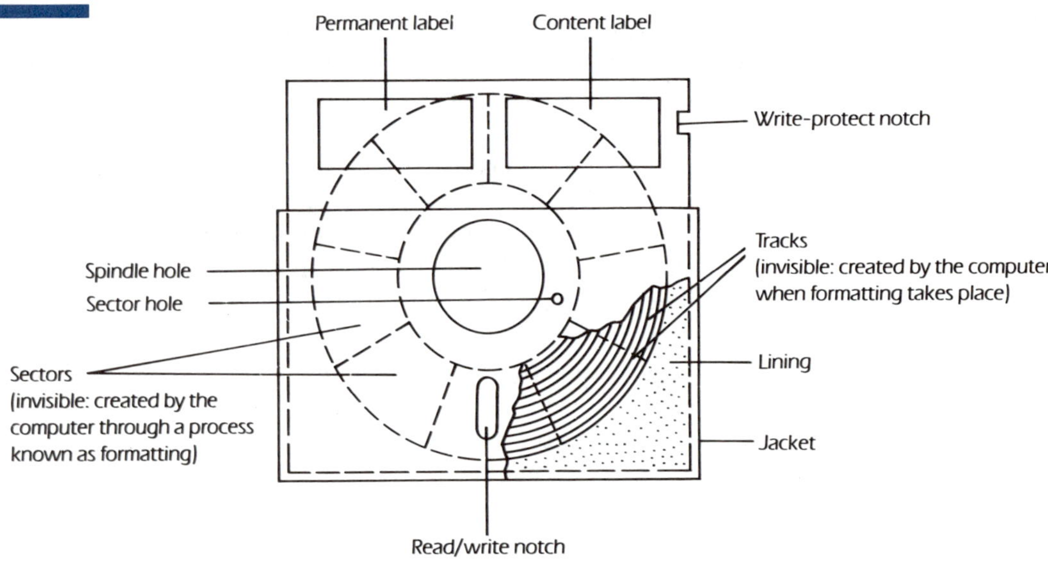

2. Connect the CRT to the computer if this has not already been done.

3. Connect the printer (if available) to the computer.

4. Plug the computer, CRT, and printer (if available) into an electrical outlet.

5. Turn on the CRT.

6. Insert the master diskette into the disk drive and close the disk drive door. If your computer has two disk drives, use the one on the left. (The master diskette contains the computer's operating system as well as the BASIC programming language!)

7. Turn on the IBM PC, using the switch on the right side of the computer housing.

8. After a few seconds, the "current date" will be shown on the CRT, followed by a request to enter a new date. The screen will look like this:

```
Current date is Tue 1-01-1980
Enter new date:
```

   If you are writing a new program or modifying an existing program, you should enter the date so that you can keep track of the most recent version of the program. Use the same format shown by the computer. For example, if you are writing the program on June 20, 1984, enter 6-20-1984. If you simply want to run programs, there is no reason to enter the date. Therefore, you just press and release the ENTER key, which is marked with the following arrow: 

   The computer will respond by printing the current time (hours : minutes : seconds . hundredths of a second) and asking for a new time.

```
Current time is 0:00:14.38
Enter new time:
```

   Again, unless you have a special reason to enter a new time, simply press and release the ENTER key.

9. The computer will now display this message (or a similar one) on the CRT:

```
The IBM Personal Computer DOS
Version 2.00 (c) Copyright IBM CORP., 1981, 1982, 1983

A>
```

   Actually, you may be using another version, such as version 1.10. Whatever version you are using, the A> is called the system prompt. No difference in response will be required for any of the different versions. The A indicates that the computer expects you to be using the first disk drive. If you have only one disk drive, that drive will automatically be the A drive. If you have two disk drives, the one on the left (facing the computer) will be the A drive, and the one on the right will be the B drive. You can switch drives easily. If the system prompt is A> and you want to use the B drive, simply type B: after the prompt, press and release the ENTER key.

```
A>B:
```

The screen will now show:

```
B>
```

To switch back to the A drive, type A: after the prompt, then press and release the ENTER key.

```
B>A:
```

The screen will now show:

```
A>
```

Select the prompt that is appropriate to the disk drive that you intend to use. If you only have one disk drive, it will be drive A, of course.

10. After the prompt A〉, type BASICA, so that the screen now shows:

```
A> Basica
```

Press/release the ENTER key after typing BASICA.

11. The computer will respond by putting this message on the screen:

```
The IBM Personal Computer Basic
Version D2.00 Copyright IBM Corp. 1981, 1982
60865 Bytes free

Ok
```

Note: The word *bytes* refers to a unit of measurement of the computer's available memory. It takes one byte to store a single character such as the letter m or the number 9. A kilobyte (K) is approximately equal to 1,000 bytes (actually 1,024 bytes). Therefore, a computer whose memory is advertised to be 256K can store roughly 256,000 characters in its memory. The DOS takes up to 30K from the available memory. BASIC can address only 64K of memory at a time, no matter how large the available memory is.

12. Remove the master diskette from the disk drive.

13. Since most of us feel more at ease with capital letters when writing a program, push/release the CAPS LOCK key. The computer will now print capital letters, and you are ready to begin programming.

14. To start a new program, type NEW, then press and release the ENTER key.

Before writing any program, however, remember that new diskettes must be prepared, or formatted, before they can receive programming that is to be saved.

Formatting a Diskette for the IBM PC

A new diskette is blank; that is, it does not contain the tracks and sectors required by the computer to find specific locations ("addresses") on the diskette. The computer enters these features onto such storage devices in the process called formatting, which requires the following procedures:

1. Turn on the computer and complete steps 1 through 9 in the preceding section. The system prompt should show:

   ```
   A>
   ```

2. If you have already completed all the steps in the preceding section, you will see the prompt:

   ```
   OK
   ```

   Now return to the system prompt by typing:

   ```
   SYSTEM
   ```

   and press and release the ENTER key. The system prompt:

   ```
   A>
   ```

   will appear again.

3. Insert the master diskette in the disk drive and type:

   ```
   FORMAT A:/S
   ```

   then push/release the ENTER key. The A indicates that the diskette is located in the A disk drive. The /S will put the COMMAND program on the diskette so that you can use various system commands (If you have two disk drives, you can leave the master diskette in disk drive A, put the new diskette in disk drive B, and type FORMAT B:/S).

4. If you are using drive A, the computer will print:

   ```
   Insert new diskette for drive A:
   and strike any key when ready
   ```

5. As soon as the disk drive light is OFF, take out the master diskette and insert the new diskette.

NOTE

Never insert or withdraw a diskette when the disk drive is operating. This could damage the disk drive read head!

6. Press the space bar.

7. The computer will now print:

```
Formatting...
```

   on the CRT while the diskette spins.

8. After some seconds the disk drive light will go off and you will see the following message or a similar one:

```
Formatting...Format Complete
System transferred

      362496 bytes total disk space
       40960 bytes used by system
      321536 bytes available on disk

Format another (Y/N)?
```

   If you had used DOS version 1.10, you would have seen a smaller number of total disk space bytes because version 1.10 formats the disk with only eight sectors.

9. Unless you want to format another diskette, type N.

10. The system prompt A> will now show up again, even if you have been using the disk drive B.

11. Complete steps 10 through 14 in the preceding section.

You are now ready to write and save programs on your IBM computer.

NOTE

The formatting process is used *only* on blank (new) diskettes or on diskettes that do not contain anything you want to save. Once you have formatted a diskette and have saved programs on it, do *not* format that diskette again. The formatting process will wipe the diskette clean!

1.2 Programming Fundamentals

Numeric Values and Strings

Now that the computer is ready for our first program instructions, we need to know the various components of a program. Consider the way a computer keeps track of a checking account balance. Each month, it produces an account activity summary that includes the dates of checks, names of recipients, amounts, and a running account balance. To perform this service, the computer must process two types of information.

First, it processes each check amount, subtracting it from the previous balance and calculating the remaining balance. Such calculations clearly involve **numeric values** (numbers). Second, the computer must be able to keep track of dates and names. A date such as May 15, 1983, is *nonnumeric* information. Even rewritten as 5/15/83, the information remains nonnumeric, since it cannot be used in the performance of the usual numeric activities, such as adding, subtracting, multiplying, or dividing. After all, the subtraction (5/15/83–7/12/82) does not yield a meaningful answer. The check recipient is also a nonnumeric item. It is not possible to perform mathematical activity with the information John K. Doe. Such nonnumeric information is referred to as a **string.**

To receive information, the computer must receive an indication of the type of information to be processed. Quotation marks signal the use of a string. Anything enclosed in quotes is a string, including letters, spaces, numbers, and symbols. By contrast, a numeric value is generally composed of numbers only or, in special cases, an E. A numeric value containing the letter E is said to be written in scientific notation. Such notation expresses the numeric value in terms of the power of 10. For example, the numeric value 556 may be written in scientific notation as 5.56×10^2 or 5.56E2. The E2 (E for *exponent*) is used instead of $\times 10^2$ because it's simpler. Numeric values are never enclosed in quotes and use no symbols except a decimal point, a plus (+) sign, or a minus (−) sign. Numeric values do not use commas. For example, do not write 2,100,325 to enter a numeric value. Use 2100325 instead. Table 1.1 illustrates the distinction between numeric values and strings.

Variables and Constants

Our checking account example uses four general categories of information: date, check recipient, check amount, and balance. Within each of these categories, specific information can vary. For example, any date is possible, and since checks are written for different amounts, the amount can vary. Any information that is free to vary within its category is called a **variable.** The categories DATE, CHECK RECIPIENT, CHECK AMOUNT, and REMAINING BALANCE are all variables.

table 1.1
SOME EXAMPLES OF NUMERIC VALUES AND STRINGS

Numeric Values	Strings
.128	"MICROCOMPUTER"
2100325	"J. Q. DOE"
.0039	"A-25/2B9K-3"
2100.827	"************"
123.8	"123.8"
1283.75	"1,283.75"
1.26875E11	"??*//+−"

By contrast, a general category within which specific information cannot vary is termed a **constant.** For example, if all checks are written on the same account, the account number never changes. Therefore, the category ACCOUNT NUMBER is a constant.

To identify information precisely, we can use two different types of information: strings and numeric values. Since DATE and CHECK RECIPIENT are strings that are also variables, they can be described more precisely as *string variables*. The categories CHECK AMOUNT and BALANCE are called *numeric variables*. Similarly, constants may be either *string constants* or *numeric constants*.

Naming Variables and Constants

There are some rules to remember in **naming variables or constants:**

1. The name must start with a letter of the alphabet.

2. Up to 40 characters may be used to identify a variable.

3. String names always end with a dollar symbol ($). Any name followed by a dollar symbol is, therefore, a string name. Names not ending with a dollar symbol always identify numeric values.

4. While strings are enclosed in quotes, string names are not. The string name is identified by the dollar symbol, instead.

5. The name cannot contain a blank.

6. The name cannot contain symbols other than letters or numbers. Symbols (e.g., * ! / + ? : ; −) are not permitted.

The application of these rules is illustrated in Table 1.2.

Having named the variables, most people use the variable name and the variable it represents interchangeably: D$ is referred to as a string variable and C as a numeric variable. This book follows the same procedure.

table 1.2
EXAMPLES OF NAMES USED TO IDENTIFY STRING AND NUMERIC VARIABLES OR CONSTANTS

Type	Name	OK?	Correction	Comment
String	DAY$	Yes	None	
Numeric	AVERAGE	Yes	None	
String	DAY	No	DAY$	See rule 3
String	D$	Yes	None	
Numeric	PT VALUE	No	PTVALUE	See rule 5
Numeric	K5	Yes	None	
Numeric	8D	No	D8	See rule 1
String	"CREDIT"$	No	CREDIT$	See rule 4
String	DAY**$	No	DAY$	See rule 6
String	A4$	Yes	None	
Numeric	A	Yes	None	
String	A$	Yes	None	
Numeric	A+	No	A	See rule 6
Numeric	P 4	No	P4	See rule 5

Before we begin assigning names to variables, a word of caution is in order. While "long" names such as AVERAGE, DEPTH, and CREDIT$ are quite acceptable, we want to avoid accidentally using a **reserved word**—that is, any word that causes the computer to perform a specific function. Words such as READ, OPEN, CLOSE, END, TO, NEXT, STOP, IF, NAME, DATE, and FOR mean only one thing to the microcomputer and, when they are used in names, may produce error messages or unintended results. Programming experts are familiar with all the reserved words and can avoid using them in names. Since we are not experts yet, we may find it useful to let "short" names label the variables and constants. In addition, typing longer names each time a variable or constant is identified takes longer and gives rise to typing errors. (Would you rather type B or BALANCE?) Therefore, we generally use such names as A, A$, K9, and D8$, in the next few chapters. When you gain more experience on the IBM PC you will learn many of the reserved words. You will then be able to create longer (more descriptive) names without accidentally using a reserved word.

Assigning the Variable Names

The procedure for **assigning variable names** to numeric values and strings is simple: Put the variable name on the left side of an equality sign, and the numeric value or string on the right. For instance, we can assign the name D9 to the numeric value 5.128 by writing:

```
LET D9 = 5.128
```

Similarly, we can assign the name Q3$ to the string MASTER by writing:

```
LET Q3$ = "MASTER"
```

table 1.3
ASSIGNING NAMES TO NUMERIC VALUES AND STRINGS

Numeric Values

Sequence	Correct?	Correction
A9 = 1.28	Yes	None
C$ = 5.7	No	C = 5.7
K = 12.9	Yes	None
3Q = 9	No	Q3 = 9
Z = 8,229	No	Z = 8229
8.3 = A	No	A = 8.3

Strings

Sequence	Correct?	Correction
K$ = "ABC"	Yes	None
P = PRICE	No	P$ = "PRICE"
P$ = "12.3"	Yes	None
L$ = ITEM	No	L$ = "ITEM"
D$ = "K-5/2"	Yes	None
"ABC" = T$	No	T$ = "ABC"

The word LET is optional. For example, we could have written:

```
D9 = 5.128
Q3$ = "MASTER"
```

The examples in Table 1.3 do not use the optional LET.

1.3 Writing Your First Program

The Function of the Program

To use the microcomputer as a practical tool, we have to be able to communicate with it. Unlike humans, computers cannot "read between the lines." The question "You know what I mean?" is not relevant to the computer. Communication with a computer requires a precise set of instructions (a program), written in a language (in this text, BASIC) that the computer can translate into activity.

Computer programs have a variety of applications, ranging from arcade games to utility bills. Banks, factories, and numerous service industries depend on computer programs. Schools use computers to help students learn through programs that perform computer-aided instruction (CAI). Engineers use programs in computer-assisted design (CAD), and manufacturers use programs for computer-assisted manufacturing (CAM). Without programs that initiate and control its activity, the computer is a useless piece of equipment.

Writing a program involves many simple rules that must be followed scrupulously: Any minor deviation from these rules results in an error. The rules for naming string variables and numeric variables are important because most of the computer's activities involve the processing of such variables. How can the computer do its job unless variables are defined and named properly? Therefore, many programs begin by defining the numeric and/or string variables. Next, the program must instruct the computer what to do with the strings and numeric values.

Writing Program Lines

Each program consists of a collection of program lines. A **program line** is, as the name implies, a line in a computer program. In referring to programs, this book uses the terms "program lines" and "lines" interchangeably. To be a recognizable part of a program, EACH DEFINITION OR INSTRUCTION MUST BE PART OF A PROGRAM LINE THAT IS PRECEDED BY A LINE NUMBER. To let the computer know, for example, that the numeric value 123.9 uses the name Q, we write the program line:

```
20   LET Q = 123.9
```

To enter the program line into the computer's memory and to get ready for the next line, press and release the ENTER key marked ↵ on the IBM PC's keyboard.

Now the computer knows exactly what Q represents. Or we can write a program line defining a string by writing:

```
40   LET K$ = "PRODUCT CODE"
```

Remember, the word LET is optional; we could have written the program lines:

```
20   Q = 123.9
40   K$ = "PRODUCT CODE"
```

and the microcomputer would have known exactly what we wanted to define. The optional LET is not used in the programs that follow.

The PRINT Command

Now that we have defined a value and a string, we can manipulate this information. The simplest manipulation involves displaying the information on the CRT. For example, we could use the **PRINT** command to add two lines to the existing lines 20 and 40 shown in the preceding section, giving us the program shown in Example 1.1.

example 1.1

```
20   Q = 123.9
40   K$ = "PRODUCT CODE"
60   PRINT Q
80   PRINT K$
```

The LPRINT Command

The use of the PRINT command in lines 60 and 80 (Example 1.1) will cause the program's results to be displayed on the CRT. If we want to put the program's results (output) in **hard copy** form—that is, on paper rather than on the screen—we must substitute **LPRINT** for PRINT. Lines 60 and 80 will then read:

```
60   LPRINT Q
80   LPRINT K$
```

When we use LPRINT, the computer requires that the printer be turned on. The results of the program's activities will show up only on paper: The CRT will not display any of the output.

Using an END Line

The program in Example 1.1 will work well. Nevertheless, many programmers feel that ending the program with an END statement is good practice. Later in this book we write programs that will execute activities only under specified conditions. Then the END statement is used to terminate the program's activities if the specified conditions are not met. Since the END statement will not harm the program and because it sometimes turns out to be essential, we generally use END to terminate a program's activities:

example 1.2

```
20    Q = 123.9
40    K$ = "PRODUCT CODE"
60    PRINT Q
80    PRINT K$
100   END
```

Numbering the Program Lines: A Word of Advice

Reexamining the program in Example 1.2, we note that the line numbers are 20, 40, 60, 80, and 100. If the lines were numbered 1, 2, 3, 4, we could not insert another instruction between the second and third lines without rewriting almost the whole program. By labeling the first two line numbers 20 and 40, we have allowed room for additional line numbers. Leaving a lot of room between the line numbers gives the program more flexibility by making inserts easier. (We learn to renumber lines in Chapter 2, but avoiding the need for renumbering will save time and effort.)

1.4 Useful System Procedures

Listing the Program

Having typed the program (Example 1.2) on the computer keyboard, we can use the **LIST** command to get a listing of the program as it is stored in the computer's memory by typing:

```
LIST
```

Next, press and release the ENTER key. The computer will show the program in Example 1.2 on the CRT. The **LLIST** command will result in a printed copy of the program listing; we simply turn on the printer and type:

```
LLIST
```

Adding Program Lines

While we still have program Example 1.2 in the computer's memory, suppose we now type in two new lines:

```
90   PRINT "END OF PROGRAM RUN"
50   PRINT "START OF PROGRAM RUN"
```

The line numbers that we have typed are clearly out of sequence. However, if we use the LIST procedure again, we will discover that the lines 50 and 90 have automatically has been inserted into their proper place in the numbers sequence, as shown in Example 1.3.

example 1.3

```
20   Q = 123.9
40   K$ = "PRODUCT CODE"
50   PRINT "START OF PROGRAM RUN"
60   PRINT Q
80   PRINT K$
90   PRINT "END OF PROGRAM RUN"
100   END
```

Running the Program

The computer will perform the operations specified in Example 1.3 when you give the **RUN** command. After you have typed:

```
RUN
```

press and release the ENTER key again. The computer will respond by showing the following result on the CRT:

```
START OF PROGRAM RUN
 123.9
PRODUCT CODE
END OF PROGRAM RUN
```

Note that the number 123.9 is not flush with the left margin. The computer has automatically reserved a space for the (unprinted) positive sign of the number.

Deleting Program Lines

A single program line may be deleted by simply typing in the program line, then pressing and releasing the ENTER key marked  on the IBM PC. For example, to delete program line 90 from the program in Example 1.3, type:

```
90                                                    <ENTER>
```

NOTE

From now on the notation ⟨ENTER⟩ indicates that you are to press and release the ENTER key. Do not type word ENTER!

You may add line 90 back to the program by retyping the line number and its content:

```
90   PRINT "END OF PROGRAM RUN"                      <ENTER>
```

Another way of deleting the program line is to use the **DELETE** command, followed by the line number to be deleted:

```
DELETE 90                                             <ENTER>
```

This procedure is especially useful when several lines are to be deleted.

For example, if we wish to delete program lines 50 through 100 in program Example 1.3, we may use:

```
DELETE 50-100                                          <ENTER>
```

The program now contains only lines 20 and 40:

```
20   Q = 123.9
40   K$ = "PRODUCT CODE"
```

To get back to the original program, we would have to type in the entire section just deleted.

Suppose program Example 1.3 has not yet been altered and we want to delete line 50 and lines 80 and 90. We would not use DELETE 50–90 because this would delete all the line numbers 50 through 90, inclusive. Instead, we might use:

```
50                                                     <ENTER>
DELETE 80-90                                           <ENTER>
```

Or we could type each line number individually:

```
50                                                     <ENTER>
80                                                     <ENTER>
90                                                     <ENTER>
```

By now you must be tired of having to retype the entire program each time you experiment with the DELETE commands. Saving the original program on a diskette appears to be a very good idea at this point. Before we can save a program, however, we must give it a name.

Naming the Program

To find the program later, we must name it. Program names are limited by the following rules:

1. Maximum length of 8 characters.
2. No blank spaces allowed.
3. A three-place extension is allowed. Any three letters may be used, but 'BAS' and 'DTA' are often used to denote BASIC and DATA, respectively. An extension is typed after a dot (decimal point).
4. The first character must be a letter.
5. Remaining characters may be numbers or any of these symbols: $#! %() '- _<>{}@^&~\:

6. Do NOT use any other symbols, such as +*/:,

Examples:
```
SAMPLEPR
SAMPLEPR.BAS
X9-5-1.BAS
AB##.TXT
C12ATC.DBA
MASTER.KPD
```

Despite the obvious range of possibilities, it is best to save a program under a name that reminds the user of its function. For example, a telephone list might be stored under the name "TELPHON" or "TELPHON.DTA".

Saving the Program

Make sure you have inserted a formatted diskette in the disk drive currently in use. A program may be saved on the formatted diskette by using the command **SAVE,** followed by the program name in quotes. For example, a program named AIRBILL may be saved by:

```
SAVE "AIRBILL"                                        <ENTER>
```

Similarly, you may save the program shown in Example 1.3 by naming the program EX1-3.BAS and typing:

```
SAVE "EX1-3.BAS"                                      <ENTER>
```

While this saving procedure works well, it may be better to save the program in the so-called ASCII format. (The acronym ASCII stands for American Standard Code for Information Interchange.)

```
SAVE "EX1-3.BAS",A                                    <ENTER>
```

Similarly, a program named AIRBILL would be saved in the ASCII format by using:

```
SAVE "AIRBILL.BAS",A
```

The reason for using the ASCII format is simple: Several very useful disk drive procedures, to be discussed in subsequent chapters, will not be available if we have not saved the programs in ASCII format.

Checking the Diskette's Contents: FILES

If we are still in the Basic or Basica mode (Ok prompt), we can find out what programs are on the diskette by typing:

```
FILES                                                 <ENTER>
```

Assuming that the program EX1-3.BAS is the only program you have saved thus far, command **FILES** will cause the CRT to show:

```
COMMAND .COM EX1-3    .BAS
```

The COMMAND program was put on the diskette by the computer when the diskette was formatted. Note that the program EX1-3.BAS shows three blank spaces between the 3 and the decimal. The computer automatically reserves up to eight spaces for each program name, plus a possible three-place extension.

Checking the Diskette's Contents: DIR

We can get a much more detailed look at the diskette's contents if we use the system command **DIR.** If we are currently in the Basic or Basica mode (Ok prompt), we save the program, then return to the system mode (A⟩ prompt) by typing:

```
SYSTEM                                  <ENTER>
```

We should now get the system prompt A⟩, or we can convert the A⟩ to B⟩ as shown earlier in the chapter. Be sure your diskette is in the disk drive shown in the prompt. Then type:

```
DIR                                     <ENTER>
```

The computer will show the following information on the CRT:

```
COMMAND   COM   4959   5-07-82   12:00p
EX1-3     BAS    256   3-19-84   10:34a
        2 File(s)
A>
```

By looking at the screen we can see how many bytes were used by the program, when the program was created, and at what time. (Date and time would have been entered as we started the computer.)

To continue programming activities, remember to return to Basica. If we type BASICA after the A⟩, we will see the message:

```
Bad command or file name
```

The reason for this error message is simple: Basica is located on the master diskette. Therefore, take out the program diskette currently in disk drive A and insert the master diskette. Now type BASICA after the system prompt:

```
A>BASICA                                <ENTER>
```

The computer will now return to the Basic mode and show the BASIC prompt

```
OK
_
```

Now take the master diskette out of the disk drive and return the program diskette to the disk drive. You are once again ready to write a program or to use the LIST, RUN, SAVE, FILES, and other BASIC computer commands.

Saving a Duplicate of Your Program

Since you will probably want to experiment with various program options, it is a good idea to save either the original program or the modifications under another name. For example, if program EX-1.BAS has already been loaded into memory, you can save another copy of it under the name EX-1A.BAS (or by any other legal name you want, of course). If you now use the FILES command, the CRT will show:

```
COMMAND .COM EX-1     .BAS EX-1A    .BAS
```

You may now save all modifications to the program under a different name, keeping the original copy intact. You will discover that it is very wise to have a duplicate copy of a program that works: Sometimes our experiments do not work out well! In fact, it is a very good idea to save a copy of your program on a separate disk.

Retrieving the Program from the Diskette

Suppose you want to use a program you have saved on the diskette. Before the program can be used, it must be loaded from the diskette into the computer's memory with the command **LOAD.** For example, the program named EX1-2.BAS would be retrieved by:

```
LOAD "EX1-2.BAS"                                    <ENTER>
```

The same LOAD command would be used if we had saved the program in the ASCII format: The specification ,A is not part of the program name.

After the disk drive has stopped, the program will be in the computer's memory. You may now run the program by typing:

```
RUN                                                 <ENTER>
```

Or, if you simply want to see the program itself, type:

```
LIST                                                <ENTER>
```

Copying a Diskette

NOTE

Diskettes are to be copied for personal use only. Be sure that you do not violate copyright laws!

Since the contents of a diskette may be very important, we like to be able to make copies. Fortunately, the IBM PC performs a copy function easily.

The diskette to be copied will be the *source* diskette. The diskette that receives the copy will be the *destination* diskette, or the *target* diskette.

If you are already in the Basic or Basica mode, type SYSTEM, then press and release the ENTER key. This command will cause the

```
A>
```

prompt to be displayed. (If you have just turned on the computer and have not yet selected the Basic or Basica, you will still be in the A⟩ mode.)

Next, insert the master (DOS) diskette in the number-one disk drive and type:

```
DISKCOPY
```

and press/release the ENTER key. After the disk copy feature has been loaded, the computer will display this message:

```
INSERT SOURCE DISKETTE IN DRIVE A

STRIKE ANY KEY WHEN READY
```

Before touching any key, remove the master diskette (unless you are trying to copy it!) and insert the source diskette. Press/release any key. After the computer has finished reading a section of the source diskette, it will print:

```
INSERT TARGET DISKETTE IN DRIVE A

STRIKE ANY KEY WHEN READY
```

Just follow these directions. The sequence will be repeated many times. When the entire diskette contents have been copied, the computer will print:

```
COPY COMPLETE

COPY ANOTHER (Y/N)?
```

Select N if you are finished. If you select Y, the entire sequence will be repeated.

If you have the good fortune of owning two disk drives, type:

```
DISKCOPY A: B:
```

and press/release the ENTER key. The source diskette should be put in drive A and the target diskette in drive B. You will not need to switch diskettes back and forth. Just relax until the computer indicates that it is done.

NOTE

Remember Murphy's law: Anything that can go wrong will go wrong! To protect yourself against the possibility of accidentally writing over your source diskette, cover the source diskette's write protect notch (see Figure 1.2) with a piece of metallic tape. Metallic tape strips are supplied with each box of diskettes. Remove the tape after you have copied the diskette's contents so that you can save programs on the diskette again.

1.5 Additional Programming Procedures

More About the PRINT Command

Examples 1.1 through 1.3 show that the PRINT command causes the computer to print out the specified values or strings. However, PRINT can also be used to skip a line (if we do not type anything at all after the word PRINT), or to print a message not already defined as a string. For example, the command PRINT "PRODUCT CODE" would yield the same result as PRINT K$, if we had defined K$ = "PRODUCT CODE". We can, therefore, use the PRINT command to print a heading for the program without first defining the heading as a string. In fact, anything put in quotes after a print command will be printed. So, on the basis of this information, let us modify program Example 1.3:

example 1.4

```
20    Q = 123.9
40    K$ = "PRODUCT CODE"
60    PRINT
80    PRINT "VALUE OF Q AND K$"
100   PRINT
120   PRINT Q
140   PRINT K$
160   END
```

When this program is run, line 60 results in a blank line, line 80 prints the heading, line 100 prints another blank line, and lines 120 and 140 print 123.9 and PRODUCT CODE, respectively.

```
VALUE OF Q AND K$

 123.9
PRODUCT CODE
```

Multiple Statements

Thus far, our program has been written so that each line number is followed by a single definition or instruction. Each of those definitions or instructions is generally referred to as a line statement or, more briefly, a **statement.** For example, line 20 in the preceding program, which defines the value of Q, contains the single (line) statement Q = 123.9. Similarly, line 100 gives a single instruction (PRINT). Using a single statement per line is considered to be good practice by many programmers. Programs consisting of single-statement program lines are often easier to read, and errors in such programs are usually easier to find and to correct.

If we examine professionally written software, however, we see that commercial programmers seldom write single-statement program lines. Good reasons for abandoning the single-statement programming style include efficiency and structure. It is more efficient to write **multiple statements per line** because programs with more than one statement in each line require less space to reproduce. The amount of space used by a program is especially important to authors and publishers because a program that can be listed on one page is far cheaper to reproduce than one listed on three pages. Multiple-line statements also require slightly less RAM.

The decision to emphasize efficiency over style is a matter of preference. Given the very rapid increase in available computer memory (128K or even 256K RAM capacities are now common), saving RAM space is no longer as important as it was for microcomputers with a 4K RAM. Therefore, efficiency generally means being able to show more of a program on the CRT at one time (very convenient) and being able to use less paper to print the program (cheaper if the program is copied for distribution). One of the joys of programming is developing an individual style while working within a rigidly defined set of rules. Because this text contains so many complete programs, it uses the multiple-statement technique to keep book size (and therefore cost) under control.

The second (and more important) reason for using multiple statements per line is program structure. Many of the more complex programming procedures cannot be accomplished easily without the multiple-statement approach. Using single statements per line can, under some circumstances, make it difficult to follow the program's logic.

Clearly, there are some good reasons for using multiple statements. Unfortunately, some programmers are so convinced of the merit of the multiple-statement technique that they cram many statements into a single line even if there is no sound reason for doing so. The result is an unreadable and difficult-to-modify program that is often described as "alphabet soup." The point is simple: Use the multiple-statement technique when necessary but don't engage in overkill.

Using Colons

Writing multiple-line statements is simple: Merely insert a **colon** (:) between the line statements. For example, if we want to "skip" 4 lines, we can write

```
10  PRINT:PRINT:PRINT:PRINT
```

The single-statement style would require us to write:

```
2  PRINT
4  PRINT
6  PRINT
8  PRINT
```

Applying the multiple-statement technique to the program shown in Example 1.4, we would write the program shown in Example 1.5.

example 1.5

```
20  Q = 123.9 : K$ = "PRODUCT CODE" : PRINT
40  PRINT "VALUE OF Q AND K$" : PRINT
60  PRINT Q : PRINT K$
80  END
```

Running this shorter program (Don't forget to delete the original lines 100, 120, 140, and 160!) will, of course, produce identical results. It is possible to condense the program even further, but reproducing that program would be impossible on this page. (A single-line equivalent of the 4 lines shown in Example 1.5 would not fit the width of this page.) The computer, too, places a limit on how many items can be crammed into one line. Many microcomputers are limited to 250 or fewer characters per line, and too many statements per line make a program difficult to read. Therefore, the use of multiple statements per line should be tempered with judgment.

Remember that anything put in quotes after a print command will be printed. If we write PRINT : PRINT we will skip 2 lines, but writing PRINT "PRINT" will produce the word PRINT. The IBM PC will even print string constants if the second quote is omitted. Try these two versions:

```
PRINT "PRINT": PRINT
PRINT "PRINT: PRINT
```

To avoid surprises, make sure you use that second quote!

Using Semicolons

We may use the **semicolon** (;) to continue a statement or a print command. For example, the sequence:

```
80    PRINT : PRINT "THIS IS THE ";
100   PRINT "END OF THE PROGRAM!"
```

added to the preceding program would skip one line, then would print:

```
THIS IS THE END OF THE PROGRAM!
```

Note the space that was left between the word THE and the right-hand quote in line 80! If this had not been done, the words THE END would have been stuck together: THEEND. If we had omitted the semicolon at the end of line 80, the result would have been:

```
THIS IS THE
END OF THE PROGRAM!
```

Similarly, we could have modified line 60 in Example 1.5 to read:

```
60   PRINT Q; K$
```

The result would have been the output:

```
 123.9 PRODUCT CODE
```

The value 123.9 and the string "PRODUCT CODE" are packed closely together this way. We could have had the same results, of course, by writing:

```
60   PRINT Q;
70   PRINT K$
```

The first line 60 is more efficient, so, unless special circumstances require the second approach, we will stick with the original line 60.

Spaces between the semicolon and the next name will not matter. For example, there is no difference between the following statements:

```
60   PRINT Q;K$
70   PRINT Q;           K$
```

A space is important only when it is used inside a set of quotes. For example, if we had written:

```
70   PRINT Q;"    ";K$
```

three spaces would have been skipped between Q and K$. Similarly, we could have inserted 10 blank spaces by putting 10 blanks inside the quotes.

Using Commas

The **comma** (,) is also used for spacing purposes. However, using a comma signals the computer to divide the available line space into segments called **print zones** or **print fields.** The 80-column CRT is divided into five print fields of 16 columns each. In any case, using the comma usually results in far wider spacing than using the semicolon does. For example, if we modify line 60 to read:

```
60   PRINT Q, K$
```

the result would be:

```
 123.9                    PRODUCT CODE
```

Again the spacing between the comma and the next name does not matter. The statements:

```
80   PRINT Q,K$
90   PRINT Q,            K$
```

yield identical results.

Of course, we can add spaces by inserting a blank encased in quotes. For example, the program line:

```
60   PRINT Q," ",K$
```

will cause the computer to put Q in the first print field, insert a blank in the second print field, and put K$ in the third print field. The result will look like this:

```
 123.9                                             PRODUCT CODE
```

Colons, Semicolons, and Commas

Now that we have discussed the effects of using semicolons and commas for spacing purposes, let us put both types of spacing in our program to make direct comparisons. The modifications are shown in Example 1.6.

example 1.6

```
20    Q = 123.9 : K$ = "PRODUCT CODE" : PRINT
40    PRINT "VALUE OF Q AND K$" : PRINT
60    PRINT Q; K$
80    PRINT Q, K$
```

```
100   PRINT : PRINT "THIS IS THE ";
120   PRINT "END OF THE PROGRAM!"
140   END
```

This program results in the following output:

```
VALUE OF Q AND K$

 123.9 PRODUCT CODE
 123.9                PRODUCT CODE

THIS IS THE END OF THE PROGRAM!
```

One final word of advice: It is a good idea to give the END statement a very high line number. This practice ensures that the END statement is not accidentally eliminated by modifying the program. For example, the line:

```
30000   END
```

is not likely to be eliminated accidentally. (Of course, we would delete line 140 from the preceding program.)

1.6 Simple Mathematical Manipulations

One of the functions that a computer performs very well is the mathematical manipulation of numbers. For example, we may want to calculate the cost of purchasing 708 items that cost $1.53 each. The cost would be, of course, the number of items purchased times the cost per item. We can let the computer do the multiplication by using the symbol * in Example 1.7, line 20.

example 1.7

```
20      P = 1.53 : Q = 708 : C = P * Q
40      PRINT : PRINT "THE COST OF";Q;"UNITS AT"
60      PRINT "$";P;"EACH IS $";C
30000   END
```

If we run this little program, the resulting output will be:

```
THE COST OF 708 UNITS AT
$ 1.53 EACH IS $ 1083.24
```

Note the order of the events in the preceding program. Remember: Numeric values that have not yet been defined are assigned a value of zero. Therefore, if we rewrite line 20 to read:

```
20 P = 1.53: C = P*Q: Q = 708
```

table 1.4
THE USE OF COMMON MATHEMATICAL SYMBOLS

Symbol	Operation	Example
*	Multiplication	A = P * Q
+	Addition	A1 = P + Q
−	Subtraction	A2 = P − Q
/	Division	A3 = P/Q

the output will be:

```
THE COST OF 708 UNITS AT
$ 1.53 EACH IS $ 0
```

The reason for this result is simple: We had not yet defined Q when we tried to calculate C; therefore, C turned out to be C = P TIMES ZERO, which is, of course, zero. The *order* in which we write definitions and procedures is very important.

1.7 Additional Mathematical Procedures

Basic Mathematical Symbols

Just as the symbol * represents multiplication, other symbols represent division, addition, and so on. Table 1.4 summarizes the use of various symbols. The use of these mathematical symbols is illustrated by Example 1.8.

NOTE

Suppose you have just finished writing the program in Example 1.7 and are getting ready to start writing the program in Example 1.8. Make sure that you have saved Example 1.7 if you want to keep it; then type:

```
NEW                          <ENTER>
```

before you start typing the program lines for Example 1.8. The NEW command clears the memory, thereby ensuring that the program lines for the various programs you may be writing in a single session will not be mixed up. Use NEW any time you want to start a new program.

example 1.8

```
20    A = 5 : B = 10 : C = A*B : D = A+B: E = A/B
40    PRINT : PRINT "A =";A
60    PRINT "B =";B
```

```
80    PRINT "A+B =";D
100   PRINT "A/B =";E
120   PRINT "A*B =";C
30000  END
```

If we run this program, we get the following results:

```
A = 5
B = 10
A+B = 15
A/B = .5
A*B = 50
```

Using the multiple-statement technique discussed earlier, we can modify the preceding program as shown in Example 1.9.

example 1.9

```
20    A = 5 : B = 10
40    PRINT : PRINT "A =";A: PRINT "B =";B : PRINT "A+B =";A+B
60    PRINT "A/B =";A/B : PRINT "A*B =";A*B
30000  END
```

Using Mathematical Symbols

Let us now take the use of the mathematical symbols one step further by applying what we learned to the problem of computing gross pay, net pay, and net pay as a percentage of gross pay for a worker named J. A. Simmons who worked 38 hours this week. The following definitions will be used to calculate gross and net pay:

G = Gross pay
N = Net pay
W = Wage rate
H = Number of hours worked
F = Social Security (FICA) tax rate
I = Insurance premium
T = Federal tax rate

Gross pay is calculated by:

$$G = H \times W$$

Net pay is calculated by subtracting the taxes and the insurance premium from the gross pay:

$N = G - (F \times G) - I - (T \times G)$

We can use these definitions and procedures to write the program shown in Example 1.10.

example 1.10

```
20    H = 38
40    W = 6: F = .0725: T = .2: I = 39.72
60    W$ = "J. A. SIMMONS"
80    G = H*W
100   N = G - F*G - I - T*G
120   N1 = N/G * 100
130   PRINT : PRINT "GROSS PAY FOR ";W$;" IS $";G
140   PRINT "NET PAY FOR ";W$;" IS $";N
160   PRINT "NET PAY AS A % OF GROSS PAY IS";N1;"%"
30000  END
```

When we run this program, we get the following results:

```
GROSS PAY FOR J. A. SIMMONS IS $ 228
NET PAY FOR J. A. SIMMONS IS $ 126.15
NET PAY AS A % OF GROSS PAY IS 55.329%
```

A quick reading of the preceding program yields several points. First, since we isolated the hours worked (*H*) in line 20, we can modify the program very quickly if J. A. Simmons works some other number of hours. Second, although we have defined each of the conditions with a symbol in line 40, we can omit this line by writing lines 80 and 100 as follows:

```
80    G = H * 6
100   N = G - .0725*G - 39.72 - .2*G
```

The result will be the same, and the program more efficient. However, the program may also be harder to modify and to read. Third, the program does not allow for overtime payment, although this is a common payroll feature. To allow for overtime, the computer must be told under what circumstances such compensation will be paid. For example, we may pay overtime IF the worker has worked more than 40 hours. The use of such logical IF statements is discussed in Chapter 2.

Using Undefined Variables

Suppose we had written the program shown in Example 1.11, in which neither A nor A$ is defined.

example 1.11

```
20   Q = 123.9 : K$ = "PRODUCT CODE"
40   PRINT Q : PRINT K$
60   PRINT A : PRINT A$
100   END
```

If we run this program, we will discover that a numeric variable that has not yet been defined is assigned a value of zero, and a string variable that has not yet been defined is a "null" string. (A null or empty string is a string containing no characters at all.) Therefore, the program yields this output:

```
123.9
PRODUCT CODE
0
```

As expected, the value for A turns out to be zero. The string A$ shows up as a blank. Having illustrated this point, let us now delete line 60.

Bugs

As we write more complicated programs, chances are that they will contain unexpected error(s). A program error is called a **bug** in programming jargon. The process of finding and correcting bugs is called **debugging.** If we try to run a program containing a bug, it produces an unintended output; or, if a programming rule has been violated, the output is an error message. The most frequently occurring error message is **syntax error,** indicating a mistake in BASIC grammar. Such errors are generally easy to find and correct because the computer usually prints the line number in which the error occurred. Whatever the source of output problems, the RUN command provides very quick feedback on how well the program is written.

We sometimes find out how well we constructed a program when we try to run it.

Finding a bug in your software is a matter of *thorough searching.*

Using the Computer in Immediate Mode

If a line number does not precede a statement, the computer is said to be in immediate mode. The immediate mode is especially useful when a program contains a bug because we can check the status of variable and constant values currently in memory. For instance, if we have run the program in Example 1.10, we may check the value of the federal tax (F*G) by typing:

```
PRINT F*G
```

Pressing and releasing the ENTER key will yield an immediate answer. (Remember, run the program in Example 1.10 first. Otherwise the F and G are not currently in memory and your answer will be zero!) Similarly, we can check the value of the total hours worked by typing PRINT H, or we can check the name currently in memory by typing PRINT W$.

The computer can also be used as an expensive calculator in immediate mode or to print any string. For example, try:

```
PRINT 1.258*45.72                              <ENTER>
PRINT 10/5                                     <ENTER>
PRINT "2 + 6 ="; 2+6                           <ENTER>
PRINT "COMPUTER"                               <ENTER>
A = 5: B = 10: PRINT A*B                       <ENTER>
```

Chapter Review

This chapter provided operational definitions of numeric values, strings, variables, and constants. It explained the procedure for naming variables and assigning those names. The variable name is on the left of an equality sign and the variable value is on the right. String names always end in a dollar symbol.

To see the effects of a BASIC instruction, we used the command PRINT. The printed results (output) can be spaced by using semicolons or commas. The semicolon serves as a continuation statement, in addition to spacing output. Commas divide the available space into print zones.

To write a program, we must start each program line with a line number. The line number may be followed by a single statement or by multiple statements. The multiple statements are separated by colons.

Before writing a new program, clear the computer's memory by typing NEW. When you are satisfied that your program runs properly, save it by using SAVE. A program named SAMPLE may be saved by typing SAVE "SAMPLE" or by typing SAVE "SAMPLE.BAS", A. The latter procedure is referred to as saving in the ASCII format. The ASCII saving format is recommended because it enables you to use many more of the IBM PC's features.

You may load a program from the diskette into the memory by typing LOAD, followed by the program name in quotes; for example, LOAD "SAMPLE.BAS". The program may then be run by typing RUN. The program currently in memory may be listed by typing LIST.

Key Terms and Concepts

disk operating system (DOS)
BASIC
CRT
diskette
boot
system prompt
byte
kilobyte
formatting (a diskette)
numeric value
string
variable
constant
naming variables or constants
reserved word
assigning variable names
program line
PRINT
hard copy
LPRINT
LIST
LLIST
RUN
DELETE
SAVE
ASCII
FILES
DIR
LOAD
statement
multiple statements per line
colon (use of)
semicolon (use of)
comma (use of)
print zone (print field)
bug
debugging
syntax error

Common Errors

1. Misuse of the continuation symbol.

Correct:

```
20 A$ = "$": B = 5.72
40 PRINT A$; B
```

Alternatively:

```
20 A$ = "$": B = 5.72
40 PRINT A$;
60 PRINT B
```

Incorrect:

```
20 A$ = "$": B = 5.72
40 PRINT A$; PRINT B
```

2. Failure to include a space between strings. (Note the space after HAVE in line 20!)

Correct:

```
20 A$ = "I HAVE "
40 B$ = "A CAR"
60 PRINT A$;B$
```

Result:

```
I HAVE A CAR
```

Incorrect:

```
20 A$ = "I HAVE"
40 B$ = "A CAR"
60 PRINT A$;B$
```

```
I HAVEA CAR
```

Correction: Add a space after HAVE in the string A$, insert a space before the A in B$, or write line 60 as follows:

```
60 PRINT A$;" ";B$
```

3. Failure to define string variables or numeric variables before using them.

Correct:

```
20 A = 5.2: C = 2
40 B = A * C
60 PRINT "B =";B
```

Output:

```
B = 10.4
```

Incorrect:

```
20 A = 5.2: B = A * C
40 C = 2
60 PRINT "B =";B
```

```
B = 0
```

Exercises

1. Correct, if necessary, the following program lines, then predict what your output will look like. Next, run the program and compare your prediction with the actual result. Were you right?

```
20    PRINT:PRINT "THIS IS AN EXERCISE":PRINT
40    PRINT K$
60    P = $2.53
80    M$ = "DOLLARS"
100   PRINT "THE PRICE IS ";
120   PRINT P;M$
140   PRINT,PRINT THAT'S CHEAP
30000  PRINT END
```

2. Correct, if necessary, the following program, then predict the output for the corrected program. Next, run the program and compare the results with those you predicted. Were you right?

```
20   K$ = 259.97
40    P = 2,500
60    PRINT "HOW MUCH WILL IT COST?":PRINT
80    PRINT "IT WILL COST ";
100   PRINT K$;
120   PRINT " FOR";P;" UNITS."
30000  END
```

The program output should look like this:

```
HOW MUCH WILL IT COST?
IT WILL COST $ 259.97 FOR 2500 UNITS.
```

3. Starting with the program in Exercise 2, combine program lines 80, 100, and 120 into a single line 80, which will produce the same output.

4. If we define T7$ = "REPEAT", where T8$ = "MESSAGE" and P2$ = "PLEASE", write a program that uses these string definitions and some PRINT commands to produce an output that says:

```
REPEAT THE MESSAGE, PLEASE.
```

5. Now produce the output in Exercise 4 with a single PRINT command, without first defining T7$ and P2$. Remember, anything put in quotes after a PRINT command will be printed.

6. Using the following numeric value and string definitions, finish writing the program:

```
20   Q = 1
40   K$ = "I HAVE"
60   K2$ = "CAR"
```

to produce the output:

```
I HAVE 1 CAR!
```

7. Write a program that produces the following output, using the numeric value definition T = 7, the numeric value definition T1 = 4, and the string definition B$ = "3 +". Use semicolons, colons, and a PRINT statement. The output should look like this:

```
3 + 4 = 7
```

8. Produce the same output as that produced in Exercise 7, without first defining T, T1, and B$; this time use a single PRINT statement. *Hint:* Anything put in quotes behind a PRINT statement will be printed.

9. Complete a program that will compute the area of a rectangle 20 feet long by 10 feet wide. The area is calculated by multiplying the length and the width.

```
THE AREA OF A RECTANGLE WHOSE WIDTH
IS 10 FEET AND WHOSE LENGTH IS 20 FEET
IS EQUAL TO 200 SQUARE FEET.
```

A portion of the program has already been written. Unfortunately, some errors were made. Correct the errors and complete the program.

```
20     L = 20 FEET
40     W$ = 10
60     PRINT THE AREA OF A RECTANGLE WHOSE WIDTH;
80     PRINT "IS;W;"AND WHOSE LENGTH IS";L;"FEET"
```

10. Using colons, combine the information in the following lines into a single multiple-statement line.

```
20     A = 25.7
40     K$ = "IS LARGER THAN"
60     B7 = 18.3
```

11. Using the results of Exercise 10, write a program that will print:

```
25.7 IS LARGER THAN 18.3
```

12. If Q = .28 and T5 = 14.1, rewrite the following lines to produce the same results in a single line.

```
40     Q = .28 : T5 = 14.1
60     PRINT Q;
80     PRINT "IS SMALLER THAN";
100    PRINT T5
```

13. Predict the output that will result from the use of the following program.

```
20     W8 = 12 : W2 = 10 : W9 = W8 + W2
40     PRINT W8;"PLUS";W2;"IS EQUAL TO";W9
30000  END
```

Now run the program. Was your prediction correct?

14. Using the program in Exercise 13, what would happen if you had written the first line as:

```
20    W8 = 12 : W2 = 10
```

and the rest of the program remained unchanged? Why? You could eliminate the problem in two different ways. Try each way and check the results by running the program.

15. Suppose you have a microcomputer that will not accept multiple statements on one line. How would you rewrite the following line? (Put each of the four statements in its own line.)

```
20    A = 2.92: A$ = "A IS: ": K9 = 1.28:   Q1 = 9305
```

16. Write a computer program that will calculate the results of $(4 \times 3) - (2 \times 5) + (4 \times 2) - 2/4$ by using the definitions of P and Q shown in the following line 20.

```
20    P = 2 : Q = 5
```

Hint: $4 = P*P$, so we do not need to define the value 4. Similarly, the value 3 is defined by $(Q - P)$.

17. What will be the value of K, if K is defined by:

```
20    K= 2*5 - 3 + 3*3*3 + 2/5
```

18. What will be the difference in output, if any, for the next five programs?

```
PROGRAM 1

20    P = 5
40    PRINT P
60    PRINT P
80    PRINT P
30000   END
```

```
PROGRAM 2

20    P = 5
40    PRINT P;
60    PRINT P;
80    PRINT P
30000   END
```

```
PROGRAM 3

20    P = 5
40    PRINT P,
60    PRINT P,
80    PRINT P
30000   END
```

```
PROGRAM 4

20    P = 5
60    PRINT P;P;P
30000   END
```

```
PROGRAM 5

20    PRINT 5;5;5
30000   END
```

Now run each program to check your answer.

2

Objectives

- To use conditional statements based on the logical IF.
- To write program documentation using REM statements.
- To use mathematical comparison symbols.
- To write a program that uses GOTO commands.
- To learn the use of KILL, RENUM, and MERGE commands.
- To learn editing procedures with the EDIT command.

WRITING MORE COMPLEX PROGRAMS: COMPARISONS AND LOOPS

In Chapter 1 we learned to boot the system and we wrote our first programs, identifying numeric and string variables and printing the output. Output spacing based on semicolons and commas was introduced. The objective was to build basic programming skills rather than solve complex problems.

In this chapter, we will begin to use some features that make the computer a powerful problem-solving tool. For example, we will learn to make logical comparisons with the help of the logical IF statement. We will also learn to take advantage of the computer's ability to perform repetitive tasks by means of the GOTO command.

2.1 IF Statements: Giving the Computer Choices

Many programs involve selecting one of several alternatives. For example, the program used in Example 1.10 leads to the question of overtime, to be paid if the number of hours worked in any week exceeds 40. The word **IF,** in other words, provides a key to the activity: Will we pay overtime or not? Any time we use the conditional IF in conversation, we use an *if statement* to communicate to the computer. The use of IF in a conditional clause is natural and common: "If it rains, we will hold the reception indoors." "If I get the promotion, I will go on vacation." The computer uses IF in the same way. However, the word THEN is always used in conjunction with IF. For example, we can deal with the overtime condition by saying: "IF J. A. Simmons has worked more than 40 hours, THEN compute the overtime pay."

Mathematical Comparisons in IF Statements

Using the symbol for "more than" (>) can change the program given in Example 1.10 as follows. First, define V to be the overtime hours, the number of hours past 40. Since H represents the actual number of hours worked, we can write V = actual hours worked − 40, or $V = H - 40$. If overtime is paid, V is greater than zero; that is, $V > 0$. If no overtime pay exists, V is less than or equal to zero. The condition "less than or equal to" is defined by the symbol <=. Therefore, no overtime exists if $V <= 0$.

Programming IF Statements

Having defined the procedures to be used, we can add them to the program shown in Example 1.10. To start, we specify the overtime calculation procedure. Assuming that overtime compensation is time-and-a-half pay for hours over 40, we can compute this amount by multiplying the number of hours over 40 times 1.5 times the base pay of $6.00. Since the base pay was defined by $W = 6.00$, we can add lines 70 and 75 to the program shown in Example 1.10.

```
70   V = H-40
75   IF V > 0 THEN P1 = V*.5*W : P2 = V*1.5*W
```

Remember that the IF condition governs all statements following it, even the statements that are separated by a colon (:). Therefore, line 75 is equivalent to the two IF statements:

```
IF V > 0 THEN P1 = V*.5*W
IF V > 0 THEN P2 = V*1.5*W
```

Line 75 tells the computer that if *V* is greater than zero, then overtime pay is computed. This condition occurs only if *H* is greater than 40. The statements in line 75 are explained as follows:

1. If overtime has been worked ($V > 0$), the total overtime pay is 1.5 times each hour over 40 times the wage rate; that is, $P2 = V*1.5*W$. For example, if 42 hours were logged, total overtime is 2*1.5*6.00 = $18.

2. Using the example of a 42-hour week, total pay not including overtime is calculated by the total number of hours ($H = 42$) times the wage rate ($W = 6.00$). Therefore, total pay without overtime is H*W = 42*6.00 = $252. Remember that the additional 2 hours was paid at the rate of $6.00 per hour.

3. The time over 40 (i.e., 2 hours) already has been paid at the regular rate, and the amount to be added for overtime is half the standard hourly wage for every hour past 40. Therefore, $P1 = V*.5*W = 2*.5*6.00 =$ $6.00.

Total (gross) pay including overtime is calculated by $G = H*W + P1$. In this case, $G = 252 + 6 =$ $258. Line 80 in the preceding program should be changed to reflect the new calculation. (We would, of course, calculate the same gross pay by 40*6.00 + 2*1.5*6 = 240 + 18 = $258.)

Naturally, if no overtime is worked, line 75 is not executed, and *P1* is not defined. Remember that a numeric value has a value of zero if it has not been defined. Unless we encounter an overtime condition ($V > 0$), both *P1* and *P2* are zero. Consequently, a "no overtime" condition leads to a calculation $G = H*W + 0$, or $G = H*W$, in line 80. If, on the other hand, an overtime condition exists, *P1* will be defined properly in line 75, with *G* adjusted accordingly. The program will, therefore, always calculate gross pay properly. Finally, add a line to show the results of the overtime pay calculations.

```
180   PRINT "OVERTIME PAY IS ";P1
```

Then run the program again. Remember that *H* is still defined to be 38 in line 20, so the overtime pay should be $0. Now modify line 20 to reflect a change in hours to 42 hours:

```
20    H = 42
```

and rerun the program. The overtime pay should be $18, reflecting 2 hours over 40 at 1.5 times the base pay of $6.00 per hour. Net pay has increased by less than that, of course, to reflect the Social Security (FICA) and federal income taxes that were withheld.

Example 2.1 displays the final program with all its modifications and its output. Be sure to review the definitions used in writing the program before studying the example.

G = Gross pay
N = Net pay
W = Wage rate
H = Number of hours worked
F = Social Security (FICA) tax rate
I = Insurance premium
T = Federal tax rate
P2 = Total overtime pay
N1 = Net pay as percentage of gross pay

example 2.1

```
20    H = 42
40    W = 6 : F = .0725 : I = 39.72 : T = .2
60    W$ = "J. A. SIMMONS"
70    V = H-40
75    IF V > 0 THEN P1 = V*.5*W : P2 = V*1.5*W
80    G = H*W+P1
100   N = G-F*G-I-T*G
120   N1 = N/G*100
130   PRINT : PRINT "GROSS PAY FOR ";W$;" IS $";G
140   PRINT "NET PAY FOR ";W$;" IS $";N
160   PRINT "NET PAY AS A % OF GROSS PAY IS";N1;"%"
180   PRINT "OVERTIME PAY IS $";P2
30000   END

RUN

GROSS PAY FOR J. A. SIMMONS IS $ 258
NET PAY FOR J. A. SIMMONS IS $ 147.975
NET PAY AS A % OF GROSS PAY IS 57.3546512 %
OVERTIME PAY IS $ 18
```

Note especially that all statements after IF are executed in line 75, even though the use of colons makes line 75 a multiple-statement line.

2.2 REMark Statements

The program in Example 2.1 is fairly simple. Yet to remember what each symbol represents, we must keep reviewing a list of definitions that is not part of the program. As programs become longer and more complicated, we cannot tolerate such an inconvenience. Worse, we may lose the list of definitions and/or explanations that allows us to follow the logic and structure of the program.

Subsequent program modifications will be far more time-consuming if we cannot easily trace the symbols and definitions. We need a way to write notes to the humans who read the program. Since these notes (REMARKS) are not meant to be read by the computer, we can tell the computer to ignore such notes by inserting **REM** before any REMark that we insert into the program.

By creating multiple-line statements with colons, we can attach the REM statements directly following the program statements. For example, we can write line 20 like this:

```
20   H = 42: REM ** HOURS WORKED **
```

Note: In this example asterisks are used to make the remark more noticeable. Any symbol may be chosen, or the programmer may decide not to use such attention-getting devices at all. In fact, we could modify the whole program by rewriting it as shown in Example 2.2. Note that the second set of asterisks is lined up to match the longest lines, 77 and 120, in order to improve the program's presentation.

example 2.2

```
20    H = 42 : REM **   HOURS WORKED                         **
40    W = 6 : REM **   WAGE RATE                             **
42    F = .0725 : REM **   SOC. SECURITY TAX RATE            **
44    I = 39.72 : REM **   INSURANCE PREMIUM                 **
46    T = .2 : REM **   FEDERAL INCOME TAX RATE              **
60    W$ = "J. A. SIMMONS" : REM **   WORKER NAME            **
70    V = H-40 : REM **   OVERTIME HOURS                     **
75    IF V > 0 THEN P1 = V*.5*W : P2 = V*1.5*W
77    REM **   P1 = PAY OVER BASE, P2 = TOTAL OVERTIME **
80    G = H*W + P1 : REM **   GROSS PAY                      **
100   N = G-F*G-I-T*G : REM ** NET PAY                       **
120   N1 = N/G*100 : REM **   NET PAY AS % OF GROSS PAY **
140   PRINT : PRINT "NET PAY FOR";W$;"IS $";N
160   PRINT "NET PAY AS A % OF GROSS PAY IS"; N1;"%"
180   PRINT "OVERTIME PAY IS $";P2
30000   END
```

The program is now easier to read; if modifications are necessary later, it will be less difficult to see what was done where. But don't go overboard: It is not necessary to REM the most obvious conditions.

2.3 Mathematical Comparisons

We often compare values to determine which value is smaller, greater than, or equal to another. The computer can make comparisons of values if we use the proper symbols. Table 2.1 summarizes the conditions we encounter most often and gives the **basic mathematical comparison symbols.**

table 2.1
BASIC MATHEMATICAL CONDITIONS

Symbol Used	Meaning	Sample Use
=	Equal to	`IF A = B THEN PRINT "="`
<	Less than	`IF A < B THEN PRINT "<"`
<=	Less than, or equal to	`IF A <= B THEN PRINT "<="`
>	Greater than	`IF A > B THEN PRINT ">"`
>=	Greater than, or equal to	`IF A >= B THEN PRINT ">="`
<>	Not equal to	`IF A <> B THEN PRINT "<>"`

In Example 2.2 we saw how a "greater than" condition was combined with an IF statement to decide whether to calculate and print overtime pay. From time to time, we may use other mathematical conditions to make decisions about whether to print or not to print, to calculate or not to calculate, or simply to end a program. Such capabilities are very useful for checking for errors in the program, too.

Multiple IF Comparisons: Using AND and OR

Instead of the simple IF conditions just described, we occasionally have two or more limit conditions. For instance, suppose that we are required to produce steel pipe with a wall thickness not less than .175 inch. AND not more than .178 inch. There are, in short, two limits to consider in this case: To be acceptable, the pipe wall thickness must be greater than or equal to .175 inch. AND it also must be less than or equal to .178 inch. Such a requirement is traced in the program shown in Example 2.3.

example 2.3

```
20   W = .179 : REM ** ACTUAL MEASURED VALUE    **
25   L = .175 : REM ** LOWER ACCEPTANCE LIMIT  **
30   U = .178 : REM ** UPPER ACCEPTANCE LIMIT  **
40   IF W >= L AND W <= U THEN PRINT "ACCEPTABLE"
60   IF W < L OR W > U THEN PRINT "UNACCEPTABLE"
30000   END
```

The pipe wall thickness is not acceptable when either one of two conditions exists. It is not acceptable if the value of *W* is less than .175 OR if the value of *W* is greater than .178. The value .179 lies outside the required range when the program is run, the computer will print out the message:

```
UNACCEPTABLE
```

If we use a value for *W* that falls inside the range defined in line 40, the program will, of course, print:

```
ACCEPTABLE
```

Try, for example, running this program after changing line 20 to:

```
20   W = .176
```

The IF . . . THEN . . . ELSE Procedure

In the program of Example 2.3, lines 40 and 60, the conditional IF was used to print one of two possible messages. The two IF statements may be replaced by a single IF, coupled with an ELSE statement as shown next:

```
40    IF W >= L AND W <= U THEN PRINT "ACCEPTABLE"
      ELSE PRINT "UNACCEPTABLE"
```

Note: The space bar was used to position the ELSE under the IF to make the long line more readable. Do NOT use the ENTER key! (Using the ENTER key would signal the beginning of a new line rather than the continuation of a line. Don't forget to delete line 60 in Example 2.3!)

The use of ELSE is particularly useful when the program uses many different IF statements, leading to any one of two possible actions or conclusions.

2.4 GOTO Commands: Loops and Counters

We can provide the computer directions on where to go in the program to perform a particular function. The "where to go" command, **GOTO,** is very useful because it enables us to jump across program lines or to repeat sequences. For example, we could write the following program to print the message HI THERE! indefinitely. In fact, the microcomputer will print the message until we interrupt the program by pressing the Ctrl and Break keys simultaneously.

```
20    PRINT "HI THERE!"
40    GOTO 20
```

Since the program keeps "**loop**ing" back to line 20 each time line 40 is executed, the two statements form what is known as an **infinite loop.**

To avoid printing the same thing over and over, we need to add a condition to the printing exercise. We can create a device called a **counter,** to keep track of the number of times the message has been printed. When the counter reaches a selected value, the program is stopped. This procedure is demonstrated in Example 2.4.

example 2.4

```
10    C = 0 : REM ** INITIALIZE COUNTER        **
20    PRINT "HI THERE!"
30    C = C + 1 : IF C = 10 THEN GOTO 30000
40    GOTO 20
30000  END
```

When line 30 is passed the first time, the value C = 0 + 1 = 1. The second time through the loop, C is already 1, so C = 1 + 1 = 2. The third time through the loop, the value C is already 2, so C will now equal 2 + 1 = 3, and so on. As soon as C reaches 10, the IF statement causes the computer to end the program. The message HI THERE! will, therefore, be printed 10 times. (Actually, since an undefined numeric value is automatically set at 0, the program in Example 2.4 will run well even if you delete line 10.)

A Word of Caution About GOTO

Line 30 may be written in several different ways. For example, line 30 may be written as follows:

```
30   C = C + 1: IF C = 10 THEN 30000
```

Or line 30 may be written like this:

```
30   C = C + 1: IF C = 10 THEN END
```

Line 30000 may then be eliminated. In fact, the latter approach is preferred because it does not use an actual or an implied GOTO command. You will learn later that it is best to minimize the use of the GOTO commands. Too many GOTOs crisscrossing a program can make the program hard to read.

Indenting Loops

To make loops more visible in a program, we should indent the program lines inside the loop. Therefore, the final version of the program in Example 2.4 will look like the following:

```
20 PRINT "HI THERE!"
40     C = C + 1: IF C = 10 THEN END
60 GOTO 20
```

As programs become more complex, you will discover that good visibility of loops in those programs will be very useful. Therefore, we will indent all loops from now on.

Passes

Since we have limited the number of times the computer completes the loop, we note that the GOTO statement is no longer an infinite loop, but constitutes a simple loop, instead. Each time we go through the loop we complete a **pass.** We can check on our passes by writing a program that looks like this:

```
20   A = A + 1
40       IF A = 3 THEN END
60       PRINT "PASS NUMBER";A
80   GOTO 20
```

When this program is run, it produces the following output:

```
PASS NUMBER 1
PASS NUMBER 2
```

The message PASS NUMBER 3 is not printed because the program ends before the PRINT command in line 60 is reached.

If the message is to be printed three times, we must either let A be 4 or delete line 40 and place the same message in line 70 instead. The program:

```
20   A = A + 1
60       PRINT "PASS NUMBER";A
70       IF A = 3 THEN END
80   GOTO 20
```

will print the following message three times:

```
PASS NUMBER 1
PASS NUMBER 2
PASS NUMBER 3
```

So where you put your IF statement does make a difference: Think carefully before placing counters and IF statements!

2.5 Additional Useful Procedures

Renumbering Program Lines

Suppose we have written the following program (Example 2.5):

example 2.5

```
1  PRINT "LINE 1"
2  PRINT "LINE 3"
3  PRINT "LINE 4"
```

We now decide to insert a PRINT "LINE 2" between lines 1 and 2. Clearly, the line numbers that have been used do not allow us to make the insertion. The entire program would have to be rewritten . . . or we could let the computer perform the miracle of renumbering the program lines for us. To activate the renumbering procedure, we use the command:

```
RENUM <new starting line number >,<original starting
        line number >,<line increment>
```

For instance, if we decide to renumber the program lines in Example 2.5 so that the first line will be 20 rather than 1, using a line increment of 10, we would type:

```
RENUM  20,1,10                                    <ENTER>
```

Remember, you do not type ⟨ENTER⟩. Instead, push/release the ENTER key!

If we now type:

```
LIST                                              <ENTER>
```

we will discover that the computer has renumbered the program for us, as follows:

```
20   PRINT "LINE 1"
30   PRINT "LINE 3"
40   PRINT "LINE 4"
```

We may now insert the line:

```
25   PRINT "LINE 2"
```

so that the complete program reads:

```
20   PRINT "LINE 1"
25   PRINT "LINE 2"
30   PRINT "LINE 3"
40   PRINT "LINE 4"
```

To save the revised program, using the ASCII procedure, we name it EX2-5.BAS and type:

```
SAVE "EX2-5.BAS",A                                <ENTER>
```

Note that the renumbering procedure only renumbered the program stored in memory. Therefore, to save the renumbered program on disk, we must remember to use the SAVE procedure. If we save the program by using the original program name, the original program will be replaced by the updated version. If we want to save the original program, we must use a different program name for the updated version, perhaps naming it (in this case) EX2-5A.BAS. Most of the time, however, there is no reason to save the original, so we simply save the updated program by the original name.

Merging Programs

Suppose we had a program (Example 2.6) named EX2-6.BAS stored on disk:

example 2.6

```
10   PRINT "LINE 5"
20   PRINT "LINE 6"
```

We may put this program into memory by typing:

```
LOAD "EX2-5.BAS"                                  <ENTER>
```

To combine the program in memory with the program EX2-5.BAS stored on disk, we first renumber EX2-6.BAS, because the latter's program lines (10 and 20) are not compatible with the program lines in EX2-5.BAS. Since EX2-6.BAS has already been placed in memory, we can renumber it by using:

```
RENUM <new line>,<start line>,<increment>
```

Suppose we want to change the line numbers in Example 2.6 so that the renumbered lines start with 50, using increments of 10. The original program's first line number is 10, so we type

```
RENUM 50,10,10                                    <ENTER>
```

The **RENUM** command causes the lines in program Example 2.6 to be renumbered as shown:

```
50   PRINT "LINE 5"
60   PRINT "LINE 6"
```

We may now combine the program in memory with any program stored on disk by using the command:

```
MERGE "program stored on disk"
```

For example, if we want to combine the program EX2-6.BAS currently in memory with the program EX2-5.BAS we saved on disk, we type:

```
MERGE "EX2-5.BAS"                                 <ENTER>
```

The result of this command will be:

```
10   PRINT "LINE 1"
25   PRINT "LINE 2"
30   PRINT "LINE 3"
40   PRINT "LINE 4"
50   PRINT "LINE 5"
60   PRINT "LINE 6"
```

We may add a final program line:

```
30000 END
```

The result may be saved to disk by typing:

```
SAVE "EX2-7.BAS",A                                   <ENTER>
```

The **MERGE** command is extremely useful at different times and/or by different programmers. But remember, the MERGE command will not work if the program to be merged was not saved in the ASCII format!

Deleting Programs from a Disk

Having completed the procedures in the preceding section, we now have three new programs on disk:

```
EX2-5.BAS
EX2-6.BAS
EX2-7.BAS
```

If we intend to keep only EX2-7.BAS, we must remove the other two programs from the disk, to save disk space for additional programs. Programs may be removed from disk by using the **KILL** command. For example, we may remove program EX2-5.BAS by typing:

```
KILL "EX2-5.BAS"                                     <ENTER>
```

Similarly, program EX2-6.BAS may be deleted from disk by typing:

```
KILL "EX2-6.BAS"                                     <ENTER>
```

NOTE

Even if we had saved the program as EX2-6 the computer would have automatically added .BAS to the program name. Therefore, the KILL command would have to include the .BAS extension.

Correcting Program Lines with EDIT

The IBM PC has numerous useful system features. Perhaps the **EDIT** command will turn out to be most popular with novice programmers. The EDIT command allows us to make corrections in any program line by using:

```
EDIT program line                                    <ENTER>
```

Note the space between the command EDIT and the program line number. To see the EDIT command in action, suppose we had written the program line:

```
100   PRINT "PREGAM LINE"
```

The line has two errors in it: Since PREGAM is misspelled, we must change the E to an O and insert an R.

We begin the correction by typing:

```
EDIT 100                                  ENTER
```

Line 100 will appear on screen with the cursor (the blinking dash) under the 1 of the line number, 100. The cursor is moved with the left and right arrow keys, on the numeric pad on the right-hand side of the keyboard. The "arrow" keys are called cursor controls.

NOTE

If you have (accidentally or on purpose) used the [Num Lock] key to lock in the numbers on the numeric key pad, pressing and releasing the cursor control keys will cause a series of numbers to be printed when you merely intended to move the cursor. To get rid of the series of numbers and enable the cursor, press and release the Num Lock key, then correct the line before pressing the ENTER key.

Since we want to move to the right, we push the right arrow key several times to position the cursor under the E in PREGAM. (Alternatively, hold the right arrow key down and let the cursor move to the right automatically—until it reaches the E. Then release the key. Try it!) When the cursor is under the E, we simply type the letter O, and the E will be replaced by O. The word now is PROGAM. We move the cursor to the A, then press/release the INSERT key. The cursor will change from a thin line to a blinking square. Now type the letter R and the computer will insert the R before the A, leaving the word PROGRAM. Since no additional changes are necessary, simply press/release the ENTER key and the line has been completely corrected:

```
100   PRINT "PROGRAM LINE"
```

Note that an insert is made before the letter under which the cursor is placed. For example, to add NUMBER 100 after the word LINE in 100, place the cursor under the right-hand quotation mark, press/release the INSERT key, press/

release the SPACE bar (to insert a space after LINE), and type NUMBER 100. The line will now read:

```
100   PRINT "PROGRAM LINE NUMBER 100"
```

Remember that the changes are made in the memory only at this point: If you want to save the changes on disk, you must use the SAVE procedure again!

Deletions may be made in the EDIT mode by positioning the cursor under the character to be deleted and pressing/releasing the DELETE key. Each time the DELETE key is depressed, another character is deleted. For example, to delete the 100 at the end of the program line statement, use EDIT 100, position the cursor under the space after the word NUMBER (we want to delete the space, too!), and press/release the DELETE key several times. The result will be:

```
100   PRINT "PROGRAM LINE NUMBER"
```

You should realize that none of the edited changes are actually stored in memory until the ENTER key has been pressed and released. In addition, the edited changes are not stored on the diskette until the program in which the changes have been made has been re-saved through the use of the SAVE procedure discussed in Chapter 1.

Go ahead and experiment a little: The EDIT procedure will save you a lot of keypunching time.

Chapter Review

Many programming applications are based on giving the computer logical choices. Such choices are based on the logical IF in BASIC. Since many alternative courses of action are based on mathematical comparisons, the mathematical symbols ⟩, ⟨, ⟨⟩, ⟨=, and ⟩= were introduced.

Computers often perform functions that are repetitive. Such tasks may be performed inside a loop. One technique used to make a loop is based on the GOTO statement. An IF statement, combined with a counter that keeps track of the number of times a procedure is performed, is usually used to terminate the loop. Failure to terminate a loop causes the computer to perform the same task "infinitely" or until the computer's actions are interrupted outside the program. A loop that is not terminated by the program itself is called an infinite loop.

Common Errors

1. Not realizing that an IF statement governs all statements following it in that line.

example
```
20   T = 28: REM ** CURRENT STOCK      **
40   T$ = "OK"
60   IF T < 20 THEN T$ = "LOW": C = 15
80   PRINT "STOCK CONDITION IS";T$
100  PRINT "CRITICAL STOCK AMOUNT IS";C
30000  END
```

Running the program yields the output:

```
STOCK CONDITION IS OK
CRITICAL STOCK AMOUNT IS 0
```

The program writer apparently meant to say that the critical stock amount is 15; but line 60 never is executed, since 28 > 20. Therefore, the critical stock amount C is never defined!

2. Improper termination of a loop.

example: Suppose you want to write a program to produce the output:

```
LINE 1
LINE 2
LINE 3
```

The program that follows will NOT do the job:

```
20   C = C + 1
40        IF C = 3 THEN 30000
60        PRINT "LINE";C
80   GOTO 20
30000  END
```

Correction: Either change line 40 to read IF C = 4 THEN 30000 or switch the program lines 40 and 60:

```
20   C = C + 1
40        PRINT "LINE";C
60        IF C = 3 THEN 30000
80   GOTO 20
30000  END
```

Better yet, write line 60 this way:

```
60   IF C = 3 THEN END
```

and delete line 30000.

Key Terms and Concepts

IF
REM
program documentation
basic mathematical comparison symbols
GOTO
loop
infinite loop
counter
pass
RENUM
MERGE
KILL
EDIT

Exercises

1. Write a program that produces the following output by using GOTO statements, counters, and an IF statement.

```
VALUE NUMBER 1 = 2
VALUE NUMBER 2 = 4
VALUE NUMBER 3 = 6
VALUE NUMBER 4 = 8
```

   Hint: Notice that the values 2, 4, 6, and 8 are always twice as large as the counter value.

2. Write a program that produces the following output by using GOTO statements, counters, and an IF statement. The resulting values are the result of a multiplication sequence: Each product number after the first is twice as large as the preceding one.

```
PRODUCT NUMBER 1 = 1
PRODUCT NUMBER 2 = 2
PRODUCT NUMBER 3 = 4
PRODUCT NUMBER 4 = 8
```

3. Using IF, GOTO, and a counter, finish the program listed below so that it will print five address labels for you. Insert your own name and address inside the quotes.

```
20    N$ = "YOUR NAME"
40    A$ = "STREET AND NUMBER"
60    C$ = "TOWN, STATE, AND ZIP CODE"
80    PRINT : PRINT N$ : PRINT A$ : PRINT C$
100   Q = Q + 1 : REM  **  COUNTER   **
 .
 .
 .
```

4. Finish the program listed below so that it will produce a multiplication table for the value 7. Stop when the value of 70 has been reached.

```
20    V = 7 :PRINT "MULTIPLICATION TABLE" : PRINT
40    C = C + 1 : REM  ** COUNTER  **
60   V1 = C*V
```

The output will consist of the following:

```
MULTIPLICATION TABLE

1 TIMES 7 = 7
2 TIMES 7 = 14
.
.
.
10 TIMES 7 = 70
```

5. Using the basic approach used in Exercise 4, write a program for an addition table having an output that looks like this:

```
ADDITION TABLE

 1 PLUS 1 = 2
 2 PLUS 2 = 4
 3 PLUS 3 = 6
 .
 .
 .
10 PLUS 10 = 20
```

6. The grade in a course is determined by reference to the following scale:

Total Points (%)	Grade
90 and over	A
80–89	B
70–79	C
60–69	D
Below 60	F

Suppose that you scored 73 out of a possible 100 points on the midterm examination; you scored 130 out of 150 points on the final examination; and you earned 56 out of a possible 70 quiz points. Write a program that produces the output shown below. *Hint:* First let the program add up all the points earned (73 + 130 + 56), then add up all the possible points (100 + 150 + 70). The percentage grade will be the first sum divided by the second sum; the result of this division will be multiplied by 100 to get the percentage value. Then use IF statements to assign the grade.

Required output:

```
YOUR % GRADE IS 80.9375
YOUR LETTER GRADE IS B
```

The program is partially written below. Finish it to produce the required output.

```
20  T1 = 73: REM ** FIRST GRADE                              **
40  T2 = 130: REM ** SECOND TEST GRADE                       **
60  T3 = 56: REM ** THIRD TEST GRADE                         **
80  T4 = T1 + T2 + T3: REM ** TOTAL POINTS EARNED            **
```

```
100   REM
120   P1 = 100: REM ** TOTAL POINTS POSSIBLE, 1ST TEST          **
140   P2 = 150: REM ** TOTAL POINTS POSSIBLE, 2ND TEST          **
160   P3 = 70: REM ** TOTAL POINTS POSSIBLE, 3RD TEST           **
180   P4 = P1 + P2 + P3: REM ** SUM OF ALL POSSIBLE POINTS      **
200   REM
220   G = T4/P4*100: REM ** PERCENTAGE GRADE EARNED             **
240   REM
260   IF G >= 90 THEN G$ = "A"
```

7. The following program is only partially completed.

```
20   C = C + 1
40   IF C = 1 THEN A = 1 : GOTO 100
60   IF C = 2 THEN A = 2 : GOTO 100
80   A = A*A
 .
 .
 .
```

Use GOTO statements and an IF statement to complete the program so that it will produce the following output:

```
VALUE 1 = 1
VALUE 2 = 2
VALUE 3 = 4
VALUE 4 = 16
VALUE 5 = 256
```

8. Starting with the following partially completed program, write some lines to produce an error message if the value of *K* is less than zero or greater than 10. Run the program four times. Each time the program is run, change the value of *K* in line 20. The appropriate error message should follow.

```
VALUE OF K       ERROR MESSAGE
----------       -------------
 2               NONE
-3               TOO SMALL
 4               NONE
 11              TOO LARGE
```

The partially completed program follows.

```
20    K = 2
40    PRINT "VALUE OF K","ERROR MESSAGE"
60    PRINT "----------","-------------":PRINT
 .
 .
 .
```

9. Define the temperature in degrees Fahrenheit in line 20 of the partially completed program shown below. The responses to be made to the temperatures are listed in the table. Try using several different temperatures in line 20 to check whether the program works as intended.

Temperature Range	Required Comment
Less than 32	BRRRR!!!
32 and under 60	Could be worse
60 and under 85	Nice!!!
85 and over	Too hot!!!

A typical program output will look like this:

```
TEMP. IS 64 DEGREES F.     NICE!!!
```

Or if you change the value in line 20 to be 87 degrees:

```
TEMP. IS 87 DEGREES F.     TOO HOT!!!
```

. . . and so on.

```
20   T = 38 : REM ** ACTUAL TEMPERATURE **
40   IF T < 32 THEN T$ = "BRRRR!!!"
.
.
.
120 PRINT "TEMP. IS";T;"DEGREES F.       ";T$
30000  END
```

10. Finish the partially completed program shown below. The program will print a ticket whose price is dependent on the person's age (line 20). A person who is younger than 6 years old is admitted free of charge. A person whose age is between 6 and 12, inclusive, pays \$3.25, and a person who is older than 12 years pays \$4.95.

```
20   A = 14 : REM ** PERSON'S AGE **
40   IF A < 6 THEN P = 0
.
.
.
100 PRINT : PRINT
120 PRINT "XXXXXXXXXXXXXXXX"
140 PRINT "     ADMIT ONE"
160 PRINT "PRICE IS $";P
180 PRINT "XXXXXXXXXXXXXXXX"
30000  END
```

Run the program several times, using different ages in line 20, to check whether it works as intended.

11. What would the output be for the program shown below?

```
20   PRINT "*";
40      C = C + 1 : IF C = 5 THEN END
60   GOTO 20
```

Hint: Remember the use of the semicolon as a continuation statement.

12. What would the output be for the program shown in Exercise 11 if the semicolon were omitted from line 20?

13. What would the output be for the following program?

```
10  C = C+1: IF C = 5 THEN END
20      PRINT "*";
60  GOTO 10
```

3

Objectives

- To write a program that uses the INPUT command.
- To write a simple "interactive" program that will make the microcomputer a teaching device.
- To save data by making them part of the program, using READ and DATA statements.

CONVERSATIONS WITH THE MICRO

Chapter 2 discussed writing programs that allow the computer to make logical comparisons and to print results based on those comparisons. Because the variable values used in processing were part of the program, it was necessary to modify the program each time the variable values were changed.

This chapter introduces two additional ways to enter variable values into the computer's memory. The INPUT command is used to enter variable values directly from the keyboard. It allows interactive computing, in which the user supplies variable values in response to the computer's request. The READ (DATA) sequence can be used to supply variable values that are stored in a part of the program identified by data lines.

3.1 Talking to the Micro: The INPUT Command

Thus far, we have written programs that do not involve any communication with the computer during program execution: After completing the program, we could only instruct the computer to RUN the program and PRINT the output. With the **INPUT** command, which directs the user to put information into the computer, it is possible to enter values and strings into the memory from the keyboard. The program, if written properly, then processes the INPUT information.

An example of an INPUT command is:

```
20  INPUT A
```

This line causes the computer to stop execution and ask us to enter a numeric value for A. The computer will not accept a string in response to line 20. Similarly, the command:

```
40  INPUT A$
```

requires the user to enter a string.

Prompting

Unfortunately, a program line that says no more than INPUT A does not indicate to the program's user what is to be entered. The screen will show only a question mark. Does the question mark mean that a numeric value or a string should be entered? If a value is to be entered, what kind of value—a dollar amount, an age, the number of units sold? If a string is to be entered, what kind of string—a name, a product code, or what? Just writing INPUT A or INPUT A$ is not very satisfactory.

Suppose we want to write a program that will ask for a purchaser's name and a purchase amount. We could write:

```
20   INPUT N$
40   INPUT P
30000   END
```

When this program is run, only the person who wrote the program will know how to respond to the question mark on the CRT. To prompt the user about the kind of response required, we can write the instruction as part of the INPUT statement. The program can be modified to:

```
20   INPUT "ENTER YOUR NAME ==============> ";N$
40   INPUT "ENTER THE PURCHASE AMOUNT ====> ";P
30000   END
```

If this program is run by Jane Q. Doe, who purchased a product for $8.95, the result will be:

```
ENTER YOUR NAME ==============> ?JANE Q. DOE
ENTER THE PURCHASE AMOUNT ====> ?8.95
```

Note that the semicolon after the instructions in lines 20 and 40 produced two results:

1. The response is typed right after the instruction because the semicolon is a continuation symbol.

2. The semicolon, when used with an INPUT instruction, causes the computer to print a question mark after the instruction is printed. If you want to eliminate the question mark, use a comma instead of a semicolon. For example, if you write line 20 like this:

   ```
   20   INPUT "ENTER YOUR NAME =========> ",N$
   ```

   you will get this input sequence

   ```
   ENTER YOUR NAME =========> JANE Q. DOE
   ```

   when you run the program.

Combining PRINT and INPUT Statements

The same results can be achieved by mixing PRINT and INPUT statements. The preceding program can be rewritten:

```
10   PRINT "ENTER YOUR NAME ==============> ";
20   INPUT N$
30   PRINT "ENTER THE PURCHASE AMOUNT ====> ";
40   INPUT P
30000  END
```

This is the only way to get the desired results on older and less sophisticated microcomputers, or when lengthy instructions are involved. Let us run this program to see what happens, typing the response immediately after the question mark. The INPUT prompts and responses will look like this:

```
ENTER YOUR NAME ==============> ? JOHN Q. DOE
ENTER THE PURCHASE AMOUNT ====> ? 12.34
```

Remember, since an amount is a numeric value, it is incorrect to use symbols other than numerals and a decimal point when entering it. For example, entering $12.34, which uses a nonnumeric symbol ($), would produce an error message. Similarly, the amount $1,256.27 is entered as 1256.27, not as 1,256.27, since a numeric value cannot contain a comma.

If neither a semicolon nor a comma was used at the end of lines 10 and 30 in the preceding program, the question mark would have appeared below the input request. The INPUT requests and responses would look like this:

```
ENTER YOUR NAME ==============>
? JOHN Q. DOE
ENTER THE PURCHASE AMOUNT ====>
? 12.34
```

Note that the response is typed after the question mark. Since the program works as well without the semicolon, using this punctuation depends on the needs or whims of the user.

We can respond to the request for the name (a string variable) either by typing the string in quotes or by leaving off the quotes, assuming that the string does not contain a comma. The entries "J. Q. DOE" and J. Q. DOE are both correct on the IBM PC. The quotes may be left off because the $ in the input variable request already defines a string. However, if we tried to enter the string J. Q. DOE, MD, we would have to use quotes because the computer will see J. Q. DOE and MD as two separate strings. Remember, if a string does not contain a comma, it may be entered with or without quotes. If the string does contain a comma, use quotes. For example, we would enter "J. Q. DOE, MD" in quotes, as shown.

3.2 Applying the INPUT/Response Sequence

The preceding programs showed how the INPUT command works. Since we did not instruct the computer to do anything with the input, nothing happens when we run the programs. In the following program, Example 3.1, we give the computer something to do with the information. For example, let us calculate the bill for the customer Jane L. Doe, who has bought 5 pounds of nails costing $1.75 per pound. Make sure you have used the CAPS LOCK key so that you enter only capital letters. The computer regards "yes" and "YES" as two different answers. Therefore, the IF statement in line 200 will not perform its function properly if we type our response in lowercase letters ("yes"). Later you will learn to write line 200 so that the program will accept either upper- or lowercase letters.

example 3.1

```
20      INPUT "CUSTOMER NAME ";N$
40      INPUT "NUMBER OF UNITS BOUGHT"; U
60      INPUT "PRICE PER UNIT";P
80      PRINT : PRINT
100     C = U*P
120     PRINT N$;", PLEASE PAY $";C
140     PRINT "THANK YOU."
160     PRINT: PRINT "DO YOU WANT TO PROCESS ANOTHER"
180     PRINT "CUSTOMER? (YES/NO)";
200     INPUT K$ : IF K$ = "YES" THEN 20
30000   END
```

Running this program will produce some action! The input and output are reproduced next, with responses entered after the question mark.

```
CUSTOMER NAME? JANE L. DOE
NUMBER OF UNITS BOUGHT? 5
PRICE PER UNIT? 1.75

JANE L. DOE, PLEASE PAY $ 8.75
THANK YOU

DO YOU WANT TO PROCESS ANOTHER
CUSTOMER? (YES/NO)? NO
```

Much later in this text we learn programming techniques that use such information to manage customer charge accounts, inventories, and so on.

We can use INPUT statements to do some very interesting things because the input feature allows **interactive use** of the computer: We can talk to the computer directly, and it can answer through the PRINT command. Using these features, plus some of the material discussed earlier in this chapter, we can make the computer a teaching tool. For example, we may write a program to teach multiplication to our younger brothers and sisters.

Programs like the one in Example 3.2 are very successful in motivating kids to learn arithmetic. (After you have typed the program into the microcomputer's memory, save it on a diskette and try it out on someone.) This interactive technique is also effective for higher level training.

example 3.2

```
20    PRINT : PRINT "THIS PROGRAM CHECKS YOUR ABILITY TO"
40    PRINT "MULTIPLY TWO NUMBERS. HAVE FUN!"
60    PRINT
80       INPUT "ENTER A VALUE";V1
100      INPUT "ENTER ANOTHER VALUE";V2
120      PRINT: PRINT "OK, SO HOW MUCH IS";V1;"TIMES";V2;
140      INPUT V3
160      V4 = V1*V2: REM ** CALCULATE THE PRODUCT **
180      IF V3 < V4 THEN PRINT "NO, YOUR ANSWER IS TOO SMALL !!!!"
200      IF V3 > V4 THEN PRINT "NO, YOUR ANSWER IS TOO LARGE !!!!"
220      IF V3 = V4 THEN PRINT "YOU ARE RIGHT!!!!!!!!"
240      PRINT : PRINT "WANT TO TRY ANOTHER ONE (YES OR NO)";
260      INPUT Y$
280   IF Y$ = "YES" THEN 60
30000  END
```

Now run this program, comparing the input and output (the information printed out by the computer) to the program lines to understand how the program works. Make sure you type YES or NO in capital letters; the computer does not see "YES" and "yes" as the same response! (Note: You should now be able to work Exercises 1–4 at the end of the chapter.)

3.3 Saving Data

So far, we are losing the information in the program as soon as it is processed. Look at the program in Example 3.3.

example 3.3

```
20    INPUT "ENTER A VALUE";X
30       PRINT "X =";X
40       PRINT "WANT TO ENTER ANOTHER VALUE? (YES/NO)";
60       INPUT Y$
80    IF Y$ = "YES" THEN 20
30000 END
```

Suppose that we run this program and enter a value 12.5; that is, X = 12.5. If we run the program again and enter the value 18.2, X = 12.5 will be replaced by X = 18.2. The first X value has been lost. Of course, if we turn off the computer or decide to run another program, the second value of *X* is also eliminated, since it is not part of the program. This condition prevents the user from saving the information that has been entered.

Using DATA Lines to Save Numeric Information

One way to store information is to use a READ command coupled with a DATA line. The **READ** command, illustrated in program Example 3.4, line 20, causes the computer to start looking for program lines identified as DATA, shown in line 80. Having found the data in the **DATA line,** the computer places the value(s) in its memory and processes these values as though they had been INPUT. With this technique, the information (data) becomes part of the program and is saved. For example, suppose that we want to print three numbers, whose values are 5, 6, and 3:

example 3.4

```
20    READ X
40        PRINT "X =";X
60    GOTO 20
80    DATA 5,6,3
30000   END
```

This program will produce an **OUT OF DATA** error: If we run it, the X values will be listed as follows:

```
X = 5
X = 6
X = 3
Out of DATA in 20
```

Examining the preceding program reveals two items of interest: First, the different X values in the DATA line (80) are separated by commas, although there is no comma after the last value. Second, we get an error message, because once X has been READ three times, there are no additional data, even though the loop created by line 60 tries to keep on reading data.

We can avoid the error message by not using an infinite loop (discussed in Chapter 2). An infinite loop may be eliminated by restricting the number of times a loop is executed. Such a restriction usually involves a counter and an IF statement, as shown in lines 50 and 55 in Example 3.5.

example 3.5

```
20    READ X
40        PRINT "X =";X
50        A = A + 1 : REM ** COUNTER **
55        IF A = 3 THEN 30000
60    GOTO 20
80    DATA 5,6,3
30000   END
```

The program now runs without an error message because it ends its activity when A = 3, that is, after the third—and last—data value has been printed.

A special note is in order at this point. As programs become longer and more complex, too many GOTO statements are likely to cause confusion. We should strive to keep the number of GOTO statements to a minimum. Therefore, Example 3.5 should be modified by changing line 55 to read:

```
55   IF A = 3 THEN END
```

Line 30000 may then be deleted.

Unfortunately, the program in Example 3.5 requires the user to know the number of items in the data line. If data are added or deleted, line 55 must be changed, too. A minor modification seems to be in order: Instead of using a counter, we could use an IF statement and a "fake" value called a **dummy variable.** The dummy is not a real value to be processed, but it will help trigger a response in a program like the one in Example 3.6. (We usually pick a value not likely to be encountered as a "real" value, such as −999.)

example 3.6

```
20    READ X
30        IF X = -999 THEN END
40        PRINT "X =";X
60    GOTO 20
80    DATA 5,6,3,-999
```

Whether a programmer uses this procedure or a counter and an IF statement depends on individual needs or style. Counters are often chosen because they enable users to keep track of where they are in the READ loop.

We are not required to store the data in the example on one line. The program's execution would not be affected if we substituted the DATA lines:

```
80    DATA 5,6
100   DATA 3
120   DATA -999
```

DATA lines can be placed anywhere in the program, but it is good practice to keep the DATA section at the end of the program, using high line numbers. This way it is less likely that data will be eliminated accidentally when program lines are added. The dummy value should be as close to the end of the program as possible, as shown in Example 3.7.

example 3.7

```
20    READ X
30        IF X = -999 THEN END
40        PRINT "X =";X
60    GOTO 20
10000  DATA 3,8,7,10,2,3,4,5
10020  DATA 4,4,3,5,2,4,3
30000  DATA -999
```

Each DATA line may contain more than one value, and we may use more than one DATA line. Values in a DATA line are separated by commas. However, the last DATA value in a DATA line is NOT followed by a comma. Programmers usually put a dummy value by itself to avoid confusing it with other data, generally in the next-to-last line (line 30000).

Assigning Strings

We can assign strings just as easily as we did numeric information. For instance, look at Example 3.8.

example 3.8

```
20    READ N$
40        IF N$ = "LAST NAME" THEN END
60        PRINT "THE NAME IS "; N$
80    GOTO 20
10000  DATA "JANE K. EMERY", "JOHN B. CLURE"
10020  DATA "WILLIAM A. CALVERT", "ELIZABETH D. YORKS"
30000  DATA "LAST NAME"
```

Running this program yields the following results:

```
THE NAME IS JANE K. EMERY
THE NAME IS JOHN B. CLURE
THE NAME IS WILLIAM A. CALVERT
THE NAME IS ELIZABETH D. YORKS
```

Or we can use a counter as we do with numeric values. Example 3.9 illustrates this technique.

example 3.9

```
20    READ N$
40        IF N$ = "LAST NAME" THEN END
50        D = D + 1 : REM ** COUNTER **
60        PRINT "NAME #";D;N$
80    GOTO 20
10000  DATA "JANE K. EMERY","JOHN B. CLURE"
10020  DATA "WILLIAM A. CALVERT","ELIZABETH D. YORKS"
```

The output resulting from this program looks like this:

```
NAME # 1 JANE K. EMERY
NAME # 2 JOHN B. CLURE
NAME # 3 WILLIAM A. CALVERT
NAME # 4 ELIZABETH D. YORKS
```

By running this program we will know how many names are saved in the DATA lines. Again, depending on particular needs, there are always several ways to accomplish a given task. Such flexibility allows programmers to develop individual programming styles and keeps programming interesting.

Finally, string variables may be saved in a data line either in quotes or without quotes. Since the command READ N$ in the preceding program already specifies the string variable N$, the computer will accept the following data line:

```
10000  DATA JANE K. EMERY, JOHN B. CLURE
```

However, since we know that the comma separates the strings from each other, we realize that if we use a name like Jane K. Emery, MD, the computer will see the name as two separate strings. A good rule to follow is this: If a string contains a comma, put the string in quotes.

3.4 Reading More Than One Variable

In the preceding examples, we read only one variable at a time, either a value or a string. For **reading more than one variable,** we list the different variable names after the READ statement, separating each by a comma. For example, we can write:

```
20    READ N$, X
```

Line 20 now reads the string (N$) first and the numeric variable (X) next. Since no additional variables will be read, do not place a comma after X. To read variables Q, A$, P, T$, Q1, B, and K, write line 20 as follows:

```
20    READ Q,A$,P,T$,Q1,B,K
```

Again, since K is the last variable read, do not put a comma after K.

We must write the values in the data line in exactly the same order as the variables in the READ statement. If the same order is not maintained, we will read the wrong values; or, if the program tries to read a numeric value and finds a string, it will produce an error message. It is helpful to write REMarks as reminders of which variables are being read and processed.

Let us now combine what we have learned in this chapter with the lessons of Chapters 1 and 2 to write a program that prints the names and salaries for four people, followed by the sum of the salaries paid and the average salary paid. The program output should look like this:

```
NAME                    SALARY ($)

JOHN Q. ATTAR           1209.85
JANE E. SUTTON          1258.7
WILL D. MARK            1140.25
CYNTHIA A. LI           1208.6

TOTAL SALARIES PAID: $ 4817.4
AVERAGE SALARY PAID: $ 1204.35
```

The program reads a name and a salary value, prints the name and the corresponding value, accumulates the salaries in preparation for the TOTAL SALARIES PAID and the AVERAGE SALARY PAID, reads the next data set, and repeats the process until all data values have been read and processed.

example 3.10

```
20    PRINT: PRINT "NAME","SALARY ($)":PRINT
40    REM ** N$ DEFINES NAMES AND M DEFINES SALARY **
60    P = P+1: REM ** COUNTER                      **
80       READ N$,M
100      IF N$ = "LAST RECORD" THEN 180
120      M1 = M1+M : REM ** SUM THE SALARIES       **
140      PRINT N$,M
160   GOTO 60
180   PRINT:PRINT "TOTAL SALARIES PAID: $";M1
200   N = P-1: REM ** NUMBER OF VALUES PROCESSED   **
220   PRINT "AVERAGE SALARY PAID: $";M1/N
10000  DATA "JOHN Q. ATTAR", 1209.85,"JANE E. SUTTON", 1258.70
10020  DATA "WILL D. MARK", 1140.25,"CYNTHIA A. LI",1208.60
29000  DATA "LAST RECORD",-999
30000  END
```

The program shown in Example 3.10 has a feature based on the earlier discussion of variable initialization. We can, for example, add the following program line:

```
10   M1 = 0: REM ** INITIALIZE SALARY TOTAL **
```

However, as discussed in Chapter 2, the BASIC used by most microcomputers automatically makes undefined numeric variables equal to zero. Therefore, the program works just as well if it is run without line 10. Given that M1 = 0 when line 120 is encountered the first time, M1 = 0 + 1209.85. (The first salary value is 1209.85.) The second time through the GOTO loop, the salary amount is 1258.70, so M1 is recalculated to be M1 = 1209.85 + 1258.70, or M1 = 2468.55. The process continues until the last salary value has been added. The sequence is illustrated as follows, with *P* the counter value in line 60.

```
P = 1      M1 = 0       + 1209.85 = 1209.85
P = 2      M1 = 1209.85 + 1258.70 = 2468.55
P = 3      M1 = 2468.55 + 1140.25 = 3608.80
P = 4      M1 = 3608.80 + 1208.60 = 4817.40
```

The last M1 value is the sum of all the salaries paid to the four people in this example.

Another point of particular interest is found in line 200, where the number of values is defined. The reason for defining the number of values by $N = P - 1$ is simple: We add 1 to the counter (in line 60) each time we execute line 160. Therefore, the value *P* goes to 5 before we encounter the last record. The value

P will always be 1 larger than the number of actual values, so we must subtract 1 to get the right number. We could avoid this problem by deleting line 60, placing the counter in line 110, using N instead of P, and changing line 160 to read GOTO 80. Line 200 can then be deleted. Also, note that we go to line 180 when we encounter the last record, rather than the end. We have, after all, some values to print.

Practice working with READ and DATA statements by solving the problems in Exercise 1. You will also have a chance to use some techniques learned earlier.

3.5 The RESTORE Command

Once the data have been read and processed, we no longer have access to the values in the DATA lines unless the RESTORE command is used. As the name implies, the **RESTORE** command puts the data back so that they can be read again. The use of RESTORE is illustrated in line 100 of Example 3.11.

example 3.11

```
20    READ X
40       IF X = -999 THEN 100
60       PRINT X
80    GOTO 20
100   RESTORE
120   READ X
140      IF X = -999 THEN END
160      PRINT X
180   GOTO 120
10000   DATA 2,4,6
29000   DATA -999
30000   END
```

Failure to use the RESTORE statement in the preceding program example will yield an "out of data" error. (Try running the program without line 100 and changing line 40 to use THEN 120.)

The RESTORE command is particularly useful in many calculation sequences. For example, if we first calculate an average value for a set of numbers, we cannot print the numbers themselves after leaving the GOTO loop. Such a problem is encountered in the next program, Example 3.12, in which an average for a set of three numbers is subtracted from each of the numbers. Without the RESTORE statement in line 140, the output shown below the program would be impossible to obtain.

In addition to the use of the RESTORE statement, the following program demonstrates the use of several important programming features we have encountered before. Note, for example, the blanks (lines 5, 10, 15, 260, and 290) and semicolons (lines 260, 300, and 320) that are used to help space the output. In addition, the use of the counter (line 80), the "flag" that terminates the READ activity (lines 40 and 170), and the REM statements are of special interest. Finally, since the 'S' was used to designate summation in line 60, the 'S' variable must be set back to zero before the symbol is used again (line 150). Failure to include line 150 will cause the program to keep adding the newly restored X values to the original total of 15. Note, incidentally, that the sum of the X values (TOTAL) is equal to the last of the CUMULATIVE SUM OF X values.

example 3.12

```
5      PRINT "                              CUMULATIVE"
10     PRINT "                    X VALUE   SUM OF X      (X-M)"
15     PRINT "                    -------   ----------    -----": PRINT
20     READ X
40        IF X = -999 THEN 120
60        S = S + X: REM ** SUM THE X VALUES                       **
80        N = N + 1: REM ** COUNT THE NUMBER OF X VALUES           **
100    GOTO 20
120    M = S/N: REM ** CALCULATE THE AVERAGE OF THE X VALUES       **
140    RESTORE
150    S = 0: REM ** SET THE SUM OF X BACK TO ZERO                 **
160    READ X
170       IF X = -999 THEN 290
180       S = S + X: REM ** SUM THE X VALUES AGAIN IN ORDER        **
200       REM ** TO PRINT THE CUMULATIVE VALUES                    **
220       X1 = X - M: REM ** SUBTRACT THE AVERAGE FROM X           **
240       S1 = S1 + X1: REM ** SUM THE (X - M) VALUES              **
260       PRINT "                   ";X;"          ";S;"         ";X1
280    GOTO 160
290    PRINT "                        ---                       ---"
300    PRINT: PRINT "TOTAL =====> ";S;" ==============> ";S1
320    PRINT "AVERAGE ===>   ";M
1000   DATA 5,6,4
29000  DATA -999
30000  END

RUN

                              CUMULATIVE
                    X VALUE   SUM OF X      (X-M)
                    -------   ----------    -----

                       5          5           0
                       6         11           1
                       4         15          -1
                      ---                    ---

TOTAL =====>  15   ==============> 0
AVERAGE ===>   5
```

Chapter Review

This chapter introduced two additional ways to enter values and strings into memory: the INPUT command and the READ (DATA) sequence.

The INPUT command enters values or strings directly from the keyboard; the values or strings are not part of the program. The advantages of using the INPUT command include flexibility (the programs do not have to be changed to accommodate different values or strings) and the ability to perform interactive computing. The latter feature is especially desirable when the microcomputer is used as a training tool. The disadvantage of the INPUT command is that the variables are volatile: They are lost when the computer is turned off, when another program is run, and when the same program is rerun.

The READ (DATA) sequence stores numeric values or strings (data) in special DATA lines, which can go anywhere in the program but are best placed at the end, to prevent accidental line replacement when the program is modified. The READ (DATA) procedure is especially useful when relatively large amounts of data are to be used. Since the DATA lines are part of the program, the data are saved for future use. The disadvantage of the READ (DATA) procedure is that the data are part of the program. Therefore, data changes require program modification in the data lines.

Key Terms and Concepts

INPUT
interactive use
READ
DATA line
OUT OF DATA error
dummy variable
reading more than one variable
RESTORE

Common Errors

1. Failure to use sufficient INPUT prompting, thereby causing confusion about the expected response.

Correct:

```
20   INPUT "TYPE YOUR NAME";N$
```

Incorrect:

```
20   INPUT N$
```

2. Forgetting to terminate a READ loop.

Correct:

```
20   READ X$,Q
40       IF X$ =  "XXX" THEN 90
60       S = S + Q: C = C + 1
80   GOTO 20
90   A = S/C
10000 DATA ERASER,259,PENCIL,292
20000 DATA XXX,999
30000 END
```

Incorrect:

```
20   READ X$,Q
40       S = S + Q: C = C + 1
60   GOTO 20
80   A = S/C
10000 DATA ERASER,259,PENCIL,292
30000 END
```

3. Improper mix of READ statements. The variables are read in exactly the same order as they appear in the READ line.

Correct:

```
20    READ A$
40    READ B
60        IF B = -999 THEN 120
80        C = C + 1: S = S + B
100   GOTO 40
120   PRINT "AVERAGE FOR ";A$;
140   PRINT "IS";S/C
10000 DATA J. Q. DOE,78,42,95
29000 DATA -999
30000 END
```

Incorrect:

```
20    READ A$,B
40        IF B = -999 THEN 100
60        C = C + 1: S = S + B
80    GOTO 20
100   PRINT "AVERAGE FOR ";A$;
120   PRINT "IS";S/C
10000 DATA J. Q. DOE,78,42,95
29000 DATA -999
30000 END
```

Exercises

1. Modify the program in Example 3.2 by modifying line 180 and deleting line 200 to produce the following input and output. (Assume that the user has INPUT the values 3 and 6, giving a wrong answer of 20.)

```
ENTER A VALUE? 3
ENTER ANOTHER VALUE? 6

OK, SO HOW MUCH IS 3 TIMES 6? 20
NO, THAT'S WRONG. THE CORRECT ANSWER IS 18

WANT TO TRY ANOTHER ONE? (YES OR NO)? NO
```

2. Now take the program that resulted from the modifications you just made to give the user a choice between additions and multiplications. Naturally, the "heading" produced in lines 20 and 40 will have to be changed to reflect this choice. The input and output look like this:

```
PLEASE SELECT ONE OF THE FOLLOWING:

       1. ADD TWO VALUES
       2. MULTIPLY TWO VALUES

PLEASE SELECT THE OPTION BY
TYPING IN THE SELECTED NUMBER? 1

ENTER A VALUE? 12
ENTER ANOTHER VALUE? 7

OK, SO HOW MUCH IS 12 PLUS 7? 19
YOU ARE RIGHT !!!!!
```

If the user had (incorrectly) answered 20, the output should have been:

```
NO, THAT'S WRONG. THE CORRECT ANSWER IS 19
```

Similar output should be obtained by selecting the multiplication. The input/output combinations would look like this:

```
PLEASE SELECT ONE OF THE FOLLOWING:

       1. ADD TWO VALUES
       2. MULTIPLY TWO VALUES

PLEASE SELECT THE OPTION BY TYPING IN THE SELECTED NUMBER? 2

ENTER A VALUE? 4
ENTER ANOTHER VALUE? 7

OK, SO HOW MUCH IS 4 TIMES 7? 28
YOU ARE RIGHT !!!!!!!!
```

If the program user had answered incorrectly, the computer would respond by printing

```
NO, THAT'S WRONG. THE CORRECT ANSWER IS 28
```

3. Write a program that results in the following input and output: Guess a whole number (integer) between 0 and 10. If the program's user fails to pick a number between 0 and 10, inclusive, the computer should print the message THE NUMBER IS SUPPOSED TO BE BETWEEN 0 AND 10, INCLUSIVE, REMEMBER? A choice outside the range will not be considered to be an appropriate guess, and the computer will not count such a guess if it is made the first time the program is run. Only five guesses are allowed. The computer should end the program after five incorrect guesses by printing:

```
YOU ONLY GET 5 TRIES. THE CORRECT NUMBER IS 3

WHAT'S THE NUMBER? 2
TOO SMALL!!!
WHAT'S THE NUMBER? 5
TOO LARGE!!!
WHAT'S THE NUMBER? 3
RIGHT!!!

IT TOOK YOU 3 TRIES!
```

The program has been started below. You may change the value of *G* each time the game is played.

```
20   G = 3
40   PRINT "GUESS A WHOLE NUMBER (INTEGER) BETWEEN"
60   PRINT "0 AND 10, INCLUSIVE." : PRINT
80   INPUT "WHAT'S THE NUMBER";N
.
.
.
```

4. Suppose your checking account has a current balance of $328.20. You are planning to write five checks. Each time a check is written, the program should calculate a new balance. If you overdraw the account, the program prints the message YOU'RE OVERDRAWN! and terminates. You may INPUT any amounts. A sample input and output follow.

```
OPENING BALANCE IS $ 328.20
WHAT IS THE VALUE OF CHECK #1? 120.15
     NEW BALANCE = $ 208.05
WHAT IS THE VALUE OF CHECK #2? 98.05
     NEW BALANCE = $ 110.00
WHAT IS THE VALUE OF CHECK #3? 153.41
     YOU'RE OVERDRAWN!
```

The program has been started below; go ahead and finish it.

```
20    PRINT : PRINT "OPENING BALANCE IS $";B
40    C = C+1
60    PRINT "WHAT IS THE VALUE OF CHECK #";C;
80    INPUT V
.
.
.
```

5. Suppose you own a computer store. You sell both hardware (computers) and software (programs, books, etc.). During the past 5 weeks you have kept track of sales records in hardware and software. Using READ and DATA statements, write the program that produced the following output. Use dummy values (−999,−999) to terminate the READ portion, a counter to keep track of the number of values processed, and appropriate calculations to compute the total sales.

```
FIVE-WEEK SALES SUMMARY

HARDWARE        SOFTWARE
SALES ($)       SALES ($)
---------       ---------

 10347.20        14379.47
 12966.54        18422.72
 11429.46        16328.19
 14338.77        19422.28
 14390.39        20879.41

HARDWARE TOTAL $ 63472.36
TOTAL SOFTWARE $ 89432.06
```

6. Now modify the program you wrote in Exercise 5 to calculate the average sales of hardware and software. The last four output lines will now read:

```
HARDWARE TOTAL $ 63472.36
AVERAGE HARDWARE $ 12694.472

TOTAL SOFTWARE $ 89432.07
AVERAGE SOFTWARE $ 17886.414
```

7. Suppose you are trying to keep track of weekly sales for several products. You want the product and its sales printed only if the weekly value exceeds $200. This week's data are as follows:

Product Code	Sales ($)
KRT-5	100.85
KT8-2	284.21
CCK-5R	189.43
A-3C-4	202.49
D5-5B/1	93.64

The partially completed program is shown below:

```
.
.
.
80    READ P$,S
100   IF P$ = "LAST RECORD" THEN END
.
.
.
```

After the program has been completed, its output should look like this:

```
PRODUCTS WITH SALES OVER $200
-----------------------------

PRODUCT              SALES($)
-------              --------

KT8-2                 284.21
A-3C-4                202.49
```

8. Using READ and DATA statements, print a picture of the arrow shown below. Remember, we can define anything to be a string and anything—including blanks—may be inserted in the quotes.

```
        *
       ***
      *****
     *******
    *********
       ***
       ***
       ***
       ***
```

9. Now modify the program in Exercise 10 to produce two arrows, side by side. *Hint:* Remember what a semicolon will do after a variable name. Also, make sure you incorporate both leading and trailing blanks in your string definitions. For example, the first asterisk location may be defined as:

```
A1$ = "     *     "
```

The second line of asterisks may be defined as:

```
A2$ = "    ***    "
```

. . . and so on.

The final output should look like this:

```
        *           *
       ***         ***
      *****       *****
     *******     *******
    *********   *********
       ***         ***
       ***         ***
       ***         ***
       ***         ***
```

4

Objectives

- To explore program structure by examining loops created with FOR/NEXT and WHILE/WEND techniques.
- To use the STEP command.
- To use subscripted variables, thereby (temporarily) saving such variables in the computer's RAM.
- To reserve RAM space for subscripted variables by using DIM statements.
- To space output on the CRT by using the LOCATE command or the TAB function.
- To clear the screen with the CLS command.
- To develop a printer/screen option.

PROGRAM STRUCTURE AND I/O CONTROL

One of the strengths of the computer is its ability to perform repetitive tasks, and this ability is dependent on our knowledge of creating loops. While the GOTO procedure may be used to create single loops, using GOTO may cause problems when programs become more complex. Therefore, an alternative FOR/NEXT procedure is introduced in this chapter. Finally, the PC is able to create loops with a WHILE (condition)/WEND procedure. As long as the condition after WHILE is true, the loop statements and procedures are executed until the WEND statement is encountered.

Chapter 4 also introduces the subscripted variable within a loop. Subscripts allow us to save variable values in the computer's memory, thereby making it possible to recall such values when necessary. The recall ability becomes especially important when comparisons must be made, or when the original values in a summation sequence are to be printed after the calculations have been made. Memory space for subscripted variables is reserved with a DIM statement.

As we generate more complex programs with the help of loops and subscripted variables, we will discover a need for better input/output placement on the screen. The screen location may be defined with the help of a TAB function or, alternatively, with a LOCATE command. Producing a more professional-looking output also requires that we clear the screen between program runs, using the clearing command CLS. The prompting at the bottom of the screen may be eliminated by using the command KEY OFF. To turn the prompting on again, we will use KEY ON.

To help position output and to make its presentation more attractive, we should learn to format numbers and strings. We will use the PRINT USING command to achieve this end.

Finally, you will learn to write some program lines that will allow you to send output either to the screen or to the printer.

4.1 Developing Program Structure

GOTO Procedures Reviewed

Thus far, we have learned to create a loop with the help of a GOTO statement. In Example 4.1, we see a simple counting program created by a GOTO statement in line 80. Another (implied) GOTO statement is used (line 60) to terminate the program run when the counter value reaches 3.

example 4.1

```
20  C = C+1 : REM **  COUNTER  **
40      PRINT "THE COUNT IS";C
60      IF C = 3 THEN END
80  GOTO 20
```

Running the program yields the output

```
THE COUNT IS 1
THE COUNT IS 2
THE COUNT IS 3
```

Program Structure and GOTO

Since we use GOTO in our everyday language (go to the store, go to class, etc.), it is not surprising that many programmers adopted GOTO as an intuitively obvious way to create loops or to jump back and forth across program lines. The problem with such an approach is that programs containing many GOTOs can create an incredible logical tangle. Such programs are said to be composed of "spaghetti code." (You'll understand why we use the term *spaghetti code* if you look at a bowl of spaghetti and try visually to separate each strand.) Spaghetti code is likely to help the programmer create errors ("bugs") and those bugs are much harder to find, making corrections ("debugging") more difficult.

Even if a program containing many GOTOs works well, it will be difficult to define. Therefore, it will become more difficult to modify the program, especially if the modifying programmer is not the original programmer. Because programs often "grow" with the demand for those programs, the lack of structure that is partially caused by too many GOTOs is perhaps the best reason to minimize the use of the GOTO command. Therefore, we will examine some alternative ways to create loops.

The FOR/NEXT Loop

The loop created by the GOTO statement in line 80 of the program shown in Example 4.1 can also be created by using a **FOR/NEXT** procedure. The FOR/NEXT loop always starts with the word FOR and is completed with the word NEXT. For instance, the program in Example 4.2 yields the same output as the preceding programs.

example 4.2

```
20   FOR C = 1 TO 3
40      PRINT "THE COUNT IS";C
60   NEXT C
30000   END
```

In this case, the loop is created by lines 20 (FOR) and 60 (NEXT). As you can see, the program's output is identical to the output shown earlier.

GOTO Versus FOR/NEXT

When we examine the GOTO controversy, we will discover that there may be a difference between the demands of program *users* and program *writers.* Although the program writers' task can be done more efficiently by using FOR/NEXT loops, users may find such efficient programs harder to run. For instance, compare the two programs in Example 4.3. Note that the user does not have to know how many X values are to be read when the GOTO procedure is used, whereas the user must respond by typing the value 5 when the FOR/NEXT technique is employed. The program on the right, which requires no prior information on the user's part, is more user-oriented.

example 4.3

```
10 INPUT "NUMBER OF VALUES";N
20 FOR I = 1 TO N
40      READ X
60      PRINT X
80 NEXT I
100 PRINT "THERE WERE";I-1;"VALUES."
1000 DATA 8,4,6,3,9
30000 END


RUN
NUMBER OF VALUES? 5
 8
 4
 6
 3
 9
THERE WERE 5 VALUES.
```

```
20 READ X
40     IF X = -999 THEN 100
60     PRINT X
70     I = I + 1
80 GOTO 20
100 PRINT "THERE WERE";I;"VALUES."
1000 DATA 8,4,6,3,9
29000 DATA -999
30000 END

RUN
 8
 4
 6
 3
 9
THERE WERE 5 VALUES.
```

(Note an important feature in the FOR/NEXT loop. Line 80 actually increments I by one before the program reaches line 100. Therefore, line 100 requires that we use $I-1$ to define the number of values.)

The FOR/NEXT loop is structurally sound. And, in many applications, its use makes the program very flexible. Therefore, you will see the FOR/NEXT loop applied frequently.

STEP Commands

The count in the FOR/NEXT loop automatically increases by 1 each time we complete a pass through the loop in Example 4.3. The user can increase or decrease the size of the jumps by using a **STEP** command (Example 4.4). For instance, if we write:

example 4.4

```
20   FOR C = 0 TO 6 STEP 2
40       PRINT "THE COUNT IS";C
60   NEXT C
30000   END
```

we get the following output:

```
THE COUNT IS 0
THE COUNT IS 2
THE COUNT IS 4
THE COUNT IS 6
```

Programmers are not limited to increasing counts; the count can be run backward by using a negative STEP command. For example, we could write a program like this:

```
20   FOR C = 6 TO 0 STEP -2
40       PRINT "THE COUNT IS";C
60   NEXT C
30000   END
```

This program provides the following output:

```
THE COUNT IS 6
THE COUNT IS 4
THE COUNT IS 2
THE COUNT IS 0
```

The STEP function is not restricted to the use of integers. For example, the following program contains a quite acceptable STEP statement in line 20.

```
20   FOR B = 3.2 TO 2.8 STEP -.1
40       PRINT B
60   NEXT B
30000   END
```

Running this program yields the following output:

```
3.2
3.1
3
2.9
2.8
```

Occasionally you will be surprised by the appearance of strange-looking numbers. For instance, take a look at program Example 4.5, and its output.

example 4.5

```
20 FOR I = 2.5 TO 3.3 STEP .1
40      PRINT I
60 NEXT I

RUN
 2.5
 2.6
 2.7
 2.8
 2.9
 3
 3.1
 3.199999
 3.299999
```

We would have expected the last two output values to be 3.2 and 3.3, respectively, instead of 3.199999 and 3.299999.

What happened? The reason for the unexpected results turns out to be a simple one. The computer uses a so-called binary code system to convert the numbers into a series of electronic on/off switches before it can process these numbers. Since our numbers are based on the decimal system, the binary conversion will not always give a precise equivalent. When the binary code is translated into the decimal value again, the computer may "truncate" (cut off) the decimal conversion, leaving 9s, as shown in Example 4.5. You will learn to correct the problem later in this chapter.

FOR/NEXT Loops: Some Examples

The program in Example 4.6 creates a set of address labels for a person named J. B. Coffe. Note the loop created in lines 40 and 120 with the aid of the FOR/NEXT sequence.

example 4.6

```
20 INPUT "HOW MANY ADDRESS LABELS WOULD YOU LIKE TO PRINT";N
40 FOR I = 1 TO N
60        PRINT "J .B. COFFE"
80        PRINT "200 N. EXECUTIVE PLAZA"
100       PRINT "ANYTOWN, TN 30189"
110       PRINT: PRINT: PRINT
120   NEXT I
30000   END
```

When this program is run, we find that it is very simple to use. The user responds to the question by typing in the number of labels to be printed, and the computer does the rest. Of course, to make labels for another name, the user has to change program lines 60–100. To improve the flexibility of the address labeling program, an INPUT format can be used for the complete address (Example 4.7).

example 4.7

```
20   INPUT "HOW MANY LABELS ";N
40   INPUT "NAME";N$
60   INPUT "STREET AND NUMBER";A$
80   INPUT "CITY, STATE, ZIP CODE";Z$
100   FOR I = 1 TO N
120       PRINT N$:PRINT A$:PRINT Z$:PRINT:PRINT:PRINT
140   NEXT I
30000   END
```

Before running this program, remember that a string is always enclosed in quotes when it is part of the program. However, a response to an INPUT is not part of the program itself. Most microcomputers accept an INPUT string without quotes. Therefore, we may respond to the question generated by line 40 simply by typing a name without using quotes, as follows:

```
NAME? J. Q. DOE
```

The computer expects to receive a single string (N$) in line 40 and assumes that whatever is entered is a single string. There is, unfortunately, a catch to letting the computer make this assumption: If we use a comma in the INPUT string, the computer will ignore whatever comes after the comma. The comma, as it turns out, signals the end of one string and the beginning of another. Therefore, if we respond to line 40 as illustrated:

```
NAME? J. Q. DOE, MD
```

the computer will interpret MD as a second string. However, since line 40 tells the computer to expect only one string (N$), it will respond with an error message. The IBM PC will print

```
REDO FROM START
```

If program line 40 is written as:

```
40   INPUT "NAME, TITLE"; N$,T$
```

the computer accepts, without question, J. Q. Doe, MD as two separate strings (N$ and T$). There is no conflict between the INPUT and the computer's expectations. Of course, since line 40 is not written this way, we must make sure that only one string is entered. If we now remember that anything enclosed by quotes is a string, we can easily overcome the problem by responding to the question NAME? by entering the string in quotes:

```
NAME? "J. Q. DOE, MD"
```

Based on this experience, we can formulate a simple rule: To enter a single string containing one or more commas, that string must be enclosed in quotes. If the string contains no commas, we can enter it without quotes.

The comments in line 40 in the preceding program (Example 4.7) are just as valid with respect to line 80. Again a single string (Z$) is expected, so we respond by enclosing our response in quotes. Let us now run the program, responding as shown. (Remember that the response follows the question mark.)

```
HOW MANY LABELS? 25
NAME? S. K. BETTER
STREET AND NUMBER? 1211 OLIVER STREET
CITY, STATE, ZIP CODE? "ANYTOWN, TN 37132"
```

Note that the last entry is enclosed in quotes because it contains a comma. The output will produce 25 labels, but to save space, only one is reproduced.

```
S. K. BETTER
1211 OLIVER STREET
ANYTOWN, TN 37132
```

Adding Values Inside a Loop

The FOR/NEXT method of creating loops is not limited to printing an output. It may be used whenever a repetitive condition exists. Suppose that we need to add numbers such as 8.0, 5.3, 2.7, and 4.2. The addition sequence demands that we first add 8.0 and 5.3, storing the result as 13.3. Next, we add 2.7 to the stored value 13.3, getting a new stored value of 16.0. Finally, we add 4.2 to 16.0 to get the final result 20.2. We can accomplish this task with the program displayed in Example 4.8. While reading through the program, remember that a numeric variable that has not yet been defined has a value of zero. Therefore, when we go through the loop the first time (I = 1), we find that S = 0 + 8.0, which is, of course, equal to 8.0. In other words, S is now defined to be 8.0. The second time through the loop (I = 2), S = 8.0 + 5.3, which is 13.3, and so on.

example 4.8

```
20     INPUT "HOW MANY VALUES DO YOU WANT TO ADD";N
40     FOR I = 1 TO N
60        PRINT "VALUE";I;
80        INPUT X
100       S = S+X : REM **  SUM THE X VALUES   **
120    NEXT I
140    PRINT:PRINT "THE SUM OF THE";N;"VALUES IS";S
30000  END
```

When we run this program, we will see the following input and output. Remember, we supply the information after the question marks.

```
HOW MANY VALUES DO YOU WANT TO ADD? 4
VALUE 1? 8.0
VALUE 2? 5.3
VALUE 3? 2.7
VALUE 4? 4.2

THE SUM OF THE 4 VALUES IS 20.2
```

Unfortunately, although the program we just finished adds X values well, it also replaces X with another X value as soon as one is input. Therefore, an X value that was entered earlier cannot be retrieved. If we need to use the X values again for other calculations or to print them out after all calculations have been completed, we must find a way to save them. We can save values temporarily by storing them in an *array* (a single row or column). We can then identify each location in the array by using *subscripts*. You will learn to use subscripts in Section 4.2.

Making Loops with WHILE/WEND

The IBM PC and all the PC-compatible microcomputers allow us to create loops with a very powerful technique. The statement WHILE, followed by a condition, causes the loop to be executed as long as the condition after WHILE is true. The loop is terminated when the WEND statement is reached—that is, as soon as the condition is no longer true. The **WHILE/WEND** loop, in other words, works like a FOR/NEXT loop, except that the loop's limits are defined by a condition rather than by the use of a counter.

The WHILE/WEND technique is demonstrated in Example 4.9. Note the following features:

1. The value X is read through −999.

2. As soon as X = −999, the WEND in line 100 will terminate the loop.

3. The counter in line 70 is not reached when X = −999 because line 100 is executed. Therefore, we do not have to use (I − 1) in line 120.

example 4.9

```
10 READ X
20 WHILE X <> -999
70      I = I + 1
75      PRINT X
80      READ X
100 WEND
120 PRINT: PRINT "THERE WERE";I;"DATA VALUES."
1000 DATA 8,4,6,3,9
29000 DATA -999
30000 END
```

```
RUN
 8
 4
 6
 3
 9

THERE WERE 5 DATA VALUES.
```

Any of the looping procedures may be used on strings, too. Note the program in Example 4.10, followed by its output.

example 4.10

```
10 READ X$
20 WHILE X$ <> "XXX"
70      I = I+1
80      PRINT X$
90      READ X$
100 WEND
120 PRINT: PRINT "THERE WERE";I;"NAMES IN THE DATA LINE."
1000 DATA J. J. WHITE, S. B. DALLEEN, K. S. MARTINEZ
29000 DATA XXX
30000 END

RUN
J. J. WHITE
S. B. DALLEEN
K. S. MARTINEZ

THERE WERE 3 NAMES IN THE DATA LINE.
```

Any condition may be used to define the extent of the WHILE/WEND loop. Note that the program in Example 4.11 uses the condition Y to define the loop.

example 4.11

```
120 ANSWER$ = "Y"
140 WHILE ANSWER$ = "Y"
160     PRINT: PRINT "HELLO."
180     INPUT "WANT TO SAY HELLO AGAIN (Y/N)";ANSWER$
200 WEND


HELLO.
WANT TO SAY HELLO AGAIN (Y/N)? Y

HELLO.
WANT TO SAY HELLO AGAIN (Y/N)? N
```

4.2 Subscripts: The Array

Suppose that we want to store a single column of weekly gross incomes for four persons. These stored values are listed in Table 4.1, in a single column and four rows. Let us further suppose that we name these values X and specify that the X value in the first row is called X(1), the X value in the second row is called X(2), and so on. In other words, we keep track of the location of variable X by assigning it an index called a *subscript*. Such an indexed series of values is called an **array.**

Looking at the organization of the weekly incomes shown in Table 4.1, we quickly conclude that

X(I) = 218.63 when I = 1
X(I) = 243.22 when I = 2
X(I) = 228.97 when I = 3
X(I) = 225.08 when I = 4

The subscript (I) is, apparently, a variable between 1 and 4, inclusive. Therefore, we can store the **subscripted variable** X(I) in the computer's memory by writing the program in Example 4.12.

table 4.1
A COLUMN OF FOUR VALUES OF X, REPRESENTING WEEKLY INCOMES FOR FOUR PERSONS

Row Number	Column of X Values	Subscript Value	Subscripted X(I) Values
1	218.63	1	X(1)
2	243.22	2	X(2)
3	228.97	3	X(3)
4	225.08	4	X(4)

example 4.12

```
20   FOR I = 1 TO 4
40        PRINT "ENTER VALUE";I;
60        INPUT X(I)
80   NEXT I
30000   END
```

If we run this program, using the information from Table 4.1, we can expect the following input and output:

```
ENTER VALUE 1? 218.63
ENTER VALUE 2? 243.22
ENTER VALUE 3? 228.97
ENTER VALUE 4? 225.08
```

This program does not do anything other than store the subscripted variable X(I) in the memory. To check whether the program works, ask the computer to print any specific X(I) value after the program is run. If we now type PRINT

X(2) and push/release the ENTER key, the answer 243.22 appears on the CRT. Similarly, if we type PRINT X(1), we get the value 218.63, and so on.

There is, of course, no law that a subscript be labeled I. We can just as easily use a subscript W, writing the program in Example 4.13.

example 4.13

```
20   FOR W = 1 TO 4
40         PRINT "ENTER VALUE";W
60         INPUT X(W)
80   NEXT W
30000   END
```

Running this program yields the same results obtained earlier. The subscript can be any variable, and the input variable does not have to be labeled X. For example, the preceding program could have used P(W), K9(W), or A(W) instead of X(W). The results would be identical in all cases as long as the program is consistent internally. Thus it is easy to identify a subscripted variable by noting that if a variable is followed by a number or a variable name in parentheses, such a variable is a subscripted variable. A variable with a single subscript assumes that the values are stored in a single column or row (an *array*).

Using the preceding definition, we can easily conclude that X2 is not a subscripted variable but X(2) is. Both X2 and X(2) are variables, but only X(2) is subscripted. Similarly, T9 and T9(5) are both variables but only T9(5), which represents a value in position five of the array T9, is a subscripted variable.

Finally, we can read the values into the computer's memory by using data lines. The FOR/NEXT and WHILE/WEND procedures are shown side-by-side in Example 4.14. Note that the WHILE/WEND loop does not require the user (or the programmer!) to know the number of values in the data line. Note also the WHILE/WEND procedure used to move the values into the memory:

1. The subscript value must be initialized before the first value is read (line 100).
2. The first value must be printed (line 140) before the subscript is incremented in line 150. (If the PRINT statement were moved to line 155, only zeros would be printed!)

example 4.14

```
100 INPUT "HOW MANY VALUES";N
120 FOR I = 1 TO N
140       READ X(I)
160       PRINT X(I)
180 NEXT I
10000 DATA 218.63,243.22
10020 DATA 228.97,225.08
30000 END
```

```
100 I = 1: READ X(I)
120 WHILE X(I) <> -999
140       PRINT X(I)
150       I = I + 1
160       READ X(I)
180 WEND
10000 DATA 218.63,243.22
10020 DATA 228.97,225.08
29000 DATA -999
30000 END
```

```
RUN                                   RUN
HOW MANY VALUES? 4                     218.63
 218.63                                243.97
 243.22                                228.97
 228.97                                225.08
 225.08
```

Let us now expand the program shown in Example 4.14 to let it calculate the average weekly income for the information presented in Table 4.1. To illustrate that the subscripted variable has been saved (at least temporarily), let us print the column of X(I) values after leaving the loop defined by lines 120 and 180 (Example 4.15). Since this procedure uses techniques presented in Chapters 1, 2, and 3, you should review the uses of PRINT commands, semicolons as continuation statements, and addition procedures.

example 4.15

```
100 I = 1: READ X(I)
120 WHILE X(I) <> -999
140    S = S + X(I): REM ** SUM THE X(I) VALUES       **
150    I = I + 1: REM ** INCREMENT THE SUBSCRIPT      **
160    READ X(I)
180 WEND
200 N = I - 1: REM ** NUMBER OF DATA VALUES READ      **
220 M = S/N: REM ** AVERAGE VALUE                     **
240 PRINT: PRINT "                    ";
260 PRINT "X(I) VALUES"
280 PRINT "                     -----------": PRINT
300 FOR I = 1 TO N
320     PRINT "                    ";X(I)
340 NEXT I
360 PRINT: PRINT "TOTAL ========>";S
380 PRINT "AVERAGE ======>";M
10000 DATA 218.63,243.22
10020 DATA 228.97,225.08
29000 DATA -999
30000 END
```

```
RUN           X(I) VALUES
              -----------

               218.63
               243.22
               228.97
               225.08

TOTAL ========> 915.9
AVERAGE ======> 228.975
```

The WHILE/WEND loop has all the advantages of the GOTO loop and yet has good structure. Note that the program in Example 4.15 is very flexible: If we change the number of values in the data line, the program will automatically keep track of the changes. Unfortunately, if we try to use more than 10 values, we get an error message (SUBSCRIPT OUT OF RANGE IN 160) because RAM space must be reserved for subscripted variables if more than 10 of them are to be used.

DIM Statements: Dimensioning Numeric Variables

We reserve RAM space by dimensioning the variable. For example, if it is necessary to use as many as 100 X(I) values in the preceding program, we can reserve space for them by writing:

```
5    DIM X(100)
```

Line 5 now states that we will reserve 100 spaces for a single array of X(I) values. As long as there are 100 or fewer values, we will not receive any subscript error messages for variable X(I).

table 4.2
WEEKLY INCOMES FOR FOUR PERSONS

Name	Income/Week
J. P. Ensig	218.63
D. K. Homel	243.22
A. A. Herzg	228.97
P. C. Smith	225.08

Dimensioned and Subscripted Strings

All the comments made concerning dimensioning and subscripting numeric variables are applicable to strings. We can, for example, rewrite the preceding program to include the names of the people whose weekly gross incomes we are examining. If we want to enter and process the information in Table 4.2, we can write the program to include the string variables.

Although there are only four sets of observations here, the programmer should anticipate having to enter a larger number of data sets. We will, therefore, dimension both the name, N$(I), and the income, X(I), in the following program.

When we put multiple **DIM** statements on one line, we will have a choice of writing either:

```
20  DIM N$(100) : DIM X(100)
```

or:

```
20  DIM N$(100), X(100)
```

The program shown in Example 4.16 uses the second alternative.

example 4.16

```
20 DIM N$(100),X(100)
100 I = 1: READ N$(I),X(I)
120 WHILE X(I) <> -999
140      S = S + X(I): REM ** SUM THE X(I) VALUES     **
150      I = I + 1: REM ** INCREMENT THE SUBSCRIPT **
160      READ N$(I),X(I)
180 WEND
200 N = I - 1: REM ** NUMBER OF DATA VALUES READ    **
220 M = S/N: REM ** AVERAGE VALUE                   **
240 PRINT: PRINT"      INCOME SUMMARY": PRINT
260 PRINT "NAME"," INCOME"
280 PRINT "----"," ------": PRINT
300 FOR I = 1 TO N
320      PRINT N$(I),X(I)
340 NEXT I
360 PRINT: PRINT "TOTAL ========>";S
380 PRINT "AVERAGE ======>";M
10000 DATA J. P. ENSIG,218.63,D. K. HOMEL,243.22
10020 DATA A. A. HERZG,228.97,P. C. SMITH,225.08
29000 DATA XXX,-999
30000 END
```

Examine the input and output loops in Example 4.16 carefully. The output loop created by lines 300–340 uses the same index variable (I) as the input loop created in lines 120–180. There is no requirement that we use the same index variable. We are only required to have the same subscript values—that is, values that vary from 1 to 4. Therefore, to generate the same output as that shown, the output loop could have been written as follows:

```
300 FOR L = 1 TO T
320      PRINT N$(L),X(L)
340 NEXT L
```

Note that the subscript is now labeled L, so we also converted N$(I) and X(I) in line 320 to N$(L) and X(L). As you can see, there is some flexibility in managing subscripts and loops. Either version will yield this output:

```
     INCOME SUMMARY

NAME               INCOME
----               ------

J. P. ENSIG        218.63
D. K. HOMEL        243.22
A. A. HERZG        228.97
P. C. SMITH        225.08

TOTAL ========> 915.9
AVERAGE ======> 228.975
```

Clearing the Screen

Our programs run well, but the screen looks overcrowded and "messy" when output shares the screen with portions of previous output or program listings. We can clear the screen by typing

```
CLS
```

(Naturally, you remember to press/release the ENTER key when you want the computer to respond!)

When the **CLS** function is used as part of the program, the program then clears the screen automatically when the program is run. From now on, we will use the CLS as our first program line. Go ahead and modify program Example 4.16 by adding this line:

```
10 CLS: REM ** CLEAR THE SCREEN                            **
```

Be careful where you place the CLS. It is not wise to put CLS right after the output lines, because this would wipe out the output immediately after it appeared on the screen, without giving you time to read it!

Even if you clear the screen with CLS, the prompting at the bottom of the screen remains. If you want to remove the prompting, too, use the command KEY OFF. You can restore the prompting, if desired, by using KEY ON. The complete screen clearing could thus be accomplished by writing line 10 as

```
10 CLS: KEY OFF: REM ** CLEAR THE SCREEN                   **
```

4.3 Controlling Location

So far, we have used blanks, semicolons, or commas to space output across the page. Although these techniques work well, they often impose unacceptable limitations. For one thing, the comma defines print zones; we may not want our output spaced that way. Blanks enclosed in quotes and semicolons increase the programmer's ability to string variable values across a page or screen, but they require us to count spaces each time a procedure is performed. For example, to place a value X(I) in the tenth column, we can type:

```
100   PRINT "         ";X(I)
```

(The discussion assumes that line 100 is part of a loop. Do not try to execute this line by itself.) Line 100 works if there are nine blank spaces between the quotes, since the computer reserves a space before the numeric value. It is far easier to let the computer count the spaces by "tabbing" nine spaces and placing the variable value in the tenth space. Fortunately, we can get this result by using a TAB function.

Using the TAB Function

The TAB function puts the string or the numeric value in a selected location. For example, the statements:

```
10   A$ = "NOTICE"
20   PRINT TAB(10);A$
```

print the word NOTICE in a position starting at the tenth column. [Note that there is no space between TAB and the left-hand parenthesis. Do not use TAB (10), for instance.] Numeric values, however, are treated differently because the computer automatically reserves a sign (− or +) position in front of the number even if the sign is not printed. Therefore, the statements:

```
10   A = 11.8
20   PRINT TAB(10);A
```

cause the number represented by A to be printed in a location starting with the eleventh column, since the tenth TAB location is reserved for the number's sign, even though the sign is not printed. If we change the value of A to A = −11.8, the minus sign (−) will be printed in the tenth column, followed by the number.

We do not, incidentally, need to define the string or the numeric value as we did in line 10 of the preceding examples. The statements:

```
10   A = 11.8
20   PRINT TAB(10);A
30   PRINT TAB(10);11.8
```

would yield the same results. The TAB rules for variable printing are the same as those used in a standard PRINT statement.

Before using any microcomputer's TAB function, it may be wise to run the program in Example 4.17 to see how the TAB locations are defined.

example 4.17

```
10 PRINT "          111111111122222222223"
20 PRINT "1234567890123456789012345678901234567890"
30 PRINT
40 Q = 5.5: A$ = "LOCATION": D = -.012
50 PRINT Q: PRINT A$: PRINT D
55 PRINT
60 PRINT TAB(10);Q;TAB(15);A$;TAB(25);D
```

If this program is run on the IBM PC, we will discover that, as expected, the value 5.5 is printed in location 11 because the microcomputer "saves" a space for the sign (+), even though the sign is not printed. A simple PRINT statement, too, is governed by the same principle. Therefore, the command PRINT Q yields a value of 5.5 starting in location 2. The first print location is, as expected, reserved for the (unprinted) plus (+) sign.

```
RUN
          111111111122222222223
1234567890123456789012345678901234567890
 5.5
LOCATION
-.012

           5.5 LOCATION  -.012
```

When there is more than one variable to print, it is not necessary to repeat the PRINT command. For example, to print the string variable N$(I) in a position starting at the twelfth column and a positive numeric variable X(I) in a location starting with the twenty-fifth position, write:

```
100  PRINT TAB(12);N$(I);TAB(24);X(I)
```

Take care to use semicolons between each variable and the next TAB statement if you want the values printed on the same line. Similarly, we can print the variable Q in a location starting at column 8, K(Q) in a location starting in column 15, P(Q) in a location starting in column 20, and M$(Q) in a location starting in column 25 by typing:

```
100  PRINT TAB(7);Q;TAB(14);K(Q);TAB(19);P(Q);TAB(25);M$(Q)
```

There are, of course, no TAB location differences in using strings. Again, since line 100 contains subscripted variables, we realize that it is part of a loop. Do not try to use this single line to get an output. It only illustrates the placement of a TAB function. Try out the TAB function in the program in Example 4.18.

example 4.18

```
10 CLS: KEY OFF: REM ** CLEAR THE SCREEN                          **
20   PRINT TAB(5);"X VALUE";TAB(22);"CUMULATIVE VALUE"
40   PRINT TAB(5);"-------";TAB(22);"----------------"
60   PRINT
80   FOR I = 1 TO 4
100     READ X(I)
120     S = S + X(I):REM ** SUM THE X VALUES                      **
140     PRINT TAB(6);X(I);TAB(27);S
160  NEXT I
180  PRINT
200  PRINT "THE SUM OF THE X(I) VALUES IS";S
10000  DATA 2.4,2.3,2.5,2.3
30000  END
```

The output resulting from this program is easily predicted. Line 20 prints "X VALUE" starting in column 5 and then prints "cumulative values" starting in column 24. The remaining program lines will fit the same pattern, giving the following results:

```
X VALUE                 CUMULATIVE VALUE
-------                 ----------------

  2.4                        2.4
  2.3                        4.7
  2.5                        7.2
  2.3                        9.5

THE SUM OF THE X(I) VALUES IS 9.5
```

Using the LOCATE Function

In many applications the LOCATE function may be substituted for the TAB function. The LOCATE function works by addressing a row/column location on the screen.

The screen is divided into a grid composed of 25 rows and 80 columns. Therefore each portion of the grid may be located by specifying its row/column intersection. For example,

```
LOCATE 12,15
```

will put us on the screen at row 12, column 15. Similarly, LOCATE 20,38 will address the screen location defined by the intersection of row 20 and column 38. Note the application of the LOCATE function in Example 4.19, followed by its run.

example 4.19

```
100 CLS: KEY OFF: REM ** CLEAR THE SCREEN     **
120 LOCATE 5,15: PRINT "SCREEN CONTROL."
140 LOCATE 7,15: INPUT "ENTER A VALUE ====> ",V
160 LOCATE 10,15
180 PRINT "THE VALUE ENTERED IS";V
1000 END
```

```
              SCREEN CONTROL.

              ENTER A VALUE ====> 34.56


              THE VALUE ENTERED IS 34.56
```

While the LOCATE function is very useful for designing attractive input screens, we must handle it with caution. Unlike the TAB function, LOCATE cannot be directed to the printer. Also, we must make sure that we do not exceed the 25 × 80 screen limitation. If we do, we will see an illegal function error. For example, if we change the LOCATE in line 160 to LOCATE 10,85 and run the program again, we will see this result:

```
              SCREEN CONTROL.

              ENTER A VALUE ====> 23.4
Illegal function call in 160
```

Using LOCATE 26,15 would yield the same error message.

Special note: If you do not use CLS in line 100 of the program in Example 4.19, the material placed on the screen will stay there when you run the program again or if you list the program. It is better to use CLS until you are thoroughly familiar with the use of the LOCATE function.

4.4 Formatting the Output

Another way to control spacing and, even better, to control the output style (format) is to employ the PRINT USING function. Both numeric and string output may be formatted with the help of this function.

Numeric Formatting

IBM PC programmers have access to a **PRINT USING** function, which can be used to format numeric values. Numeric PRINT USING formatting requires the symbol #, which reserves a single space for a numeric character.

The PRINT USING function allows insertion of decimal places and commas in numeric values. For example, PRINT USING "#.##";5 yields the output 5.00, and PRINT USING "#.##";.3 yields the output 0.30. If a number has more decimal places than specified in the PRINT USING function, the output shows the rounded value. Therefore, PRINT USING "#.##";8.736 yields the output 8.74. A number that is larger than that allowed by the PRINT USING function will be printed in its entirety, but it will be preceded by a percent symbol (%) to indicate to the user that an "overflow" has occurred. If the actual value is smaller than allowed by the PRINT USING reservation, the leading "#" causes blank spaces to be printed. For example, PRINT USING "##.#";5.22 produces a blank followed by 5.2.

In addition to reserving space for numeric characters and the decimal point, the PRINT USING function allows the user to insert commas, dollar signs, and asterisks. For example, PRINT USING "$$#,###.##";8375.346 produces the output $8,375.35. Note that two dollar signs were used to request the insertion of the dollar sign. Similarly, two asterisks in combination with a single dollar symbol print two asterisks before the formatted number. In contrast, the use of a single dollar sign fixes the dollar sign in a given location. Note the effect of a single dollar sign in program Example 4.20, line 110.

The use of two dollar signs results in a "floating dollar symbol," so called because the dollar symbol always is positioned right before the first numeric value, regardless of its location. (See line 100, program Example 4.20.) The program in Example 4.20 illustrates the various options.

example 4.20

```
20   A = 1435.786
40   PRINT USING "####.###";A
60   PRINT USING "####.##";A
80   PRINT USING "#,###.##";A
100  PRINT USING "$$#,###,###.##";A
110  PRINT USING "$#,###,###.##";A
120  PRINT USING "**$#,###.##";A
140  PRINT USING "####";A
160  PRINT USING "##.###";A
30000 END

RUN

1435.786
1435.79
1,435.79
```

```
      $1,435.79
$     1,435.79
**$1,435.79
1436
%1435.786
```

The PRINT USING string may be defined before use. For example, if W$ = "##.#", we can get the formatted output by PRINT USING W$;32.78. Similarly, the program shown in Example 4.21 produces the output $4,382.75.

example 4.21

```
20    M$ = "$$#,###.##"
40    Q = 4382.748
60    PRINT USING M$;Q
30000   END
```

It is important to remember that the symbol "#" reserves a space for a number. For example, the string "###.##" reserves three spaces before and two spaces after the decimal place. If the number 5.6 is printed with the aid of this PRINT USING string, the first two reserved spaces are not needed. The computer will, therefore, leave those spaces blank. The second decimal place is not used, either. The computer will insert a zero whenever a reserved decimal place is not used. Therefore, the command:

```
PRINT USING "###.##";5.6
```

will cause the computer to print:

```
  5.60
```

Note the two blanks before the 5. Such blanks are called **leading blanks.** The zero inserted after the 6 is called a **trailing zero.** When printing a number smaller than 1, the computer will insert a zero before the decimal point. Such a zero is called a **leading zero.** Therefore, the command:

```
PRINT USING "###.##";.52
```

will cause the computer to print:

```
  0.52
```

Note the presence of two leading blanks and a leading zero. Using the same string, the values .18, 429, 14.8, and 2 would be printed as:

```
  0.18
429.00
 14.80
  2.00
```

The effects of a PRINT USING string are further illustrated in Example 4.22.

example 4.22

```
20   A = .124: B = 423.6: C = 8034.644: D = 2
40   K$ = "#,###.##"
60   PRINT USING K$;A
80   PRINT USING K$;B
100   PRINT USING K$;C
120   PRINT USING K$;D

RUN
    0.12
  423.60
8,034.64
    2.00
```

The PRINT USING string allows the insertion of positive or negative signs before any numeric value, as demonstrated in Example 4.23, line 40.

example 4.23

```
20   A = .124: B = 423.6: C = 8034.645: D = 2
30   E = -23.453
40   K$ = "+#,###.##"
60   PRINT USING K$;A
80   PRINT USING K$;B
100   PRINT USING K$;C
120   PRINT USING K$;D
140   PRINT USING K$;E

RUN

    +0.12
  +423.60
+8,034.65
    +2.00
   -23.45
```

Even though the output may be rounded by the PRINT USING function, it is important to realize that the PRINT USING function does not permanently change the number's value.

Combining the PRINT USING function with multiple TAB locations sometimes creates problems. For instance, running the program in Example 4.24 will generate the error message:

```
Syntax error in 80
```

Thus we deduce that the PRINT USING function in line 80 may not be followed by a TAB function.

example 4.24

```
20 CLS: KEY OFF: REM ** CLEAR THE SCREEN                    **
40 FOR I = 1 TO 4
60      READ A,B
80      PRINT USING "##,###.##";A; TAB(15);" ";
100     PRINT USING "##,###.##";B
120 NEXT I
10000 DATA 12045.678,123.4,198.2,2.466,14876.1,1023,34,.9
30000 END
```

We do need to print a blank in TAB position 15 to be able to start the next PRINT USING sequence at position 16, but we should place the TAB statement on its own line. Even better, it is quite legal to define a multiple PRINT USING string such as the one shown in line 40 of Example 4.25.

The program modification also includes the use of a WHILE/WEND loop. Note particularly how the WHILE/WEND loop is terminated in line 100.

example 4.25

```
20 CLS: KEY OFF: REM ** CLEAR THE SCREEN                    **
40 A$ = "##,###.##            ##,###.##"
60 READ A,B
100 WHILE A <> -999 AND B <> -999
120     PRINT USING A$;A,B
140     READ A,B
160 WEND
1000 DATA 12045.678,123.4,198.2,2.466,14876.1,1023,34,.9
29000 DATA -999,-999
30000 END
```

```
12,045.68           123.40
   198.20             2.47
14,876.10         1,023.00
    34.00             0.90
```

Not only can we insert blanks in the PRINT USING format string, we can insert messages or characters. Take a look at the program in Example 4.26.

example 4.26

```
20 CLS: KEY OFF: REM ** CLEAR THE SCREEN                    **
40 A$ = "#.# AND UNDER #.#"
60 A = 1: B = 2.9
```

```
80 PRINT USING A$;A,B
100 END
```

```
1.0 AND UNDER 2.9
```

String Formatting

The PRINT USING function can be used to format strings, as well. To perform this function, backward slashes (\) are used. The number of spaces reserved for the string is defined by the number of blanks inside the slashes plus two. In other words, the total amount of space reserved for the string(s) equals the length of the PRINT USING string. Therefore, the total reserved string space provided by two slashes enclosing three blanks is 5. Therefore,

```
PRINT USING "\   \"; "BASICALLY"
```

yields the output BASIC. Such formatting allows programmers to plan output spacing without worrying about overflow. The program in Example 4.27 illustrates the PRINT USING string formatting.

example 4.27

```
20   A$ = "JONQUILL": B$ = "AMES"
30   C$ = "ATWOOD": D$ = "FLEETWOOD"
40   M$ = "\          \"
50   M1$ = "\  \"
60   PRINT USING M$;A$
80   PRINT USING M$;B$
100  PRINT USING M$;C$
120  PRINT USING M$;D$
140  PRINT
160  PRINT USING M1$;A$
180  PRINT USING M1$;B$
200  PRINT USING M1$;C$
220  PRINT USING M1$;D$
30000  END

RUN
JONQUILL
AMES
ATWOOD
FLEETWOOD

JONQ
AMES
ATWO
FLEE
```

Combining Numeric and String Formatting

The technique used in Example 4.25 may be used to combine numeric and string formatting in a single string. The procedure is demonstrated in Example 4.28. Note particularly lines 40 and 100. We want to use a unique condition to end the WHILE/WEND loop. Chances are that no individual has the initials XXX and a classification of XX and a grade point average (GPA) of −999. Actually, a GPA of −999 is not too likely; therefore, line 100 could have been written as WHILE G <> −999 in order to terminate the loop.

example 4.28

```
20 CLS: KEY OFF: REM ** CLEAR THE SCREEN                   **
25 PRINT TAB(4);"INITIALS   CLASS   GPA"
30 PRINT TAB(4);"--------   -----   ----": PRINT
40 A$ = "        \ \       \\      #.##"
60 READ N$,C$,G
100 WHILE N$ <> "XXX" AND C$ <> "XX" AND G <> -999
120     PRINT USING A$,C$,G
140     READ N$,C$,G
160 WEND
1000 DATA ATW,Sr,2.87285,PTR,So,2.78552,JDW,Sr,3.122005
1020 DATA TTA,Fr,1.78925,JWO,Jr,2.98295
29000 DATA XXX,XX,-999
30000 END
```

```
   INITIALS   CLASS   GPA
   --------   -----   ----

      ATW       Sr    2.87
      PTR       So    2.79
      JDW       Sr    3.12
      TTA       Fr    1.79
      JWO       Jr    2.98
```

table 4.3
DECLARING NUMERIC PRECISION

Precision Symbol	Meaning	Example	Number of Significant Decimal Places
%	Integer	A%	None
!	Single precision	A!	6
#	Double precision	A#	16
None	Single precision	A	6

4.5 Defining Numeric Variable Precision

Thus far we have used numeric variable names such as A, K5, and L9 without realizing that such variable names cause the IBM PC to assume **single precision.** A single-precision number is one with up to six decimal places. By contrast, a **double-precision** number has up to 16 decimal places. The IBM PC allows users to define numeric precision by adding a symbol to the variable name, as shown in Table 4.3.

Failure to declare precision level causes the computer to assume single precision. Most of the time we do not need to declare precision levels. However, many scientific calculations are based on exact measurements and require the use of double-precision calculation. Quite clearly, calculations performed at different precision levels yield slightly different answers, as shown in Examples 4.29, 4.30, and 4.31.

example 4.29

```
20   A = 4.937554: B = 14.72779
40   PRINT " A*B =";A*B
60   PRINT TAB(8);"(SINGLE PRECISION)"
30000   END

RUN
A*B  = 72.71925
        (SINGLE PRECISION)
```

example 4.30

```
20   A# = 4.937554: B# = 14.72779
40   PRINT " A*B = ";A#*B#
60   PRINT TAB(8); (DOUBLE PRECISION)"
30000   END

RUN
A*B  = 72.71925609839264
        (DOUBLE PRECISION)
```

example 4.31

```
20   A! = 4.937554: B! = 14.72779
40   PRINT " A*B =";A!*B!
60   PRINT TAB(8);"(SINGLE PRECISION)"
30000   END

RUN
A*B  = 72.71925
        (SINGLE PRECISION)
```

Remember that undeclared numeric values are assumed to be single precision. However, we can declare any variable to be double precision by using **DEFDBL** at the "front end" of the program (Example 4.32). It is not necessary to rewrite the program to redefine the variables. (*Note:* DEFDBL A-Z defines any variable encountered as a double-precision variable. For example, A, A8, B9, Z4, and so on are all double precision after the DEFDBL A-Z command.)

example 4.32

```
10   DEFDBL A-B
20   A = 4.937554: B = 14.72779
40   PRINT " A*B ="; A*B
60   PRINT TAB(8);"(DOUBLE PRECISION)"
30000  END

RUN
A*B = 72.71925609839264
       (DOUBLE PRECISION)
```

4.6 Creating a Screen/Printer Option

Suppose you have written a program whose output is sometimes directed to the screen and sometimes to the printer. If you write the output with PRINT statements, you will have to substitute LPRINT each time you want to receive the output on the printer. Then, if you want the next run to go to the screen, you will have to change all the LPRINT statements to PRINT again. Such a procedure, to say the least, is awkward.

Of course, you could write a program with a screen/printer option as shown in Example 4.33. When the program encounters line 160, it will select either the screen portion of the program, lines 180–340, or the printer portion, lines 1000–1140. Note the END statement in line 360, we do not want to run into the LPRINT lines accidentally. The program is followed by its output.

example 4.33

```
100 CLS: KEY OFF: REM ** CLEAR THE SCREEN                  **
120 LOCATE 5,15
140 INPUT "WOULD YOU LIKE A PRINTED COPY (Y/N)";Y$
150 CLS: REM ** CLEAR THE SCREEN AGAIN                     **
160 IF Y$ = "Y" THEN 1000
180 PRINT "X" VALUE": PRINT "-------": PRINT
200 READ X
220 WHILE X <> -999
240    N = N + 1: REM ** GET THE NUMBER OF VALUES          **
250    S = S + X: REM **  REM ** SUM THE X VALUES          **
260    PRINT USING " ##.#";X
280    READ X
300 WEND
```

```
320 PRINT: PRINT "AVERAGE =";
340 PRINT USING " ##.#";S/N
360 END
1000 LPRINT "X VALUE": LPRINT "-------": LPRINT
1020 READ X
1040 WHILE X <> -999
1060     N = N + 1: REM ** GET THE NUMBER OF X VALUES    **
1070     S = S + X: REM ** SUM THE X VALUES              **
1075     LPRINT USING " ##.#";X
1080     READ X
1100 WEND
1120 LPRINT: LPRINT "AVERAGE =";
1140 LPRINT USING "##.#";S/N
10000 DATA 1.23,3.876,2.9,2,.98,1.238
29000 DATA -999
30000 END
```

```
              WOULD YOU LIKE A PRINTED COPY (Y/N)? N
```

```
X VALUE
-------

  1.2
  3.9
  2.9
  2.0
  1.0
  1.2

AVERAGE = 2.0
```

Clearly, the program in Example 4.33 works well, but it is very inefficient. In effect, we had to write the program twice: Once for the PRINT statements and once for the LPRINT statements.

Fortunately, the IBM PC and its compatibles allow us to perform the screen/printer option very efficiently if the programmer uses a little imagination. The computer's memory contains portions known as **buffers.** We can use these buffers to define the conditions under which the program operates. All we need to do is specify which buffer we want to use and define the operating conditions within that buffer. Your PC may have as many as 15 buffers available, but it is much safer to assume that you can access only 3 on a "minimum" PC.

Note how we define the operating conditions in Example 4.34. We are using buffer number 1 and, within that buffer, we specify the printer (A$ = "LPT1:")

or the screen (A$ = "SCRN:") when we request output. Line 180 tells the computer which buffer to check for output instructions. Finally, each PRINT statement is modified to reflect that it receives its marching orders from buffer number 1. Therefore, we use PRINT #1 whenever we produce output. Note especially that each PRINT statement must be followed by a comma. The comma, in this case, has nothing to do with continuation. Instead, it is an integral part of the PRINT statement. For example, if you want to skip three lines, you would write

```
PRINT #1, : PRINT #1, : PRINT #1,
```

Failure to use the comma will yield a syntax error message. Also, note that the printer width is set in line 200. In this case we have reserved up to 132 characters per line in case we have a printer capable of printing 132 characters per line. Finally, we must remember to CLOSE the buffer we opened in line 180 by typing CLOSE 1 in line 400. But *never* close a buffer until all the printing is done. For example, if you were to write CLOSE 1 in line 350, you would get an error message when line 360 is encountered.

example 4.34

```
100 CLS: KEY OFF: REM ** CLEAR THE SCREEN                        **
120 LOCATE 5,15
140 INPUT "WOULD YOU LIKE A PRINTED COPY (Y/N)";Y$
150 CLS: KEY OFF: REM ** CLEAR THE SCREEN AGAIN                  **
160 IF Y$ = "Y" OR Y$ = "y" THEN A$ = "LPT1:" ELSE A$ = "SCRN:"
180 OPEN A$ FOR OUTPUT AS 1
200 WIDTH #1, 132
220 PRINT #1, "X VALUE": PRINT #1,"-------": PRINT #1,
240 READ X
260 WHILE X <> -999
280     N = N + 1: REM ** GET THE NUMBER OF VALUES               **
300     S = S + X" REM ** SUM THE X VALUES                       **
320     PRINT #1, USING " ##.#";X
330     READ X
340 WEND
360 PRINT #1,: PRINT #1, "AVERAGE";
380 PRINT #1, USING "##.#";S/N
400 CLOSE 1
10000 DATA 1.23,3.876,2.9,2,.98,1.238
29000 DATA -999
30000 END
```

If you run this program, you will get the same output shown for Example 4.33. But this time you did not have to write the program lines twice. The procedure shown in Example 4.34 is highly recommended when you want to give the program user a print option. (*Special note:* We have made sure in line 160 that either a capital Y or a lower case Y will be acceptable.)

A final comment about the screen/printer option is in order at this point: You may use another buffer number. For example, if you want to use buffer number 2, you would write

```
180 OPEN A$ FOR OUTPUT AS 2
```

and you would use PRINT #2 in all the lines containing a PRINT statement. The printer would still be named LPT1: The "1" is part of the printer definition and not a buffer number.

Chapter Review

In this chapter we created loops by using the FOR/NEXT and WHILE/WEND procedures. The count in the FOR/NEXT loop increases by 1 with each pass through the loop, unless a STEP function is used. The STEP function allows either positive or negative steps. The count in the loop changes by the amount specified in the STEP function.

Variables used inside the loop are replaced with each pass through it unless they are subscripted. A subscripted variable uses a tag (subscript) to locate that variable's position in a single row or column (array). The subscript always follows the variable name and is enclosed in parentheses. For example, variable B may be subscripted as B(Q), where Q may have an integer value. The fourth location in the array is defined as Q = 4, so B(Q) = B(4). Subscripted variables are temporarily stored in memory so that their values may be recalled, if necessary. If more than 10 subscripted variable values are to be used, space must be reserved in memory by using a DIM statement. For example, up to 200 B(Q) values can be used if DIM B(200) is specified in the program.

Printed output may be spaced with a TAB function, which allocates the output to the designated TAB location. For example, PRINT TAB(20); A$ starts printing the string variable A$ in column 20. TAB functions may use variable locations. For example, TAB(D) spaces the output to any TAB location for which D is defined. Screen locations may also be defined with the LOCATE function. LOCATE X,Y places screen control at row X and column Y. Up to 25 rows and 80 columns may be addressed.

Output may be formatted with the help of the PRINT USING command. Numeric values are formatted through the # symbol.

```
PRINT USING "#.##";X
```

formats X values for up to two decimal places and one place before the decimal. String values are formatted with a backward slash (\) symbol.

```
PRINT USING "\    \";X$
```

reserves spaces equal to the slashes plus the blanks between the slashes. That is, if you want to reserve 5 spaces, use a slash, 3 blanks, and another slash. Numeric and string formatting may be done in a single string definition:

```
PRINT USING "\    \ ##   #,###.##";N$,X,Y
```

Numeric precision may be declared by using these symbols: % = integer, ! = single precision, and # = double precision. Undeclared variables are assumed to be single precision. Double precision may be declared by using DEFDBL.

A screen/printer option may be introduced into the program by using a buffer. While a PC may have up to 15 buffers, it is better to assume only 3 available buffers on a "minimum" PC. The screen/printer option yields a string that defines either the printer (LPT1:) or the screen (SCRN:) to direct the output location. The PRINT statement must be modified to reflect the buffer used. If buffer number 3 is used, the PRINT statements would all be modified to PRINT #3,. The comma becomes an integral part of the PRINT statement when the buffer is used to define the output device. For example, PRINT #1,: PRINT #1,: PRINT #1, USING "##";A would be used to skip two lines and to print variable A.

Key Terms and Concepts

spaghetti code
FOR/NEXT
WHILE/WEND
STEP
array
subscripted variable
DIM
prompts
CLS
KEY OFF
TAB
LOCATE
format
PRINT USING
leading blank
trailing zero
leading zero
single precision
double precision
DEFDBL
buffer
LPT1:
SCRN:

Common Errors

1. Forgetting that strings containing commas for use with either INPUT or READ statements must be entered in quotes.

```
20   INPUT "ENTER DATE (MONTH,DAY,YEAR)";D$
```

Correct response:

```
"MARCH 28, 1984"
```

Incorrect response:

```
MARCH 28, 1984
```

Failure to use the quotes will cause REDO FROM START error message.

Correct:

```
20   READ D$,A
40      IF D$ = "XXX" THEN END
60      PRINT D$,A
80   GOTO 20
10000   DATA "MARCH 28, 1984",512
10020   DATA "MARCH 29, 1984",506
29000   DATA "XXX",-999
```

Incorrect:

```
20   READ D$,A
40      IF D$ = "XXX" THEN END
60      PRINT D$,A
80   GOTO 20
10000   DATA MARCH 28, 1984,512
10020   DATA MARCH 29, 1984,506
29000   DATA XXX,-999
```

2. Failing to dimension all subscripted variables.

Correct:

```
20   DIM A(20),A1(20)
40   FOR I = 1 TO 20
60      PRINT "ENTER VALUE #";I;
80      INPUT A(I)
100     A1(I) = 2.7128*A(I)
120  NEXT I
```

Incorrect:

```
20   DIM A(20)
40   FOR I = 1 TO 20
60      PRINT "ENTER VALUE #";I;
80      INPUT A(I)
100     A1(I) = 2.7128*A(I)
120  NEXT I
```

3. Failing to read variables and print variables in an appropriate sequence when using a WHILE/WEND loop. (Note the output following each program.)

Correct:

```
100 READ X
120 WHILE X <> -999
140     PRINT USING "#.#";X
160     S = S + X
180     READ X
200 WEND
220 PRINT USING "THE SUM OF THE VALUE IS ##.#";S
10000 DATA 2,3,5.1,4.3
29000 DATA -999
30000 END
```

```
RUN
2.0
3.0
5.1
4.3
THE SUM OF THE VALUES IS 14.4
```

Incorrect: (Note that the first value printed is 0.0. The first value must be read before the WHILE condition!)

```
120 WHILE X <> -999
140     PRINT USING "#.#";X
160     S = S + X
180     READ X
200 WEND
220 PRINT USING "THE SUM OF THE VALUES IS ##.#";S
10000 DATA 2,3,5.1,4.3
29000 DATA -999
30000 END
OK
```

```
RUN
0.0
2.0
3.0
5.1
4.3
THE SUM OF THE VALUES IS 14.4
```

Also Incorrect: (Omitting line 180 means that only the first data value will be read. Therefore, the −999 is never reached and the program keeps printing 2.0 until you interrupt it with Ctrl/Break.)

```
100 READ X
120 WHILE X <> -999
140     PRINT USING "#.#";X
160     S = S + X
200 WEND
220 PRINT USING "THE SUM OF THE VALUES IS ##.#";S
10000 DATA 2,3,5.1,4.3
29000 DATA -999
30000 END
```

```
RUN
2.0
2.0
2.0
2.0
2.0
2.0
2.0
2.0

Break in 140
```

Also Incorrect: (Note the location of the READ statement. The −999 "flag" is included in the PRINT results because the WHILE condition is not encountered until *after* the −999 has been printed. Note also the PRINT using overflow: The value −999 does not fit #.#.)

```
120 WHILE X <> -999
130     READ X
140     PRINT USING "#.#";X
160     S = S + X
200 WEND
220 PRINT USING "THE SUM OF THE VALUES IS ##.#";S
10000 DATA 2,3,5.1,4.3
29000 DATA -999
30000 END
```

```
RUN
2.0
3.0
5.1
4.3
%-999.0
THE SUM OF THE VALUES IS %-984.6
```

4. Failing to initialize subscripts in a WHILE/WEND loop and failing to increment the subscript before the next variable value is read.

Correct:

```
100 DIM X(20)
110 P = 1: READ X(P)
120 WHILE X(P) <> -999
140     PRINT USING "#.#";X(P)
160     S = S + X(P)
180     P = P + 1: READ X(P)
```

```
200 WEND
220 PRINT USING "THE SUM OF THE VALUES IS ##.#";S
10000 DATA 2,3,5.1,4.3
29000 DATA -999
30000 END
```

```
RUN
2.0
3.0
5.1
4.3
THE SUM OF THE VALUES IS 14.4
```

Incorrect: Although the output *appears* to be correct, the failure to increment the subscript in line 180 means that the variable read remains X(1). Each succeeding value merely replaces the previous one; the values are not saved. Note that PRINT X/3) yields 0.

```
100 DIM X(20)
110 P = 1: READ X(P)
120 WHILE X(P) <> -999
140     PRINT USING "#.#";X(P)
160     S = S + X(P)
180     READ X(P)
200 WEND
220 PRINT USING "THE SUM OF THE VALUES IS ##.#";S
10000 DATA 2,3,5.1,4.3
29000 DATA -999
30000 END
```

```
RUN
2.0
3.0
5.1
4.3
THE SUM OF THE VALUES IS 14.4
OK
PRINT X(3)
 0
```

Incorrect: (Note that the subscript remains at 0 because it was never initialized. Therefore, each pass causes the previous X(0) value to be replaced by the next X(0) value. Take a look at the PRINT statements below the program output.)

```
100 DIM X(20)
120 WHILE X(P) <> -999
140     PRINT USING "#.#";X(P)
160     S = S + X(P)
180     READ X(P)
200 WEND
220 PRINT USING "THE SUM OF THE VALUES IS ##.#";S
10000 DATA 2,3,5.1,4.3
29000 DATA -999
30000 END



RUN
0.0
2.0
3.0
5.1
4.3
THE SUM OF THE VALUES IS 14.4

PRINT X(1)
 0
PRINT X(2)
 0
PRINT X(3)
 0
PRINT X(4)
 0
PRINT X(0)
-999
```

5. Failing to print variables in the same order as shown in the PRINT USING statement.

Correct:

```
100 N$ = "\         \    #.###     ##.###"
120 READ A$,B,C
140 PRINT USING N$;A$,B,C
10000 DATA AUTOMOTIVE ENGINEERING,.548,12.539
30000 END
Ok

RUN
AUTOMOTIV    0.548    12.539
```

Incorrect:

```
100 N$ = "\          \    #.###     ##.###"
120 READ A$,B,C
140 PRINT USING N$;B,A$,C
10000 DATA AUTOMOTIVE ENGINEERING,.548,12.539
30000 END
OK

RUN
Type mismatch in 140
```

6. Not making sure that TAB functions cannot become negative, or that TAB functions cannot exceed the screen or printer limits.

Correct:

```
20   FOR I = 1 TO 4
40        READ X
60        IF X<1 OR X>80 THEN 100
80        PRINT TAB(X);"*"
100  NEXT I
10000  DATA 231,-8,512,14
30000  END
```

Incorrect:

```
20   FOR I = 1 TO 4
40        READ X
60        PRINT TAB(X);"*"
80   NEXT I
10000  DATA 231,-8,512,14
30000  END
```

7. Not making sure that the LOCATE values are within the 25-row and 80-column limits.

Correct:

```
                                  CENTER SCREEN
OK

LIST
100 CLS: KEY OFF
120 LOCATE 12,35: PRINT "CENTER SCREEN"
30000 END
```

Incorrect:

```
Illegal function call in 120
OK

LIST
100 CLS: KEY OFF
120 LOCATE 26,35: PRINT "CENTER SCREEN"
30000 END
```

8. Using invalid subscripts. A subscript must be a positive integer.

Correct:

```
20   FOR I = .1 TO 1.8 STEP .1
40        C = C + 1
60        X(C) = I
80   NEXT I
```

Incorrect:

```
20   FOR I = .1 TO 1.8 STEP .1
40        X(I) = I
60   NEXT I
```

9. Improper user prompting. INPUT statements are not allowed directly after a semicolon, and prompts contained in INPUT statements may not contain variables.

Correct:

```
20   FOR J = 1 TO 5
40        PRINT "VALUE #";J;
60        INPUT A
80   NEXT J
```

Incorrect:

```
20   FOR J = 1 TO 5
40        INPUT "VALUE #";J;A
60   NEXT J
```

Also Incorrect:

```
20   FOR J = 1 TO 5
40        PRINT "VALUE #";J;INPUT A
60   NEXT J
```

Exercises

1. Using a loop based on a WHILE/WEND approach and spacing the output with a TAB function, write a program that produces the following input and output. There should be two spaces between the column headings.

```
         DATA SUMMARY
-------------------------

VALUE #  X VALUE  Y VALUE
-------  -------  -------

   1       28.8      14
   2       35.7      12
   3       42.8      14
   4       55.1      19

TOTAL     162.4      59
```

The program that produced this output has been started; go ahead and finish it.

```
100   CLS: KEY OFF: REM ** CLEAR THE SCREEN                              **
120   PRINT: PRINT: PRINT TAB(8);"DATA SUMMARY"
140   PRINT "-------------------------":PRINT
160   PRINT "VALUE #"; TAB(10); "X VALUE"; TAB(19); "Y VALUE"
180   PRINT "-------"; TAB(10); "-------"; TAB(19); "-------"
200   PRINT: READ X,Y
220   WHILE X <> -999 AND Y <> -999
 .
 .
 .
10000   DATA 28.8,14,35.7,12,42.8,14,55.1,19
29000   DATA -999,-999
30000   END
```

2. Now modify the program in Exercise 1 to produce the following output. Make sure you use a PRINT USING format.

```
         DATA SUMMARY
-------------------------------

VALUE #  X VALUE  Y VALUE   X+Y
-------  -------  -------  ----

   1       28.8      14    42.8
   2       35.7      12    47.7
   3       42.8      14    56.8
   4       55.1      19    74.1

TOTAL     162.4      59
```

3. Write a program that will compute the percentage of change in value over the preceding year. For example, if the first year's sales for a company are $85,000 and the second year's sales are $87,000, the change is $2,000. The percentage of change will be 2,000/85,000 times 100. Using subscripted values, the program should produce an output like the one displayed. (Use a buffer-based screen/printer option!) The option question should be placed on the screen with a LOCATE command.

```
WOULD YOU LIKE A PRINTED COPY (Y/N)? Y


                SALES SUMMARY
-------------------------------------------

YEAR    SALES,$     DOLLAR CHANGE    % CHANGE
----    -------     -------------    --------

1979     85,000               --           --
1980     87,000           +2,000        +2.35
1981     93,000           +6,000        +6.90
1982     91,000           -2,000        -2.15
```

The program should reserve space for up to 20 sales values. Remember, the percentage of change is always measured against the preceding year. The first value (1979 sales) does not have a percentage change value because we do not know the 1978 sales.

4. Suppose you have put your money into a savings account that pays 10 percent annually. Write a program that will produce the following output from the given input. **Note:** You leave the money invested, so the interest is computed on the total amount each year. For example, if you invest $100 the first year you will earn $10 at the end of the first year because 10 percent of $100 is $10. During the second year you have $110 in the savings account, so you will earn 10 percent of $110, or $11. You start the third year with $121, and so on. Limit the output to 8 years. Two sample runs are shown. (*Note:* Use buffer number 2 for your screen/printer option.)

```
WHAT IS THE INTEREST %? 10
WHAT IS THE STARTING BALANCE? 100
NUMBER OF YEARS? 3

WOULD YOU LIKE A PRINTED COPY (Y/N)? N

  SAVINGS ACCOUNT SUMMARY
---------------------------

                 END-OF-YEAR
YEAR  AMOUNT,$     INTEREST
----  --------   -----------

  1     100.00       10.00
  2     110.00       11.00
  3     121.00       12.10
```

```
WHAT IS THE INTEREST %? 13.25
WHAT IS THE STARTING BALANCE? 5000
NUMBER OF YEARS? 5

WOULD YOU LIKE A PRINTED COPY (Y/N)? N

  SAVINGS ACCOUNT SUMMARY
---------------------------

                END-OF-YEAR
YEAR  AMOUNT,$    INTEREST
----  --------  -----------

  1   5,000.00      662.50
  2   5,662.50      750.28
  3   6,412.78      849.69
  4   7,262.47      962.28
  5   8,224.75    1,089.78
```

5. Now modify the program in Exercise 4 to include the interest accumulation. The output should look like this:

```
WHAT IS THE INTEREST %? 12.25
WHAT IS THE STARTING BALANCE? 8000
NUMBER OF YEARS? 4

WOULD YOU LIKE A PRINTED COPY (Y/N)? N

        SAVINGS ACCOUNT SUMMARY
---------------------------------------

                END-OF-YEAR  CUMULATIVE
YEAR  AMOUNT,$    INTEREST    INTEREST
----  --------  -----------  ----------

  1   8,000.00     980.00       980.00
  2   8,980.00   1,100.05     2,080.05
  3  10,080.05   1,234.81     3,314.86
  4  11,314.86   1,386.07     4,700.93
```

6. What would the output for the following program look like?

```
20   FOR I = 1 TO 5
40       PRINT TAB(I);"*"
60   NEXT I
30000 END
```

   Run this short program. How do the results compare to your prediction?

7. How will the output in Exercise 6 change if we modify program line 40 to read:

```
40   PRINT TAB(2*I);"*"
```

8. What will happen if we modify the program in Exercise 6 by inserting:

```
40   PRINT TAB(I*I);"*"
```

9. What picture would result from the running of the following program?

```
20   PRINT TAB(20);"*"
40   FOR I = 1 TO 8
60       PRINT TAB(20 - I);"*";TAB(20 + I);"*"
80   NEXT I
100  PRINT TAB(11);"*******************"
30000 END
```

5

Objectives

- To write programs that use nested loops.
- To learn to organize numerical data.
- To define and illustrate the rules of mathematical precedence.
- To apply the rules of mathematical precedence to a variety of practical applications.

NESTED LOOPS AND THEIR APPLICATIONS

Chapter 4 discussed creating loops by using the GOTO, FOR/NEXT, and WHILE/WEND procedures to read data and/or to print output. We should, therefore, understand how loops work at this point.

This chapter builds on the simple FOR/NEXT loop to create nested loops. These loops within loops form the basis of much of our future programming activity. Nested loops are used in this chapter to format output, to organize information into frequency distributions, and to sort values into ascending or descending order. Quite aside from the numerous programming applications for nested loops, writing such loops emphasizes generally useful programming techniques.

Finally, as our applications programming ability improves, we must be able to work with more complex mathematical equations. Therefore, this chapter contains a brief section on mathematical procedures.

5.1 Looking at Nested Loops

A **nested loop** is defined as a loop within a loop. (Reread Chapter 4 to review loops, if necessary.) The simplest nested loop is composed of an outer loop (lines 100 and 200 in the program in Example 5.1) and an inner loop (lines 140 and 180).

example 5.1

```
100 FOR J = 1 TO 2
120     PRINT "OUTER LOOP, J =";J
140     FOR C = 1 TO 3
160         PRINT TAB(5);"INNER LOOP, C =";C
180     NEXT C
200 NEXT J
30000 END
```

If you use the WHILE/WEND technique, the value of I must be reset to 1 before each execution of the inner loop. The program would then look like this:

```
100 J = 1
120 WHILE J <= 1
140     PRINT "OUTER LOOP, J =";J
160     C = 1
180     WHILE C <= 3
200         PRINT TAB(5);"INNER LOOP, C =";C
220         C = C + 1
240     WEND
260     J = J + 1
280 WEND
30000 END
```

Either program version is structurally sound. However, the WHILE/WEND technique has the advantage of conforming to the loop structure of other high-level languages and the newer versions of BASIC.

Whatever version you prefer, the nested looping procedure works as follows:

1. The outer loop starts at a value J = 1 and prints OUTER LOOP.

2. The inner loop is completed for I = 1 TO 3; that is, the message INNER LOOP is printed three times.

3. Having completed the inner loop, we return to J = 2 for the outer loop and repeat step 2.

4. Since J = 2 is the highest outer loop value allowed, we now exit the outer loop to END the program.

In short, running the program yields the following output:

```
OUTER LOOP, J = 1
     INNER LOOP, I = 1
     INNER LOOP, I = 2
     INNER LOOP, I = 3
OUTER LOOP, J = 2
     INNER LOOP, I = 1
     INNER LOOP, I = 2
     INNER LOOP, I = 3
```

All nested loops work the same way. The inner loop is always completed for a specific outer loop condition, after which control is returned to the outer loop.

The only requirement for nested looping is that the loops do not cross. For example, Table 5.1A shows a proper nested loop; Table 5.1B shows incorrect form (because the loops cross).

table 5.1
AN ILLUSTRATION OF NESTED LOOPING PROCEDURES

A: Correct Looping	B: Incorrect Looping
20 FOR J=1 TO 2	20 FOR J=1 TO 2
40 FOR I=1 TO 3	40 FOR I=1 TO 3
...	...
100 NEXT I	100 NEXT J
120 NEXT J	120 NEXT I

There is no practical limit to the number of nested loops we can create, as long as the loops do not cross. For example, both the sets of nested loops in Table 5.2 are appropriate, even though they perform different functions.

To prevent errors in nested loops, we must be able to see their structure; this is easily done when the loops are properly indented. Such indentations are procedures incorporated in **structured programming,** a programming style in which the program's structure can easily be examined. So, to restate the advice given in Chapter 4, indent those loops!

table 5.2
ILLUSTRATIONS OF MULTIPLE NESTED LOOPS

```
20  FOR J=1 TO 3
40    FOR I=1 TO 2
60      FOR Q=1 TO 5
        ...
200     NEXT Q
220   NEXT I
240 NEXT J
```

```
20  FOR J=1 TO 3
40    FOR I=1 TO 2
      ...
100   NEXT I
120   FOR Q=1 TO 5
             ...
200   NEXT Q
220 NEXT J
```

Generating Patterns

We have seen the use of the semicolon as a continuation symbol many times. For instance, try running either version of the program Example. 5.2:

example 5.2

```
(FOR/NEXT version)

20  FOR I = 1 TO 4
40      PRINT "*"
60  NEXT I
```

```
(WHILE/WEND version)

20 I = 1
30 WHILE I <= 4
40      PRINT "*"
60      I = I + 1
80  WEND
```

yields an output of four asterisks as follows:

```
*
*
*
*
```

However, if we write a semicolon at the end of line 40:

```
40  PRINT "*";
```

the output becomes:

```
****
```

because the semicolon in line 40 represents a continuation statement. We can make use of this property to plot charts by using a nested loop. However, program Example 5.3 does not print the expected output of four bars.

example 5.3

```
(FOR/NEXT version)

20  FOR I = 1 TO 4
40    FOR J = 1 TO I
60      PRINT "*";
80    NEXT J
100 NEXT I
```

```
(WHILE/WEND version)

20   I = 1
40   WHILE I <= 4
60       J = 1
80       WHILE J <= I
100          PRINT "*";:J = J + 1
140      WEND:I = I + 1
180  WEND
```

In fact, the output for either program version looks like this:

```
**********
```

This result is not very surprising. The semicolon is a continuation statement, after all. Printing a "bar chart" requires the use of a PRINT statement to stop the continuation. By inserting a line:

```
150  PRINT
```

we can get the expected output:

```
*
**
***
****
```

The PRINT statement in line 90 terminates the continuation statement in line 60.

The preceding procedure can be used to develop a set of bars composed of asterisks to be printed for different values of a variable, F(I). Each asterisk bar represents an F(I) value. For instance, if F(I) = 4, a bar of four asterisks is printed. The program that can perform this function is shown in Example 5.4.

example 5.4

```
(FOR/NEXT version)

20   DIM F(20)
40   FOR I = 1 TO 5
60        READ F(I)
80   NEXT I
100  REM ** NOW PRINT THE 'BARS' **
120  FOR I = 1 TO 5
140       FOR J = 1 TO F(I)
160            PRINT "*";
180       NEXT J
200     PRINT
220  NEXT I
10000 DATA 2,5,9,4,1
30000 END
```

```
(WHILE/WEND version)

20   DIM F(20): I = 1
40   READ F(I)
60   WHILE F(I) <> -999
80      I = I + 1:READ F(I)
120  WEND
140  N = I - 1: I = 1
160  WHILE I <= N
180     J = 1
200     WHILE J <= F(I)
220        PRINT "*";:J = J + 1
260     WEND
280     PRINT: I = I + 1
320  WEND
10000 DATA 2,5,9,4,1
29999 DATA -999
30000 END
```

Many programmers use the WHILE/WEND loop to read the data into the computer's memory and then use the FOR/NEXT LOOP to print the results. The advantage of that approach is that we can let the computer keep track of the number of values read (N = I − 1 in line 140) and then we can start the FOR/NEXT loop by writing FOR I = 1 TO N to print the asterisks. We will use this procedure in many of the following programs.

As expected, either version of the program prints the following output:

```
**
*****
*********
****
*
```

A minor modification in the program may be accomplished by inserting this line:

```
(FOR/NEXT version)

130     PRINT TAB(5);"+";
```

```
(WHILE/WEND version)

190     PRINT TAB(5);"+";
```

The modification then prints the asterisks as shown next:

```
+**
+*****
+*********
+****
+*
```

Given this newfound "printer graphics" ability, we can begin to write programs that develop frequency patterns from information (data). Such patterns are often used to develop understanding of the general characteristics of collected data.

5.2 Organizing Numeric Information

One of the important functions that microcomputers perform involves the organization of information. Ours is the information age: Biologists collect information (data) on wildlife population density and movement; business people collect financial and marketing data; engineers develop data on machinery and industrial processes; farmers need data on crop yields and fertilizer effects; teachers develop data on their students' performance, and so on. The list of data-based applications and the professionals using them is almost endless.

However information is processed, the first task is to organize it. The most common approach to data organization is to create a **frequency distribution,** a tally of the number of times each value or group of values occurs. The pattern displayed by a frequency distribution often provides important clues to the meaning of the data on which the frequency distribution is based. Therefore, it is important to know how to write programs to create frequency distributions. Two approaches are discussed in the sections that follow.

Writing a Simple Frequency Distribution Program

Suppose a teacher gives an examination. Quite naturally, the examination results are important to that teacher. How many students receive which grades? What is the class average? These and other questions may be answered easily by using the program presented in Example 5.5, which contains some important features we should examine carefully:

First, the program allows us to use up to 200 grades—DIM X(200)—in line 40. Those grades may be organized into 10 class intervals ranging from '0 TO 10' for the first interval to '90 TO 100' for the last interval. Since the upper limit of the interval we just defined is not inclusive, each class interval is of size 10. Therefore, line 560 uses STEP 10, and line 620 adds 10 to create the upper limit for each class. Remember, the upper limit is *not* inclusive. For example, the value 10 would be put into an interval '10 TO 20' rather than in the interval '0 TO 10'.

Second, given that the upper limit of each interval is not inclusive, note how we decide which value is to be put into which interval in line 760. We add 1 to the frequency count each time a value falls inside a particular interval. Since line 760 involves a very long statement, in an indented loop we used the right arrow key (located on the numeric pad on the keyboard) to move a portion of the line to the next line, without changing line numbers. The 'uninterrupted' line would read:

```
760 IF X(I) >= L1(J) AND X(I) < U1(J) THEN F(J) = F(J)+1
```

Third, note that line 560 steps B to 100 because the upper limit in line 620 adds 10 to B, thereby making the upper limit of the last class 100 + 10 = 110. This last class is added to enable us to handle a grade of 100.

example 5.5

```
20 CLS: KEY OFF: REM ** CLEAR THE SCREEN                         **
40 DIM F(11), L1(11), U1(11), X(200)
60 N = 1:  REM ** INITIALIZE SUBSCRIPT VALUE                     **
80 READ X(N)
100 WHILE X(N) <> -999
140       S = S + X(N): REM ** SUM THE X(N) VALUES               **
160       N = N + 1: REM ** ADD 1 TO SUBSCRIPT COUNTER           **
170       READ X(N)
180 WEND
190 N = N - 1: REM ** NUMBER OF VALUES                           **
200 PRINT: PRINT
220 PRINT TAB(3);"GRADE"
240 PRINT TAB(3);"RANGE"; TAB(18);"FREQUENCY PATTERN";
260 PRINT TAB(44);"NUMBER"
280 PRINT "----------"; TAB(12);"-----------------------------";
300 PRINT TAB(44);"------";: PRINT
500 REM
520 REM ** CREATE THE INTERVALS                                  **
540 REM
560 FOR B = 0 TO 100 STEP 10
580      D = D + 1: REM ** INTERVAL SUBSCRIPT                    **
600      L1(D) = B: REM ** LOWER INTERVAL LIMIT                  **
```

```
620     U1(D) = B + 10: REM ** UPPER INTERVAL LIMIT           **
640 NEXT B
660 REM
680 REM ** CREATE FREQUENCY DISTRIBUTION                      **
700 REM
720 FOR I = 1 TO N
740     FOR J = 1 TO D
760         IF X(I) >= L1(J) AND X(I) < U1(J)
            THEN F(J) = F(J) + 1
780     NEXT J
800 NEXT I
820 REM
840 REM ** PLOT FREQUENCY DISTRIBUTION                        **
860 REM
870 A$ = "### TO ###"
880 FOR I = 1 TO D
900     PRINT USING A$;(I-1)*10,I*10;
980     PRINT TAB(12);"+";
1000        FOR J = 1 TO F(I)
1040            PRINT "*";
1060        NEXT J
1080    PRINT TAB(45);"  ";
1090    PRINT USING "##";F(I)
1100 NEXT I
1120 PRINT TAB(45);"---": PRINT: PRINT "CLASS AVERAGE IS";
1140 PRINT USING "###.##";S/N;
1160 PRINT TAB(38);"TOTAL   ";
1180 PRINT USING "###";N
10000 DATA 73,52,87,48,65,66,73,75,88,63,31,100,68,79,72,75
10020 DATA 77,76,51,98,67,68,71,79,60,72,78,58,73,81,94,66
10030 DATA 72,23,79,66,69,75,43,78,62,75,67,87,71,87,76,77
10040 DATA 83,95,58,76,78,71,59,74,78,75,92,51
29000 DATA -999
30000 END

RUN
```

Don't become impatient when you try to run this program. It will take the computer a few seconds to organize all the values.

```
 GRADE
 RANGE            FREQUENCY PATTERN            NUMBER
---------- ----------------------------------  ------

  0 TO  10 +                                      0
 10 TO  20 +                                      0
 20 TO  30 +*                                     1
 30 TO  40 +*                                     1
 40 TO  50 +**                                    2
 50 TO  60 +******                                6
 60 TO  70 +************                         12
 70 TO  80 +***************************          27
 80 TO  90 +******                                6
 90 TO 100 +****                                  4
100 TO 110 +*                                     1
                                                ---

CLASS AVERAGE IS 71.35                   TOTAL   60
```

Finding High and Low Values

You may have heard the obvious absurdity that if you stick one hand in a bucket of ice water and the other in a bucket of boiling water, on the average the hands will be comfortable. (Please don't try this!) This extreme illustration demonstrates that differences between the values from which averages are calculated are important, too. A crude, yet effective, measure of observed differences (variability) between values is the range. The range is defined as the difference between the largest and smallest values. Finding the **high and low values** is, fortunately, fairly simple. For example, what would happen if we inserted the following lines into the program shown in Example 5.5?

```
30   H = -999E20: L = 999E20
150   IF X(N) < L THEN L = X(N)
155   IF X(N) > H THEN H = X(N)
```

Going back to the data in Example 5.5, line 10000, we find that the first value is X = 73. If we now look at line 170, we note that 73 is smaller than L, which is defined to be 999E20. (Remember the scientific notation? E20 stands for 10 raised to the twentieth power, so 999E20 is a very large number.) To make sure that the first value read is smaller than L, we arbitrarily defined L to be a very large number. Therefore, during the first pass through the loop, L = X(1) = 73. When we get to line 180, X(N) is, of course, still 73. Since 73 is greater than the −999E20 value assigned to H in line 30, H is redefined to be 73 in line 150. At this point, both H and L are 73.

During the second pass through the loop, X(N) = 52. This time, we see that 52 "is less than" 73, so L is redefined to be 52 in line 170. The low value is, at this point, 52. When line 180 is encountered, 52 is not greater than 73, so H keeps its value of 73. The high value is, at this point, 73.

During the third pass through the loop, X(N) = 87. Since 87 is not less than 52, L keeps its value of 52 in line 170. The low value is, so far, still 52. However, 87 is greater than 73, which was the last defined value for H. Therefore, line 180 redefines H as 87. The high value is, so far, equal to 87. The process of comparison and replacement continues until all X(N) values have been read. If we now add the following lines to the program (Example 5.5),

```
1200   PRINT "LOWEST GRADE IS   ";
1220   PRINT USING "###";L
1240   PRINT "HIGHEST GRADE IS ";
1260   PRINT USING "###";H
```

we should get the following output when we run the modified program.

```
   GRADE
   RANGE            FREQUENCY PATTERN                NUMBER
---------- ------------------------------           ------
   0 TO  10   +                                         0
  10 TO  20   +                                         0
  20 TO  30   +*                                        1
  30 TO  40   +*                                        1
  40 TO  50   +**                                       2
  50 TO  60   +******                                   6
  60 TO  70   +************                            12
  70 TO  80   +***************************             27
  80 TO  90   +******                                   6
  90 TO 100   +****                                     4
 100 TO 110   +*                                        1
                                                      ---

CLASS AVERAGE IS  71.35                       TOTAL    60
LOWEST GRADE IS   23
HIGHEST GRADE IS 100
```

We will have to be careful about placing the new lines 150 and 155. For example, if we had used line numbers 170 and 175, instead, the lowest and highest grades would have been incorrect because the subscript would have already been changed in line 160.

5.3 Improving Program Flexibility

The program in Example 5.5 can be made even more flexible. If, for example, it is modified by adding the lines in the following sequence, any data values can be used.

```
22   INPUT "STARTING VALUE FOR 1ST INTERVAL";V1
24   INPUT "INTERVAL SIZE";V2
```

Lines 560 and 620 are then changed to read:

```
560   FOR B = V1 TO H STEP V2
620         U1(D) = B+V2
```

You should begin to start thinking in terms of designing programs that have enough flexibility for a wide variety of applications.

Using Logarithms: Sturgess's Rule

Thus far, we have arbitrarily selected the number of intervals into which to tally the values. However, the number of intervals that creates the most significant patterns is given by **Sturgess's rule:**

```
K = 1 + 3.3*LOG(N)
```

To be able to use Sturgess's rule, the programmer needs to know about **logarithms,** or logs. A log is the exponent of a number that tells the power to which that number (the base) is raised to produce a given number. Many people are used to logs to the base 10, sometimes written log(base 10). Thus, the log(base 10) of the value 100 is 2, since the base 10 squared (i.e., 10^2, or 10^2) is 100. Similarly, the log of the value 1000 is 3, since 10^3 (= 10^3) = 1000, and so on.

Most microcomputers, however, use natural logarithms, which are based (approximately) on 2.718282. For example, if we type PRINT LOG(100), we get the value 4.60517019 because 2.718282^4.60517019 = 100.

Although the natural log is common in science and engineering, business applications often use the log to the base 10. We can convert the natural log to the "base 10" log by dividing the natural log of a number by the natural log of 10. One word of caution: You cannot find the log of a negative number. For example, to calculate a log (base 10) for a number *N*, write LOG(N)/LOG(10). Therefore, to use Sturgess's rule to determine the appropriate number of intervals, we can write the program in Example 5.6.

example 5.6

```
20   INPUT "HOW MANY VALUES WILL BE USED";N
40   K = 1 + 3.3*(LOG(N)/LOG(10))
60   K = INT(K+.5): REM /// ROUND OFF TO INTEGER VALUE ///
80   PRINT:PRINT "THE NUMBER OF INTERVALS WILL BE";K
30000 END
```

The ability to determine the appropriate number of intervals can now be used to improve the flexibility of the frequency tally program shown in Example 5.5. The interval size becomes equal to (H − L)/K, rounded to the nearest tenth.

Sorting Data: The Bubble Sort

Sorting values into ascending or descending order is one of the most important and most frequently used data organization techniques. Among the more readable of the numerous articles that have been published on sorting routines are Terry Barron and George Diehe's "Sorting Algorithms for Microcomputers" (*Byte,* May 1983, pages 482–490) and H. S. Gentry's "Sorting Techniques Explained" (*Microcomputing,* November 1981, pages 156–160). Since the highest speed sorting routines are complex, we will look only at a slow but "easy" technique, known as the **bubble sort** because values that belong at the top of the sorted list "bubble up" with each pass through the sorting loop.

Examining Example 5.7, notice that the sorting process is based on a series of comparisons between data values. If there are *N* values, we need to sort only *N* − 1 such values to create an ordered sequence, as shown in line 5080. The first set of comparisons is made between X(1) and the remaining X(2) . . . X(5) values specified in the inner loop. (We have "borrowed" five data values from the program in Example 5.5, line 10000, to keep the example brief.) An explanation of the sorting procedure follows the program.

example 5.7

```
220 CLS: KEY OFF: REM ** CLEAR THE SCREEN                    **
230 DIM X(100), X1(100)
240 N = 1: READ X(N): X1(N) = X(N)
260 WHILE X(N) <> -999
280       N = N + 1: READ X(N): X1(N) = X(N)
300 WEND
320 N = N - 1: REM ** # VALUES READ FROM THE DATE LINE **
5000 REM *********************************************
5020 REM *              PERFORM THE BUBBLE SORT             *
5040 REM *********************************************
5060 C = 1
5080 WHILE C <= N - 1
5120       J = C + 1
5160       WHILE J <= N
5200             IF X(C) > X(J) THEN SWAP X(C),X(J)
```

```
5220         J = J + 1
5240     WEND
5270     C = C + 1
5300 WEND
6000 REM ***********************************************
6020 REM *   PRINT THE ORIGINAL AND SORTED DATA VALUES   *
6040 REM ***********************************************
6050 CLS
6060 PRINT "ORIGINAL"; TAB(15);"SORTED"
6080 PRINT " VALUES "; TAB(15);"VALUES"
6100 PRINT "--------"; TAB(15);"------": PRINT
6120 C = 1
6140 WHILE C <= N
6160     PRINT USING "  ###          ###";X1(C),X(C)
6180     C = C + 1
6200 WEND
10000 DATA 73,52,87,48,65
29999 DATA -999
```

```
RUN
ORIGINAL     SORTED
 VALUES      VALUES
--------     ------

   73          48
   52          52
   87          65
   48          73
   65          87
```

The SWAP command in line 5200 will do exactly that: The X(C) and X(J)values are exchanged ("swapped") whenever X(C)> X(J). The bubble sort begins by letting C = 1 (line 5060) and J = 2 (line 5160). The following sequence of events occurs next, based on an original set of values shown in the data, line 10000.

`C = 1   J = 2` Compare X(1) = 73 to X(2) = 52. Since 73 > 52, we swap X(1) and X(2). Now X(1) = 52 and X(2) = 73.

table 5.3
BUBBLE SORTING: RESULTS FOR C = 1

Original Listing	C = 1 J = 2	C = 1 J = 3	C = 1 J = 4	C = 1 J = 5
X(1) = 73	52	52	48	48
X(2) = 52	73	73	73	73
X(3) = 87	87	87	87	87
X(4) = 48	48	48	52	52
X(5) = 65	65	65	65	65

`C = 1   J = 3` Since X(1) = 52, we compare X(1) = 52 and X(3) = 87. Since 52 < 87, no changes are made.

`C = 1   J = 4` Compare X(1) = 52 to X(4) = 48. Since 52 > 48, we swap X(1) and X(4). Now X(1) = 48 and X(4) = 52.

`C = 1   J = 5` Compare X(1) = 48 to X(5) = 65. Since 48 < 65, no swap is made. No additional J values are possible. Therefore, we return to the outer loop, letting C= 2 this time.

The sequence of events we have just traced must, of course, be repeated for the conditions C= 2 and J = 3 through 5; C= 3 and J = 4 through 5, and, finally, C= 4 and J = 5. The results of the C= 1 condition, discussed above, are summarized in Table 5.3.

The results shown in Table 5.3 clearly indicate that the value 48 has "bubbled" to the top at this point. It may also occur to us that the number of value switches can be quite large. In fact, we can add a counter to the program, inserting a (temporary) addition in line 5200.

```
5200  IF X(C) > X(J) THEN SWAP X(C),X(J): N5 = N5+1
```

and adding two (temporary) lines that print the results:

```
7000  PRINT: PRINT "IT TOOK";N5;"STEPS TO COMPLETE"
7020  PRINT "THIS BUBBLE SORT ROUTINE."
```

If we run the program again, we discover that it took 10 steps to sort these five values. If we add 10 data values, for a total of 15, we discover that the number of steps has grown to 120. The number of steps required to perform a bubble sort is, apparently, enormous when dealing with a large number of values. The bubble sort technique is very slow: It takes about a minute to sort 100 values, and it takes several hours to sort 1000 values. Why, then, use a bubble sort at all? First, the bubble sort is the simplest sorting technique available; it is easy to understand and easy to write into a program. Second, if a programmer never sorts large amounts of data, it works quite well.

table 5.4
NUMBER OF STUDENTS, BY CLASSIFICATION, IN A SAMPLE OF 60

Classification	Frequency
Freshman	18
Sophomore	22
Junior	9
Senior	11

Keeping Track of Several Variables While Sorting

Suppose we have collected the data shown in Table 5.4. The objective is to sort the data set, arranging the data so that those with the highest frequency are listed first. How can a programmer keep track of the string variable to make sure that it is shifted along with the sorted frequency value?

Using the bubble sort program shown in Example 5.7, we can make the required modifications easily by changing line 5200 to read:

```
5200  IF X(C) < X(J) THEN SWAP X(C),X(J): SWAP C$(C),C$(J)
```

Note the program modifications in Example 5.8 and observe that the output keeps the sorted values paired.

example 5.8

```
220 CLS: KEY OFF: REM ** CLEAR THE SCREEN                   **
230 DIM X(100), X1(100), C$(100), C1$(100)
240 N = 1: READ C$(N),X(N): X1(N) = X(N): C1$(N) = C$(N)
260 WHILE C$(N) <> "EOF" AND X(N) <> -999
280      N = N + 1: READ C$(N),X(N)
290      C1$(N) = C$(N): X1(N) = X(N)
300 WEND
320 N = N - 1: REM ** # VALUES READ FROM THE DATE LINE **
5000 REM ************************************************
5020 REM *           PERFORM THE BUBBLE SORT             *
5040 REM ************************************************
```

```
5060 C = 1
5080 WHILE C <= N - 1
5120     J = C + 1
5160     WHILE J <= N
5200         IF X(C) < X(J) THEN SWAP X(C),X(J):
             SWAP C$(C),C$(J)
5220         J = J + 1
5240     WEND
5270     C = C + 1
5300 WEND
6000 REM ************************************************
6020 REM *   PRINT THE ORIGINAL AND SORTED DATA VALUES   *
6040 REM ************************************************
6050 CLS
6060 PRINT TAB(3);"ORIGINAL ORDER";TAB(24);"SORTED ORDER"
6080 PRINT "-----------------";TAB(22);"-----------------"
6100 PRINT TAB(3);"CLASS"; TAB(12);"NUMBER";
6120 PRINT TAB(24);"CLASS"; TAB(33);"NUMBER"
6140 PRINT "---------  ------    ---------  ------"
6160 PRINT
6180 A$ = "\       \   ###      \        \   ###"
6200 C = 1
6220 WHILE C <= N
6240     PRINT USING A$;C1$(C),X1(C),C$(C),X(C)
6260     C = C + 1
6280 WEND
10000 DATA FRESHMAN,18,SOPHOMORE,22,JUNIOR,9,SENIOR,11
29000 DATA EOF,-999
29999 DATA -999
```

```
  ORIGINAL ORDER        SORTED ORDER
-----------------     -----------------
  CLASS    NUMBER       CLASS    NUMBER
---------  ------     ---------  ------

FRESHMAN     18       SOPHOMORE    22
SOPHOMORE    22       FRESHMAN     18
JUNIOR        9       SENIOR       11
SENIOR       11       JUNIOR        9
```

5.4 More About Common Mathematical Procedures

So far, we have limited ourselves to simple addition, multiplication, division, and subtraction. We will discover quickly that we must be very careful when performing more than one of these procedures in a single calculation. Life becomes even more interesting when we add parentheses to some procedures. For example, A = 10 when we write:

```
A = 3*4-2
```

On the other hand, if we had written:

```
A = 3*(4-2)
```

we would have discovered that A = 6. Apparently, the parentheses make quite a difference.

We will also find that K = 9 if we write the equation:

```
K = 6/2*3
```

even though some may incorrectly assume that the answer is 1, because 2*3 = 6 and 6/6 = 1. However, the multiplication/division series begins on the left and proceeds to the right. (The same is true of a division series.) To get a value of 1 in the preceding example, we would have to put parentheses around a portion of the sequence. For example, by writing:

```
K = 6/(2*3)
```

we would have found the answer to be 1. Clearly, we need a set of mathematical guidelines. The rules of **mathematical precedence,** which define the order in which mathematical procedures take place, are outlined in Table 5.5.

table 5.5
RULES OF MATHEMATICAL PRECEDENCE

1. Mathematical procedures inside parentheses are always performed first.
2. Exponential operations are always performed next, starting on the left and moving to the right. (Raising a value by some power is an exponential operation.)
3. Multiplications and divisions are third.
4. In a series of multiplications and/or divisions, the procedure starts on the left. For example, the sequence 2/2*3 = 3, because 2/2 = 1 and 1*3 = 3.
5. Finally, we perform additions and subtractions, starting from the left and moving to the right.

Our interest in the mathematical processes and procedures just described is not a casual one. Many common events are based on mathematical procedures that are fairly complex. For example, home mortgage payment schedules are based

on a formidable equation. If we are putting our savings in an account that promises continuously compounded interest, we are dealing, once again, with a complex mathematical procedure. Such situations are easily examined with a microcomputer—if we can write the equations by applying the rules of precedence. Before exercising this newfound knowledge, take a quick look at Table 5.6 to review the use of the various **mathematical symbols.**

Let us now look at a few illustrations (Table 5.7) to develop an appreciation for the rules of mathematical precedence. When we are familiar with them, we can examine some useful applications.

To double-check the answers to the procedures in Table 5.7 we can use our microcomputer in **direct mode.** That is, we can get results immediately by simply typing PRINT, followed by the calculation we want to perform. No line number is used in direct mode: The computer is, in effect, used as an expensive calculator this way. For example, for an answer to the sequence (3 + 6)*4/5, we merely type:

```
PRINT (3+6)*4/5
```

and push/release the ENTER key.

table 5.6
A REVIEW OF THE USE OF MATHEMATICAL SYMBOLS

Procedure	Symbol	Example	Result
Multiply	*	X = 2*8	X = 16
Divide	/	B = 3/5	B = .6
Add	+	A = 8+2	A = 10
Subtract	-	Z = 2-7	Z = -5
Raise to the (given) power[a]	^	K = 3^2	K = 9

table 5.7
USE OF THE RULES OF MATHEMATICAL PRECEDENCE

Equation to Be Evaluated	Calculation Sequence
K = 3+4*2	K = 3 + 8 = 11
B = (3+4)*2	B = 7*2 = 14
A = (3+6)*4/5	A = 9*4/5 = 36/5 = 7.2
X = 3+6*4/5	X = 3 + 24/5 = 3 + 4.8 = 7.8
L = 3*4^2	L = 3*16 = 48
D = (3*4)^2	D = 12^2 = 144

[a]Squaring a number has the same effect as multiplying the number by itself; that is, 2^2 = 2*2, 6^2 = 6*6. Similarly, 4^3 is the same as 4*4*4 = 64, 2^5 = 2*2*2*2*2 = 32, and so on.

`E = (3+4^2)*5-2`	E = (3 + 16)*5 − 2 = 19*5 − 2 = 93
`C = 5-2^3+5*3/10`	C = 5 − 8 + 15/10 = 5 − 8 + 1.5 = −1.5
`P = (5-2)^3+5*(3-1)/(10-5)`	P = 3^3 + 5*2/5 = 27 + 10/5 = 27 + 2 = 29
`M = (1+1/5)^(5-3)`	M = (1 + .2)^2 = (1.2)^2 = 1.44
`F = (1+2*3^2)*2*5+5`	F = (1 + 2*9)*2*5 + 5 = (1 + 18)*2*5 + 5 = 19*2*5+5 = 38*5 + 5 = 190 + 5 = 195
`H = 2^3+2`	H = 8 + 2 = 10
`N = 2^3*2`	N = 8*2 = 16
`R = 2^(3*2)`	R = 2^6 = 64
`Q = ((5-2)^3+5)*(3-1)/(10-5)`	Q = (3^3 + 5)*2/5 = (27 + 5)*2/5 = 32*2/5 = 64/5 = 12.8
`T = (((2-3)*2)-2)*2`	T = ((−1*2) − 2)*2 = (−2 − 2)*2 = −4*2 = −8

5.5 Applications of the Rules of Mathematical Precedence

Computing Simple Interest

Suppose we want to find out how much we can expect to earn by investing \$5,000 at 11 percent simple interest over 3 years. The equation that provides the answer is defined by:

$A = P\,(1 + N^*I)$

where A = total amount paid back

P = amount invested

I = interest rate (expressed as a decimal: 11% = .11, 5% = .05, etc.)

N = number of years

The difference between the amount paid back (A) and the amount invested (the principal, P) is, of course, the total interest earned. We can write a sample program like the one in Example 5.9.

example 5.9

```
20   PRINT: INPUT "AMOUNT INVESTED";P: PRINT
40   INPUT "NUMBER OF YEARS INVESTED";N: PRINT
60   PRINT "WHAT IS THE INTEREST RATE? (NOTE: ENTER"
80   PRINT "THE VALUE AS A DECIMAL, FOR EXAMPLE, AN"
100  PRINT "INTEREST RATE OF 8% IS ENTERED AS .08)";
120  INPUT I
140  A = P*(1 + N*I): REM *** SIMPLE INTEREST EQUATION ***
160  PRINT: PRINT
180  PRINT "TOTAL AMOUNT PAID BACK IS $";A
200  PRINT "INTEREST EARNED IN";N;"YEARS IS $";A-P
30000  END

RUN

AMOUNT INVESTED? 5000

NUMBER OF YEARS INVESTED? 3

WHAT IS THE INTEREST RATE? (NOTE: ENTER
THE VALUE AS A DECIMAL, FOR EXAMPLE, AN
INTEREST RATE OF 8% IS ENTERED AS .08)? .11


TOTAL AMOUNT PAID BACK IS $ 6650
INTEREST EARNED IN 3 YEARS IS $ 1650
```

Computing Compound Interest

One limitation of the interest computation in Example 5.9 is that the interest rate is simple; that is, it is computed each year, and only on the amount invested. If we compound the interest, during the second year we will earn the interest over the principal plus the first year's interest; during the third year we will earn interest over the total amount to date (principal plus two years' interest); and so on. If the compounding is computed only once a year, the equation is modified as follows:

$$A = P(1 + I)^N$$

We can translate this equation into BASIC by writing:

```
A = P * (1 + I)^N
```

If we substitute this new compounding equation in line 140 of Example 5.9, we will discover that compounding makes quite a difference, especially when the investment period becomes longer. To compare the two types of interest, we can

figure 5.1
SCREEN LAYOUT FOR PROGRAM EXAMPLE 5.10

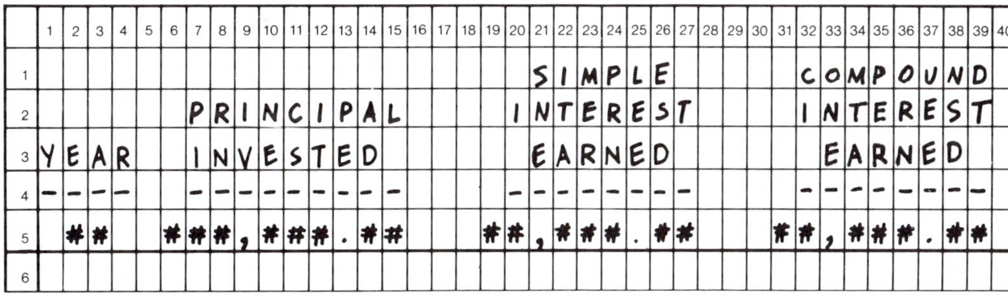

run the program in Example 5.9 several times, switching equations after each run. Or we can use both equations in the same program, as shown in Example 5.10. Note, incidentally, that the total amount of interest earned is the difference between *A* and *P*.

To write a program that shows the differences between simple and compound interest rates, we must print a few headings. It will be useful to check the necessary output spacing, since it is difficult to write TAB commands on the basis of intuition. The easiest way to plan the **screen layout,** the spacing we want on the CRT or on the printed page, is to use graph paper or "official" screen layout forms. As long as we can identify the columns easily, we can define the print positions.

The sample screen layout form in Figure 5.1 defines the print or screen locations for the program headings to be used in Example 5.10. Only a portion of the screen layout form is reproduced here, since most forms include 80 columns and 25 rows.

The column numbers on the screen layout form correspond to the TAB positions in the program shown in Example 5.10. For example, we expect the first printed heading portion to be the word SIMPLE, starting in column 21, followed by the word COMPOUND, which starts in column 32. The first heading line in Example 5.10, will, therefore, read:

```
160 PRINT TAB(21);"SIMPLE";TAB(32);"COMPOUND"
```

The remaining PRINT positions are defined in the same way. Since some of the statements are rather lengthy, we have spread the statements over two lines in some cases, to keep the margins well within this page. Remember the function of the semicolon (;) in continuation statements. (Note the semicolons at the end of lines 180, 220, and 260 in Example 5.10.)

example 5.10

```
10 CLS: KEY OFF: REM ** CLEAR THE SCREEN                          **
20 PRINT: INPUT "AMOUNT INVESTED";P
40 INPUT "NUMBER OF YEARS INVESTED";N: PRINT
60 PRINT "WHAT IS THE INTEREST RATE? ( NOTE: ENTER"
80 PRINT "THE VALUE AS A DECIMAL, FOR EXAMPLE, AN"
100 INPUT "INTEREST RATE OF 8% IS ENTERED AS .08)";I
```

```
140 PRINT: PRINT
160 PRINT TAB(21);"SIMPLE"; TAB(32);"COMPOUND"
180 PRINT TAB(7);"PRINCIPAL"; TAB(20);"INTEREST";
200 PRINT TAB(32);"INTEREST"
220 PRINT "YEAR"; TAB(7);"INVESTED"; TAB(21);"EARNED";
240 PRINT TAB(33);"EARNED"
260 PRINT "----"; TAB(7);"---------"; TAB(20)"---------";
280 PRINT TAB(32);"--------": PRINT
290 P$ = " ##   ###,###.##    ##,###.##    ##,###.##"
300 FOR D = 1 TO N
320     A1 = P*(1 + D*I): REM ** SIMPLE INTEREST EQUATION   **
340     A2 = P*(1 + I)^D: REM ** COMPOUND INTEREST EQUATION **
360     PRINT USING P$;D,P,A1-P,A2-P
380 NEXT D
30000 END
```

```
AMOUNT INVESTED? 5000
NUMBER OF YEARS INVESTED? 5

WHAT IS THE INTEREST RATE? ( NOTE: ENTER
THE VALUE AS A DECIMAL. FOR EXAMPLE, AN
INTEREST RATE OF 8% IS ENTERED AS .08)? .11

                       SIMPLE     COMPOUND
       PRINCIPAL      INTEREST    INTEREST
YEAR   INVESTED        EARNED      EARNED
----   ---------      --------    --------

  1     5,000.00        550.00      550.00
  2     5,000.00      1,100.00    1,160.50
  3     5,000.00      1,650.00    1,838.15
  4     5,000.00      2,200.00    2,590.35
  5     5,000.00      2,750.00    3,425.29
```

One point in Example 5.10 deserves emphasizing. Note that the equations in lines 320 and 340 seem to have changed. For example, although the simple interest equation was defined as $A = P\,(1 + N*I)$, the equation in line 320 uses a D in place of the N. The reason for this modification is rather straightforward: The symbol N represents a value in the Nth year. Since we are computing the interest value for each of the 10 years in the example, we let the number of years in the equation (D) vary between the first and the Nth years.

Interest equations are not, of course, limited to the two we have just examined. For example, if to compound interest not just once but Q times per year, the equation must be modified to read:

$$A = P\left(1 + \frac{I}{Q}\right)^{NQ}$$

Translated into BASIC, the preceding equation is written:

```
A = P*(1 + I/Q)^(N*Q)
```

An even more complex interest equation is used for continuous compounding. The computer will take the most complex equations in stride. There will be an opportunity to perform these and other calculations in the Exercises at the end of the chapter.

5.6 The INT Function

Any numeric value may be converted to a whole number (integer) with the help of the **INT** function. For example, INT(27.04) yields the integer 27. The same integer value will be returned when we use INT(27.99), thereby demonstrating that the INT function does *not* round the values but truncates them, instead. Take a look at the program in Example 5.11 and examine its output.

example 5.11

```
20  A = 2.0001: B = 2.9999: C = 2.0567: D = .9999: E = .0001
40  F = -2.0001: G = -.9999: H = -.0001: PRINT
60  PRINT "ORIGINAL VALUE"; TAB(20);"INTEGER VALUE"
80  PRINT "--------------"; TAB(20);"-------------": PRINT
100  PRINT TAB(4);A; TAB(25);INT(A)
120  PRINT TAB(4);B; TAB(25);INT(B)
140  PRINT TAB(4);C; TAB(25);INT(C)
160  PRINT TAB(4);D; TAB(25);INT(D)
180  PRINT TAB(4);E; TAB(25);INT(E)
200  PRINT TAB(3);F; TAB(25);INT(F)
220  PRINT TAB(3);G; TAB(25);INT(G)
240  PRINT TAB(3);H; TAB(25);INT(H)
30000  END

RUN
```

```
ORIGINAL VALUE          INTEGER VALUE
--------------          -------------

      2.0001               2
      2.9999               2
      2.0567               2
       .9999               0
       .0001               0
     -2.0001              -3
      -.9999              -1
      -.0001              -1
```

Two points are worth emphasizing. First, the positive values seem to be cut off at the decimal point. Therefore, the value 2.0001 is reduced to 2. Second, negative values appear to jump to an integer value different from the one we might expect. The integer of −2.001 is, for example, given as −3 rather than −2. The explanation of this result is quite simple. The truncation actually involves shifting the numbers' location to the left on the numeric scale. The first whole number encountered in such a shift is the integer value, as shown on the following scale. For example, the first value encountered in such a leftward shift from .9999 is 0. Similarly, the first integer value encountered in a leftward shift from −.0001 is −1.

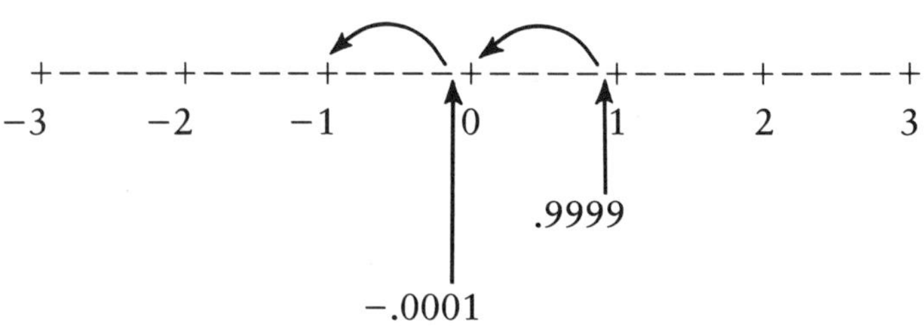

Rounding with the Help of the INTeger Function

How then can we use INT for rounding if INT truncates? A simple bit of arithmetic will show the way. Suppose that we want to round the value 2.468 to two decimal places. What will happen if we multiply it by 100, add .5, take the integer value, and divide the result by 100? The following sequence shows the effect of this operation:

```
2.468 * 100 = 246.8
246.8 + .5 = 247.3
INT(247.3) = 247
247/100 = 2.47
```

Presto: The value 2.468 has been properly rounded to two decimal places. In other words:

```
INT(2.468*100 + .5)/100
```

yields the rounded value 2.47. Since the rules of mathematical precedence dictate that a multiplication precedes an addition, the sequence:

```
INT(.5 + 2.468*100)/100
```

yields the same results. The rounding sequence is often written in this order. Using the same technique, we can round 2.468 to one decimal place by writing:

```
INT(.5 + 2.468*10)/10
```

A pattern quickly begins to emerge: **Rounding** to one decimal place involves a multiplication and division by 10. Rounding to two decimal places requires multiplication and division by 100. Rounding to three decimal places requires multiplication and division by 1,000, and so on. Example 5.12, followed by its output, demonstrates several rounding sequences. Line 200 proves that the single INT format INT(.5 + V) rounds a value to its nearest integer.

example 5.12

```
20     V = 2.526948: PRINT
40     PRINT TAB(2);"ORIGINAL";TAB(13);"ROUNDED";TAB(23);"NUMBER OF"
60     PRINT TAB(3);"VALUE";TAB(14);"VALUE";TAB(22);"DEC. PLACES"
80     PRINT TAB(2);"--------";TAB(13);"-------";TAB(22)"-----------"
100    PRINT
120    PRINT V; TAB(12);INT(.5+V*10000)/10000; TAB(26);4
140    PRINT V; TAB(12);INT(.5+V*1000)/1000; TAB(26);3
160    PRINT V; TAB(12);INT(.5+V*100)/100; TAB(26);2
180    PRINT V; TAB(12);INT(.5+V*10)/10; TAB(26);1
200    PRINT V; TAB(12);INT(.5+V*1)/1; TAB(26);0
30000   END

RUN

ORIGINAL     ROUNDED     NUMBER OF
 VALUE        VALUE     DEC. PLACES
--------     -------    -----------

2.526948     2.5269          4
2.526948     2.527           3
2.526948     2.53            2
2.526948     2.5             1
2.526948     3               0
```

The output in the preceding example can be obtained more elegantly by modifying the program as illustrated in Example 5.13. Note how the values in the loop (lines 120–180) are reset properly each time the program moves through the loop. (Check particularly the action in line 160.)

example 5.13

```
20 V = 2.526948: M1 = 10000: M2 = 4: PRINT
40 PRINT TAB(2);"ORIGINAL";TAB(13);"ROUNDED";TAB(23);"NUMBER OF"
60 PRINT TAB(3);"VALUE"; TAB(14);"VALUE";TAB(22);"DEC. PLACES"
80 PRINT TAB(2);"--------";TAB(13);"-------"TAB(22);"-----------"
100 PRINT
120 FOR I = 1 TO 5
140       PRINT V; TAB(12);INT(.5+V*M1)/M1; TAB(26); M2
160       M1 = M1/10: M2 = M2-1
180 NEXT I
30000 END
```

Chapter Review

Nested loops (loops within loops) are used in countless programming applications ranging from output formatting to data organization. A nested loop is composed of an outer loop and one or more inner loops; it is executed by starting the outer loop and completing the inner loop(s) before control is returned to the outer loop. Because crossing loops generates error messages on the computer, loops are not allowed to cross. To detect the nested loop's structure and to help prevent crossing errors, loops should be indented.

Nested loops can be used to organize data into frequency distributions showing the pattern of the data and providing clues to data behavior and meaning. When large numbers of values are recorded and little value duplication occurs, data may be tallied into intervals. The number of intervals used is a matter of choice. However, we may use Sturgess's rule to determine the number of intervals most likely to yield a significant pattern. Sturgess's Rule requires the use of logarithms (logs) to the base 10. The log given by the microcomputer is a natural log (to the base $e = 2.71828$). We may convert the natural log to a log to the base 10 by LOG(N)/LOG(10), where N is the number for which the log is taken.

Another application of nested loops is found in sorting data into ascending or descending order. Since data sorting is a common organization technique, sorting routines have received much programming attention. Many sorting routines have been developed during the past decade. The simplest sorting technique is the bubble sort, in which low (or high) values "bubble" to the top of the array with each pass through the loop. Much faster sorting techniques are available, but they are beyond the scope of this book.

The INT function converts any numeric value into an integer. Decimal places are truncated and the remaining integer value will be found to the left of the original value on the numeric scale. Therefore, INT(1.25) yields the integer 1, INT(-2.3) yields the value -3, INT(.99) yields the integer value 0, and so on.

Key Terms and Concepts

- nested loop
- structured programming
- frequency distribution
- high and low values
- Sturgess's rule
- logarithm
- bubble sort
- INT

Common Errors

1. Not indenting the nested loops so that they are easily visible.

Correct:

```
20   FOR G = 1 TO 5
40        FOR J = 1 TO 4
60             PRINT G*J
80        NEXT J
100  NEXT G
```

Incorrect:

```
20   FOR G = 1 TO 5
40   FOR J = 1 TO 4
60   PRINT G*J
80   NEXT J
100  NEXT G
```

2. Letting loops cross.

Correct:

(See program above)

Incorrect:

```
20   FOR G = 1 TO 5
40        FOR J = 1 TO 4
60             PRINT G*J
80        NEXT G
100  NEXT J
```

3. Failing to terminate the semicolon's effect in a print loop. Suppose you want to print the following asterisk pattern:

```
1 *
4 ****
9 *********
```

Note the importance of line 100 in the program. Try running the program without it!

```
20   FOR C = 1 TO 3
30   PRINT C;
40        FOR J = 1 TO C^2
60             PRINT J;"*";
80        NEXT J
100  PRINT
120  NEXT C
```

Exercises

1. Using a nested loop, write a program to print the following output.

```
I = 1       J = 1
I = 1       J = 2
I = 1       J = 3
I = 2       J = 1
I = 2       J = 2
I = 2       J = 3
```

2. Modify the program line in Exercise 1 to print the following output.

```
I = 1       J = 1
            J = 2
            J = 3
I = 2       J = 1
            J = 2
            J = 3
```

3. What is wrong with the following program?

```
20   FOR I = 1 TO 10
40        FOR J = 1 TO 5
60             PRINT I;"TIMES";J;"IS;I*J
80        NEXT I
100  NEXT J
```

4. Using a nested loop, write a program to print the following output.

```
0 1 2 3 4 5
1 2 3 4 5
2 3 4 5
3 4 5
4 5
5
```

5. Write a program that uses a nested loop to print the string "*****" in the following pattern.

```
*****  *****  *****  *****  *****  *****
*****  *****  *****  *****  *****  *****
*****  *****  *****  *****  *****  *****
```

6. Using the compounded interest equation discussed in Section 5.5, write a program that produces the following input/output. Make sure to use a nested loop to generate the end-of-year value. *Hint:* The inner loop can be written:

```
FOR J = .05 TO .15 STEP .05

WHAT AMOUNT WILL BE INVESTED? 1000
WHAT IS THE INVESTMENT PERIOD, IN YEARS? 5
NUMBER OF TIMES COMPOUNDED PER YEAR? 4
```

```
                    END-OF-YEAR-VALUE
            -------------------------------
YEAR          5%           10%          15%
----       --------     --------     ---------

  1        1,050.95     1,103.81     1,158.65
  2        1,104.49     1,218.40     1,342.47
  3        1,160.76     1,344.89     1,555.45
  4        1,219.89     1,484.51     1,802.23
  5        1,282.04     1,638.62     2,088.15
```

7. Using the following DATA line, write a program to print the asterisk pattern shown, using a nested loop. Each asterisk bar should contain the number of asterisks corresponding to the X(I) variable values in the DATA line.

```
1000 DATA 1,4,9,15,16,14,6,2
```

```
X(I) VALUE     ASTERISK PATTERN
----------     ----------------
    1          *
    4          ****
    9          *********
    15         ***************
    16         ****************
    14         **************
    6          ******
    2          **
```

8. Modify the program written in Exercise 7 to print the output shown below. **Note:** The ¦ symbol should be printed at TAB(15). The number of > symbols must be one less than the X(I) value to put the asterisk into the correct position.

```
X(I) VALUE   ASTERISK PATTERN
----------   ----------------

    1          ¦*
    4          ¦>>>*
    9          ¦>>>>>>>>*
    15         ¦>>>>>>>>>>>>>>*
    16         ¦>>>>>>>>>>>>>>>*
    14         ¦>>>>>>>>>>>>>*
    6          ¦>>>>>*
    2          ¦>*
```

9. Given the following two DATA lines, write a program that produces the frequency distribution shown below. *Hint:* Use a sort routine, then compare each sorted value to the next. If the two are equal, add 1 to the frequency. If the two are not equal, start a new frequency count.

```
10000 DATA 2.1,2.3,2.1,2.4,2.2,2.2,2.3,2.2
10020 DATA 2.2,2.3,2.2,2.2
```

Required output:

```
X(I) VALUE        FREQUENCY
----------        ---------

    2.1               2
    2.2               6
    2.3               3
    2.4               1
```

10. Modify the program written in Exercise 9 to produce this output:

```
X(I) VALUE        FREQUENCY         FREQUENCY CHART
----------        ---------         ---------------

    2.1               2             +**
    2.2               6             +******
    2.3               3             +***
    2.4               1             +*
```

11. Organize the data in Table 5.8 to produce the frequency distribution shown at the top of p. 156. The cumulative frequency represents the addition of each interval frequency value to the preceding total; the relative frequency value is the frequency value for each interval divided by the total number of values, *N*. (In other words, the relative frequency value for the first interval is 0/30; that of the second interval is 1/30; that for the third interval is 0/30; and so on.) Use a PRINT USING statement to format the output.

table 5.8
JUNE PRECIPITATION AT XYZ LOCATION (INCHES OF RAINFALL)

Year	Precipitation	Year	Precipitation	Year	Precipitation
1954	2.8	1964	3.4	1974	4.9
1955	2.3	1965	3.7	1975	2.7
1956	5.1	1966	2.9	1976	3.6
1957	2.4	1967	2.6	1977	3.1
1958	3.2	1968	3.1	1978	2.5
1959	2.9	1969	2.7	1979	3.1
1960	3.3	1970	2.6	1980	2.2
1961	.5	1971	2.3	1981	2.9
1962	4.1	1972	3.7	1982	1.8
1963	4.2	1973	1.6	1983	2.3

```
          DATA SUMMARY FOR 30 DATA VALUES

                             CUMULATIVE   RELATIVE
     INTERVAL       FREQ.    FREQUENCY    FREQUENCY
   ------------     -----    ----------   ---------

    0.0 TO 0.5        0            0        0.000
    0.5 TO 1.0        1            1        0.033
    1.0 TO 1.5        0            1        0.000
    1.5 TO 2.0        2            3        0.067
    2.0 TO 2.5        5            8        0.167
    2.5 TO 3.0        9           17        0.300
    3.0 TO 3.5        6           23        0.200
    3.5 TO 4.0        3           26        0.100
    4.0 TO 4.5        2           28        0.067
    4.5 TO 5.0        1           29        0.033
    5.0 TO 5.5        1           30        0.033

   AVERAGE RAINFALL =======>  2.95
   LOWEST RAINFALL ========>  0.50
   HIGHEST RAINFALL =======>  5.10
```

12. Modify the program in Exercise 11 to use Sturgess's rule (Section 5.3) to determine the number of intervals and the interval size. Start the first interval at the lowest X(I) value. The required output is shown below.

```
          DATA SUMMARY FOR 30 DATA VALUES

                             CUMULATIVE   RELATIVE
     INTERVAL       FREQ.    FREQUENCY    FREQUENCY
   ------------     -----    ----------   ---------

    0.5 TO 1.3        1            1        0.033
    1.3 TO 2.1        2            3        0.067
    2.1 TO 2.9       11           14        0.367
    2.9 TO 3.7       10           24        0.333
    3.7 TO 4.5        4           28        0.133
    4.5 TO 5.3        2           30        0.067

   AVERAGE RAINFALL =======>  2.95
   LOWEST RAINFALL ========>  0.50
   HIGHEST RAINFALL =======>  5.10
```

13. Now modify the program in Exercise 12 to produce the bar chart shown below. *Hint:* Use a nested loop from T= 1 TO F(J) to print the *. Note that the output was interrupted to enable the user to read the first portion of the printout before the screen is cleared and the frequency plot is shown.

```
DATA SUMMARY FOR 30 DATA VALUES

                               CUMULATIVE   RELATIVE
  INTERVAL        FREQ.   FREQUENCY    FREQUENCY
------------   -----  ----------   ---------

 0.5 TO 1.3        1          1         0.033
 1.3 TO 2.1        2          3         0.067
 2.1 TO 2.9       11         14         0.367
 2.9 TO 3.7       10         24         0.333
 3.7 TO 4.5        4         28         0.133
 4.5 TO 5.3        2         30         0.067

AVERAGE RAINFALL =======>  2.95
LOWEST RAINFALL ========>  0.50
HIGHEST RAINFALL =======>  5.10

TAP THE RETURN KEY TO CONTINUE.
```

```
                            FREQUENCY VALUES

                                      1    1    2    2    3
                            0    5    0    5    0    5    0
                            +----+----+----+----+----+----+
                           --
                           --
                            :
                    0.9     +*
                            :
  INTERVAL          1.7     +**
                            :
  MIDPOINT          2.5     +***********
                            :
   VALUES           3.3     +**********
                            :
                    4.1     +****
                            :
                    4.9     +**
```

14. Using the direct mode, evaluate the following procedures. Are the answers what you would have expected?

a. `1.5*4-6*(3-1)^2`
b. `1.5*4-6*3-1^2`
c. `1.5*(4-6*3)-1^2`
d. `3-7*2+(2+12)^2-1`
e. `2*(1+3^2)^2*2`
f. `2*(1+3^2)^(2*2)`
g. `4+2*2^3+1`
h. `4+2*2^(3+1)`

15. Translate the following mathematical procedures into BASIC; then evaluate them in a program whose output follows.
   a. $2 \times 4^2 - (5 - (3 - 5))^2 / 2 + 4 \times (2 + 3)^5$
   b. $2 \times (4^2 - (5 - (3 - 5)^2)) / (2 + 4 \times (2 + 3)^2)$
   c. $4 + 2 \times 2^{3+1}$
   d. $4 + 2 \times 2 \times 2^3 + 1$
   e. $2 - 2^{3+2} + 3^{2\times3}$
   f. $2 - 2^{3+2} + 3^2 \times 3$
   Required program output:

```
THE ANSWER TO QUESTION 15A IS 12,507.50
THE ANSWER TO QUESTION 15B IS       0.29
THE ANSWER TO QUESTION 15C IS      36.00
THE ANSWER TO QUESTION 15D IS      37.00
THE ANSWER TO QUESTION 15E IS     699.00
THE ANSWER TO QUESTION 15F IS      -3.00
```

16. The area of a circle is calculated by $A = \pi r^2$, and the circle's circumference is calculated by $C = 2\pi r$ (r = radius = half the diameter; $\pi = 3.14159$). Using this information, write a program that will calculate the circumference and the area of a circle. The input/output should be placed inside a WHILE/WEND loop.

```
WHAT IS THE CIRCLE'S RADIUS? 10

THE CIRCLE'S CIRCUMFERENCE IS ===>     62.832
THE CIRCLE'S AREA IS ============>    314.159

DO YOU WANT TO DO ANOTHER CALCULATION (Y/N)? Y


WHAT IS THE CIRCLE'S RADIUS? 14.25

THE CIRCLE'S CIRCUMFERENCE IS ===>     89.535
THE CIRCLE'S AREA IS ============>    637.939

DO YOU WANT TO DO ANOTHER CALCULATION (Y/N)? N
```

17. The volume of a cylinder is calcuated by $V = \pi r^2 H$, where H is the height or the length of the cylinder. Write a program to calculate any cylinder's volume. The input/output should look like this:

```
WHAT IS THE CYLINDER'S DIAMETER? 2.5
WHAT IS THE CYLINDER'S LENGTH (HEIGHT)? 28.3

THE CYLINDER'S VOLUME IS ===>    138.917

DO YOU WANT TO DO ANOTHER CALCULATION (Y/N)? Y
```

```
WHAT IS THE CYLINDER'S DIAMETER? 18.55
WHAT IS THE CYLINDER'S LENGTH (HEIGHT)? 16.2

THE CYLINDER'S VOLUME IS ===> 4,378.167

DO YOU WANT TO DO ANOTHER CALCULATION (Y/N)? N
```

Hint: Did you remember that the radius is half the diameter?

18. Using the interest equation for interest compounded *Q* times per year, we find that the total value of an amount *P* invested for *N* years at *I* interest, compounded *Q* times per year, is defined by:

$$A = P \times \left(1 + \frac{I}{Q}\right)^{N \times Q}$$

Translate this equation into BASIC; then write a program to produce the following input and ouput. Note that the heading automatically prints the correct values for the amount invested and the interest rate.

```
AMOUNT INVESTED (PRINCIPAL)? 7500
INTEREST RATE? (ENTER AS A DECIMAL)? .09
NUMBER OF YEARS INVESTED? 8

NUMBER OF TIMES COMPOUNDED PER YEAR? 12

WOULD YOU LIKE A PRINTED COPY (Y/N)? N

COMPOUNDED INTEREST EARNED ON
$ 7500 INVESTED AT 9%
-----------------------------

                      INTEREST
YEAR     PRINCIPAL     EARNED
----     ---------    --------

  1      7,500.00       703.56
  2      7,500.00     1,473.12
  3      7,500.00     2,314.87
  4      7,500.00     3,235.58
  5      7,500.00     4,242.66
  6      7,500.00     5,344.21
  7      7,500.00     6,549.10
  8      7,500.00     7,867.02
```

Note: A variable such as P is assumed to have only single precision (six decimal places) when the IBM PC is used. To "carry" more decimal places in calculations performed on the IBM PC, you should define a double-precision variable by using the # symbol. For example, P#, A1#, and B9# all define double-precision numeric values. The calculations done here are all based on single-precision calculations.

19. A frequently used interest equation involves continuous compounding, where the continuously compounded interest equation is defined by:

$$A = P \times E^{I \times N}$$

where I = interest rate, in decimal form
P = amount invested
N = number of years
E = base of the natural log (E = 2.71828)
A = total value of the investment

Using this equation, write a program to produce the following input and output:

```
AMOUNT INVESTED (PRINCIPAL)? 7500
INTEREST RATE? (ENTER AS A DECIMAL)? .09
NUMBER OF YEARS INVESTED? 5

WOULD YOU LIKE A PRINTED COPY (Y/N)? N

COMPOUNDED INTEREST EARNED ON
 $7,500.00 INVESTED AT 9.00%
USING CONTINUOUS COMPOUNDING
------------------------------

                          INTEREST
YEAR     PRINCIPAL         EARNED
----     ---------        --------

   1      7,500.00          706.31
   2      7,500.00        1,479.13
   3      7,500.00        2,324.73
   4      7,500.00        3,249.97
   5      7,500.00        4,262.34
```

(Note that continuous compounding makes a difference in the interest earned when compared to compounding the interest once a month, as in Exercise 18.)

20. Suppose that to finance the purchase of a new car, you must borrow $8,000, with a 36-month repayment schedule, paying $300 per month. What is the effective interest rate? The following equation is used to solve this problem:

$$I = \frac{24(M \times N - P)}{P\,(N + 1)}$$

where M = monthly payment
N = number of payments
P = loan amount

(The interest is calculated on the remaining balance of the loan.) Write a brief program that will calculate the effective interest rate, providing the following input and output.

```
LOAN AMOUNT? 8000
NUMBER OF MONTHLY PAYMENTS? 36
MONTHLY PAYMENT AMOUNT? 300

EFFECTIVE INTEREST RATE IS 22.70%
TOTAL AMOUNT PAID IS    $10,800.00
```

21. The monthly payment on a mortgage loan is often determined by using the following equation:

$$M = \frac{P \times I/12}{1 - \left(\frac{1}{1 + I/12}\right)^{(N \times 12)}}$$

where M = monthly payment
P = loan amount (principal)
N = number of years on the loan
I = interest rate

Translate this equation into BASIC, and write a program to produce the following input and output.

```
WHAT IS THE PRINCIPAL? 50000
WHAT IS THE NUMBER OF YEARS? 25
WHAT IS THE INTEREST RATE (DECIMAL FORM)? .12

THE MONTHLY PAYMENT WILL BE      $526.61
```

22. Using the data in line 10000, write a program to produce the output shown on the next page. Use LOCATE to position the question concerning the printer/screen option. (Use buffer number 2 to define the option.)

```
10000 DATA AKW,16,328.76,BBJ,14,982.45,KDB,12,477.53
```

```
                          WOULD YOU LIKE A PRINTED COPY (Y/N)? N


          BRILLIANT CORPORATION SALES REPORT
-------------------------------------------------

EMPL.     # OF      AMOUNT      % OF     AMT. SOLD
CODE      SALES      SOLD       SALES    PER SALE
-----     -----    --------     -----    ---------

 AKW        16      328.76      18.38        20.55
 BBJ        14      982.45      54.92        70.17
 KDB        12      477.53      26.70        39.79

TOTALS ====>      1,788.74     100.00
```

23. Using the data in lines 10000–10040, write a program (using PRINT USING formatting) to produce the output shown below. Do not use subscripted variables. Use buffer number 1 to format the printer/screen option.

```
10000 DATA 32000: REM ** INITIAL BUDGET                                  **
10020 DATA 04/08/84,AKX-52,585.25,4
10030 DATA 04/19/84,AKD-07,699.95,5
10040 DATA 04/20/84,QUIL/5,480.00,3
29999 DATA XX/XX/XX,XXXXXX,-999,-999
```

```
                         WOULD YOU LIKE A PRINTED COPY (Y/N)? N


INITIAL BUDGET =====>   $32,000.00

PURCHASE   ITEM    COST PER    # OF                  REMAINING
  DATE    BOUGHT     UNIT     UNITS   TOTAL COST      BUDGET
--------  ------  --------    -----   ----------    ---------

04/08/84  AKX-52    585.25      4       2,341.00    29,659.00
04/19/84  AKD-07    699.95      5       3,499.75    26,159.25
04/20/84  QUIL/5    480.00      3       1,440.00    24,719.25
```

6

Objectives

- To use nested loops to format output and to print tables of values.
- To organize numeric data into frequency distributions.
- To use a sorting technique to create an ordered sequence of numeric values or strings.

MUCH MORE ABOUT STRINGS

The preceding chapters discussed the application of several programming techniques and concepts such as loops, nested loops, logical comparisons, subscripted variables, sorting, and input/output placement through the use of TAB functions and LOCATE commands. These programming techniques were generally illustrated in programs that used numeric variables.

This chapter demonstrates that most of the techniques that work for numeric variables work just as well for string variables. In addition, string variables allow the use of special string functions, such as LEFT$, RIGHT$, MID$, STR$, LEN, and VAL. Strings may even be added through a process known as *concatenation.* (However, we cannot multiply strings, divide them, subtract them, or raise them to a power.) The string functions are used to make logical string comparisons, to help format output, and to create special print effects.

6.1 Strings Revisited: Making Comparisons

In Chapter 2 we learned to compare numbers to each other, deciding whether a particular number is equal to another number. For example, we concluded that $A <> B$ if $A = 3$ and $B = 4$. Such a comparison is used in Example 6.1.

example 6.1

```
20   INPUT "ENTER THE VALUE OF A";A
40   INPUT "ENTER THE VALUE OF B";B
60   PRINT
80   IF A = B THEN PRINT "A AND B ARE EQUAL!"
              ELSE PRINT "A IS NOT EQUAL TO B!"
30000  END
```

The **comparisons** just made for numbers can also be applied to strings. For example, we can compare the string "WILLIAM A. ROBBINS" to the string "CYNTHIA B. ARMSTRONG" and conclude that "WILLIAM A. ROBBINS" <> "CYNTHIA B. ARMSTRONG".

Such comparisons can be very useful. Suppose that a list of names and telephone numbers is to be stored for quick reference. How can we write a program that will compare a user-supplied name to the names found on the stored list? Before writing such a program, remember that the computer cannot read between the lines. For example, the computer will decide that:

```
BILL A. ROBBINS <> WILLIAM A. ROBBINS
```

Even the most minor typographical differences "confuse" the computer. In this chapter we learn some techniques that minimize this problem. In the meantime, we had better not confuse the computer by using different versions of the same name.

Let us now apply the comparison check by writing a program (Example 6.2) that yields the appropriate telephone number in response to an entered name. A phone number like 805-2619 should be read as a string because it contains a dash (-) within the series of numbers. The symbol is not a minus sign in this case because we are not trying to subtract 2619 from 805.

example 6.2

```
60   INPUT "ENTER THE NAME";N1$
80   WHILE N$ <> "END OF DATA"
100      READ N$,P$
120      IF N1$ = N$ THEN PRINT : PRINT "THE PHONE NUMBER FOR ";N1$;" IS ";P$: END
140   WEND
180   PRINT
190   PRINT "THE LIST DOES NOT INCLUDE THE NAME ";N1$: END
10000   DATA   "WILLIAM A. ROBBINS","899-3572"
10020   DATA   "SEMANTHA L. DORDON","723-1295"
10040   DATA   "CYNTHIA B. ARMSTRONG","897-3290"
10060   DATA   "EMERY G. GAFFE","998-2337"
10080   DATA   "JAMES P. KNOXX","734-2117"
30000   DATA   "END OF DATA","000-0000"
```

Before running this program we should remember the earlier caution: The user-supplied names must be spelled exactly as they appear in the data. Note, for example, that WILLIAM A. ROBBINS and WILLIAM A.ROBBINS are seen as different names by the computer because the first version had a space behind the period after the middle initial but the second name did not. The following program runs illustrate the point:

```
RUN
ENTER THE NAME?  WILLIAM A. ROBBINS

THE PHONE NUMBER FOR WILLIAM A. ROBBINS IS 899-3572

RUN
ENTER THE NAME? BILL A. ROBBINS

THE LIST DOES NOT INCLUDE THE NAME BILL A. ROBBINS

RUN
```

```
ENTER THE NAME?  WILLIAM A.ROBBINS

THE LIST DOES NOT INCLUDE THE NAME WILLIAM A.ROBBINS

RUN
ENTER THE NAME? EMERY G. GAFFE

THE PHONE NUMBER FOR EMERY G. GAFFE IS 998-2337
```

From a simple phone number search it is a relatively small step to matching a credit card number against a cardholder's current balance to decide whether credit can be extended. We can also do cross matches, entering both the name and the number and comparing the name to the one that is expected to be paired with the number. Nevertheless, the programming principles do not change. In Chapters 7 and 8 we will study files so that we can apply these programming notions in a more realistic setting.

The preceding program (Example 6.2) can be modified to perform additional tasks and to illustrate that programming techniques for numeric variables work just as well with string variables. For instance, if the variables N$ and P$ are subscripted, the data we have read can be stored temporarily.

6.2 String Functions

The LEN Function: Finding the Length of a String

Since knowing the length of a string is very helpful for planning the layout of printed headings, we are faced with the problem of variable-length strings. For example, if a programmer plans to use a maximum of 20 spaces for a name and a name with 23 spaces appears, the programmer will have to measure the length of the string before trying to insert it into the designated heading. The programmer can alert the program user to the problem, or "cut" the name to fit the space, or choose from among several other options. To find the length of a string B$, you can use the LEN function:

```
LEN(B$)
```

For example, you can write the program in Example 6.3:

example 6.3

```
20 INPUT "TYPE A NAME";B$
40 L = LEN(B$)
60 PRINT:PRINT "THE LENGTH OF THE STRING ";B$;" IS";L
30000 END
```

Running this program yields the following results:

```
TYPE A NAME? JANE Q. DOE

THE LENGTH OF THE STRING JANE Q. DOE IS 11
```

The LEN function causes the computer to count any characters in the string, blanks and periods—and any other symbols—included.

It is not necessary to define a string as a string variable before counting the number of places in it. For example, to get the length of the string "THIS IS A STRING", you can simply type:

```
PRINT LEN ("THIS IS A STRING")
```

The printed answer is equal to 16. Remember, however, to write the string in quotes *if* it is not already defined to be a string variable. Failure to put quotes around such a string will result in a **type mismatch error** because the lack of quotes causes the computer to expect a numeric value. The LEN function is strictly designed for strings: It cannot be used to measure the number of places in a number unless the number is first converted into a string. We will perform this act of magic in the section that follows.

The STR$ Conversion: Changing a Number into a String

A numeric value can be changed into a string by using the **STR$** function. The program in Example 6.4 illustrates the point. After changing the numeric value into a string, we can find its length.

example 6.4

```
20  V = 3.721
40  V$ = STR$(V)
60  K = LEN(V$)
80  PRINT : PRINT "THE VALUE OF V IS";V
100  PRINT "THE STRING V$ IS";V$
120  PRINT "THE LENGTH OF THE STRING V$ IS";K
30000  END

RUN

THE VALUE OF V IS 3.721
THE STRING V$ IS 3.721
THE LENGTH OF THE STRING V$ IS 6
```

The program's output indicates that the decimal point is counted, too. The number 3.721 contains four digits and one decimal point, plus the (unprinted) + sign, for a total of six places in the string. Being able to count spaces in a number enables us to space values across a page. For example, we can use a TAB function whose value is determined by the length of the number. By using such variable TAB functions, we can lay out a general screen spacing that would be more flexible to the program's user.

The VAL Function: Changing the String Back into a Number

Just as numbers are changed into strings, those strings can be changed back into numbers. The feat may be accomplished by using the **VAL** function. For example, if we define E$ = "3.1415", we can find the number E by using:

```
E = VAL(E$)
```

The procedure is demonstrated in Example 6.5.

example 6.5

```
20   A = 3.1415
40   E$ = STR$(A)
60   E = VAL(E$)
80   PRINT : PRINT "VARIABLE 'A' IS EQUAL TO";A
100   PRINT "VARIABLE 'E$' IS EQUAL TO";E$
120   PRINT "VARIABLE 'E' IS EQUAL TO";E
30000   END

RUN

VARIABLE 'A' IS EQUAL TO 3.1415
VARIABLE 'E$' IS EQUAL TO 3.1415
VARIABLE 'E' IS EQUAL TO 3.1415
```

The output resulting from the preceding program is the value (or the string) 3.1415 in each of the three cases. The ability to change numbers into strings and back into numbers will turn out to be handy when we begin graphing.

The LEFT$ Function

A left-hand portion of any string may be selected by using the LEFT$ command, using the format LEFT$(string, number of characters to be included). For example, the statement:

```
PRINT LEFT$("PROBABILITY",5)
```

yields the five left-most places in the string "PROBABILITY". In other words, the PRINT command yields the output:

```
PROBA
```

The string "PROBABILITY" may first be defined as a string variable, as shown in Example 6.6

example 6.6

```
20 K$ = "PROBABILITY"
40 PRINT LEFT$(K$,5)
30000 END
```

Running this program will produce the same output: We will see the word segment PROBA again.

The LEFT$ command is especially useful for writing programs for others to use and for programs in which we want a YES or NO response from the user. Perhaps the user has not read the program's prompting very well, or perhaps the programmer did not do an adequate job in writing the program. Whatever the reason, suppose that we have written the following program lines:

```
20 INPUT "PLEASE ANSWER YES OR NO (Y/N) ";A$
40 IF A$ = "Y" THEN . . .
. .
. .
```

If someone types YES in response to the question, even though program users are expected to type the single letter Y, the program will not execute properly. On the other hand, if line 40 is changed to read:

```
40 IF LEFT$(A$,1) = "Y" THEN . . .
```

responses such as Y, YES, YEAH, and YUP all lead to the desired result because the computer looks only at the left-most character in the response.

Lowercase Characters and Capitals

The preceding line 40 assumed that a capital letter Y was used in response to the question PLEASE ANSWER YES OR NO (Y/N)? If the response is made in lowercase, the statement IF LEFT$(A$,1) = "Y" THEN . . . will not be executed properly because the computer will not "see" the letters "Y" and "y" in the same way. We may fix that problem by using:

```
IF LEFT$(A$,1) = "Y" OR LEFT$(A$,1) = "y" THEN . . .
```

The MID$ Function

Given our experience with the LEFT$ function, it should not be surprising that the **MID$** function allows us to get inside the string. Usually, the MID$ function is used with three arguments: The first is the string itself, the second tells where to start in the string, and the third tells how many elements are included. Therefore, the statement:

```
MID$("PROBABILITY",4,3)
```

yields the result BAB since we start with the fourth letter and end three letters later. Similarly,

```
MID$("PROBABILITY",3,5)
```

yields the result OBABI, since the count starts at the third letter and includes five letters. Writing the following two program lines:

```
20 A$="PROBABILITY"
40 PRINT MID$(A$,3,5)
```

produces the same results.

The MID$ function may be used with two arguments:

```
PRINT MID$("PROBABILITY",4)
```

The second argument specifies only the starting place—starting at the left of the string—and the lack of a third argument indicates that all the remaining characters will be included. Therefore, the preceding PRINT command yields the string BABILITY.

The MID$ function is especially useful in a loop, allowing programmers to print strings vertically. Let us take a look at the next program (Example 6.7).

example 6.7

```
20 V$ ="VALUE"
40 FOR I = 1 TO LEN(V$)
60      PRINT MID$(V$,I,1)
80 NEXT I
30000 END
```

Running the program yields the results described in Table 6.1.

The program writes the string vertically. Such a technique is useful for labeling the vertical axis of a diagram.

table 6.1
THE EFFECT OF MID$(V$,I,1) COMMAND IN A LOOP

Value of I	MID$(V$,I,1)	Result
1	MID$(V$,1,1)	V
2	MID$(V$,2,1)	A
3	MID$(V$,3,1)	L
4	MID$(V$,4,1)	U
5	MID$(V$,5,1)	E

What was done with a word may be done with a number, after the number has been converted into a string by the STR$ command. For example, the sequence:

```
20   N = 3.1415
40   N$ = STR$(N)
60   PRINT MID$(N$,3)
```

yields the outcome .1415, since the first character is the (unprinted) + sign, the second is the digit 3, and the third character is the decimal point. We can strip numbers this way or reconfigure them in any format desired.

A number may be printed vertically just as words are printed vertically. For example, the value 3.14 is printed vertically by writing:

```
10 N = 3.14
20 N$ = STR$(N)
40 FOR I = 1 TO LEN(N$)
60      PRINT MID$(N$,I,1)
80 NEXT I
```

Running this program yields the result:

```
3
.
1
4
```

We can print this value diagonally by substituting:

```
60 PRINT TAB(I);MID$(N$,I,1)
```

into the preceding program, yielding the result:

```
 3
  .
   1
    4
```

Such formatting can be very helpful for labeling the horizontal axis of a graph when only a limited number of columns is available and the numbers are too long to fit the allotted spaces.

Counting Decimal Places with MID$

One of the useful formatting features of the MID$ function is its ability to count the number of decimal places in a number. The use of the MID$ application is shown in Example 6.8.

example 6.8

```
20   INPUT "ENTER A NUMBER ";X
40   X$ = STR$(X) : REM ** CHANGE THE NUMBER INTO A STRING    **
60   L = LEN(X$) : REM ** FIND THE LENGTH OF THE STRING       **
80   FOR I = 1 TO L
100       IF MID$(X$,I,1) = "." THEN D = L - I
120 NEXT I
130 IF D = 1 THEN A$ = "DECIMAL PLACE." ELSE A$ = "DECIMAL PLACES."
140 PRINT : PRINT "THE VALUE";X;"HAS";D;A$
30000 END
```

Suppose we run the preceding program, using X = 1.3. The program will perform the following calculations and procedures.

1. If the program is run, the value of L will be 4: the string length includes the (unprinted) sign.

2. The loop in line 80 stops, therefore, at L = 4.

3. During the first pass (I = 1) through the loop, MID$(X$,I,1) is a blank because the (unprinted sign is included). Since no decimal has been encountered, the IF statement simply allows the loop to be completed at line 120.

4. During the third pass (I = 3) through the loop, MID$(X$,I,1) = ".". Therefore, D = 4 − 3 = 1.

5. Since no additional decimals are encountered, D remains at 1.

The following program runs demonstrate that the program works as intended.

```
RUN
ENTER A NUMBER 1.3

THE VALUE 1.3 HAS 1 DECIMAL PLACE.


RUN
ENTER A NUMBER 23

THE VALUE 23 HAS 0 DECIMAL PLACES.


RUN
ENTER A NUMBER .013756

THE VALUE .013756 HAS 6 DECIMAL PLACES.
```

The ability to count decimal places is especially handy when STEP functions are used. For example, if numbers are measured to the nearest .01, the sequence from low (L) to high (H) might be written as follows:

```
FOR I = L TO H STEP .01
```

Unfortunately, if a different set of numbers is used, the step amount may no longer be appropriate. Numbers measured to the nearest .001 would require that the preceding line be rewritten. If, on the other hand, we let the computer count the decimal places as shown in Example 6.8, the line could be written as follows:

```
FOR I = L TO H STEP 10^(-D)
```

Since 10 raised to a negative power is a decimal—10ˆ(−2) = .01, for example—the line will now automatically adjust the STEP for any numbers used in the program.

The RIGHT$ Function

The **RIGHT$** function works in the same way as the LEFT$ function except that the count begins on the right instead of on the left. For example, the statement:

```
PRINT RIGHT$("I HAVE IT",2)
```

yields the result IT. Similarly, the two lines:

```
20   B$ = "JOHN D. HOPPER"
40   PRINT RIGHT$(B$,6)
```

produce the output HOPPER. The ability to isolate portions of strings is useful for searching a list of names for specified characteristics. For example, the problem of dealing with an incorrectly spelled first name (see Section 6.1) can be reduced by letting the computer check the last name, too.

The RIGHT$ function can be used in a loop with either subscripted or unsubscripted variables. The simple loop (lines 40–80) shown in Example 6.9 yields the accompanying output.

example 6.9

```
20   A$ = "VALUE"
40   FOR I = 1 TO LEN(A$)
60        PRINT RIGHT$(A$,I)
80   NEXT I
30000 END
```

```
RUN

E
UE
LUE
ALUE
VALUE
```

As with the other string commands, the RIGHT$ command can be used to format output. For example, the preceding program can be modified slightly, producing the program shown in Example 6.10 (followed by its output).

example 6.10

```
10   PRINT
20   A$ = "VALUE"
30   L = LEN(A$)
40   FOR I = 1 TO LEN(A$)
60        PRINT RIGHT$(A$,I);
65        PRINT " * ";
70        PRINT RIGHT$(A$,L+1-I)
80   NEXT I
30000   END

RUN

E * VALUE
UE * ALUE
LUE * LUE
ALUE * UE
VALUE * E
```

An argument of 0 is not allowed. Therefore, line 70 shows the addition of 1 to the length of the string L, to ensure that the last argument in the loop is 1.

6.3 Concatenation: Adding Strings

We can add strings just as we can add numbers. The addition of strings is known as **concatenation.** For example, if we define:

```
A$ = "PROBABILITY"
B$ = " "
C$ = "VALUES"
```

we can conclude that the addition sequence A$ + B$ + C$ yields the output:

```
"PROBABILITY VALUES"
```

(Note: B$ is a blank, defined as a set of quotes containing a blank space.) In program form, the procedure might look like Example 6.11.

example 6.11

```
20   A$ = "PROBABILITY": B$ = " ":C$ = "VALUES"
40   D$ = A$ + B$ + C$
60   PRINT D$
30000   END
```

Take a look at the effect of concatenation in Example 6.12, followed by its output.

example 6.12

```
20   FOR I = 1 TO 5
40        M$ = M$ + "*"
60        PRINT TAB(10);M$
80   NEXT I
30000   END
```

```
RUN
          *
          **
          ***
          ****
          *****
```

Running this program should not yield any surprises. Since M$ was not previously defined, M$ is an empty (null) string before the loop is executed. Each time the program completes a pass through the loop, an asterisk is added. The output may be changed by using a continuation symbol in line 60, rewriting the line to read:

```
60   PRINT M$;
```

The resulting output would be a string composed of 15 asterisks:

```
***************
```

If the variable M$ must be used again in a nested loop, it may be reset to a null string by using M$ = "". Note that the quotes do not contain a space.

6.4 Sorting Strings into Alphabetical Order

Sorting strings can be accomplished by the procedure used for sorting numeric variables. The explanation of the sorting procedure is identical to that given in Section 5.3. Consequently, the string sorting program (Example 6.13) is nearly identical to the program presented in Example 5.7. The only difference is that the program now reads string variables rather than numeric variables.

example 6.13

```
220 CLS: KEY OFF: REM ** CLEAR THE SCREEN                    **
230 DIM X$(100), X1$(100)
240 N = 1: READ X$(N): X1$(N) = X$(N)
260 WHILE X$(N) <> "EOF"
280     N = N + 1: READ X$(N): X1$(N) = X$(N)
300 WEND
320 N = N - 1: REM ** # VALUES READ FROM THE DATE LINE **
5000 REM ***********************************************
5020 REM *           PERFORM THE BUBBLE SORT            *
5040 REM ***********************************************
5060 C = 1
5080 WHILE C <= N - 1
5120     J = C + 1
5160     WHILE J <= N
5200         IF X$(C) > X$(J) THEN SWAP X$(C),X$(J)
5220         J = J + 1
5240     WEND
5270     C = C + 1
5300 WEND
6000 REM ***********************************************
6020 REM *   PRINT THE ORIGINAL AND SORTED DATA VALUES   *
6040 REM ***********************************************
6050 CLS
6060 PRINT "ORIGINAL"; TAB(15);"SORTED"
6080 PRINT "STRINGS"; TAB(15);"STRINGS"
6100 PRINT "--------"; TAB(15);"-------": PRINT
6120 C = 1
6140 WHILE C <= N
6160     PRINT TAB(3);X1$(C);  TAB(17);X$(C)
6180     C = C + 1
6200 WEND
10000 DATA ABE,DCB,AAC,DEA,DDA,AAA,CBB,ABA,BBB
29999 DATA EOF
30000 END
```

```
RUN

ORIGINAL      SORTED
STRINGS       STRINGS
--------      -------

  ABE           AAA
  DCB           AAC
  AAC           ABA
  DEA           ABE
  DDA           BBB
  AAA           CBB
  CBB           DCB
  ABA           DDA
  BBB           DEA
```

Running the program (Example 6.13) may yield a few minor surprises when the data are composed of strings containing a mixture of letters and numerals or symbols. Note, for example, what happens when we change the data lines and run the program again:

```
RUN

ORIGINAL      SORTED
STRINGS       STRINGS
--------      -------

  5AAA          ***A
  2AAA          ///A
  4AAA          //AA
  1AAA          1AAA
  AAAA          1ABB
  3BBB          1BBB
  //AA          2AAA
  ///A          3BBB
  ***A          4AAA
  A1AA          5AAA
  AA1A          A1AA
  1BBB          AA1A
  1ABB          AAAA
```

The numeric value that is part of the string apparently takes precedence over the letters. Therefore, the string 1AAA occurs before AAAA, and 3BBB occurs before 4AAA. Less obviously, asterisks seem to be listed before slashes—as shown in the preceding sequence. The reason for such sorting orders is found in the binary equivalent for the various characters, which is lower for an asterisk than that for a slash.

6.5 Sorting Names

Names are often stored in DATA lines or in files in the following sequence: first name, middle initial, last name. When **sorting names** in alphabetical order, however, the sorting is usually done by the last name. Fortunately, a simple program using both MID$ and RIGHT$ functions can accomplish the switch to last names easily, as shown in Example 6.14.

example 6.14

```
20 PRINT "ENTER YOUR NAME: FIRST NAME, MIDDLE"
40 PRINT "INITIAL, LAST NAME. (EXAMPLE:"
60 INPUT "JANE Q. DOE)";N$
110 PRINT: PRINT
115 PRINT " C"; TAB(7);"MID$(N$,C)"; TAB(20);"MID$(N$,C,1)"
120 PRINT: C = LEN(N$)
140 WHILE MID$(N$,C,1) <> " " AND C > 0
160     PRINT C; TAB(8); MID$(N$,C); TAB(25);MID$(N$,C,1)
180     C = C - 1
200 WEND
220 PRINT: PRINT "YOUR LAST NAME IS ";MID$(N$,C+1)
```

The same output can be generated with the help of the RIGHT$ function, starting with the last character in the last name.

Line 140 looks for a space before the last name. Other cues, such as the presence of a period (.) may be added by the programmer. The program as written is not foolproof: When a last name contains spaces (VAN DER LAAG), only a portion of the name will be printed.

```
RUN
ENTER YOUR NAME:FIRST NAME, MIDDLE
INITIAL, LAST NAME.  EXAMPLE:
JANE Q. DOE)? PETER ROB

 C    MID$(N$,C)    MID$(N$,C,1)

 9     B                 B
 8     OB                O
 7     ROB               R

YOUR LAST NAME IS ROB
```

Chapter Review

Knowing the string functions is important for several reasons. First, many of the data to be processed consist of strings rather than numeric values. Second, string functions can be used for formatting output. Third, the string functions can be used to create special print effects or printer graphics.

Many of the techniques learned in earlier chapters work equally well on string variables. However, several of these techniques—such as logical comparisons and sorting—deserve special emphasis. The logical comparisons are used to compare input strings with stored strings, thereby allowing us to search stored strings for particular variables or characteristics. The sorting techniques (of which only the bubble sort was highlighted) are included because the ability to alphabetize lists is important. Sorting routines that are faster than the bubble sort may be used, and string variables may be chosen instead of numeric variables.

The length of a string is measured by the LEN function. This function can also be used to measure the length of a number—after the number has been changed into a string by the STR$ function. The resulting string can then be changed back into a numeric value by using the VAL function. These string functions allow the user to plan output heading spacing and numeric value placement. The LEFT$, RIGHT$, and MID$ functions are all used to strip designated portions of strings, starting at the left, the right, or anywhere inside the string. These string functions play an especially important role in output formatting and special printer effects.

Common Errors

1. Using illegal string arguments. The first MID$ argument, for example, must be greater than zero.

Correct:

```
20   FOR I = 5 TO 1 STEP -1
40        PRINT MID$(F$,5+1-I,1);
60   NEXT I
```

Incorrect:

```
20   FOR I = 5 TO 1 STEP -1
40        PRINT MID$(F$,5-I,1)
60   NEXT I
```

(When I = 5, 5 − I = 0)

2. Failure to set string accumulators back to null if they are to be used again. (This is just as necessary with strings as it is for numeric counters to be set back to zero before they are reused!)

Correct:

```
20   FOR I = 1 TO 3
40        FOR J = 1 TO 5
60             M$ = M$ + "*"
80        NEXT J
100     PRINT M$
120     M$ = ""
140  NEXT I
```

Incorrect:

```
20   FOR I = 1 TO 3
40        FOR J = 1 TO 5
60             M$ = M$ + "*"
80        NEXT J
100     PRINT M$
120  NEXT I
```

3. Improper selection of string functions to find a specific character in a string. Example: Find the letter B in the string A$ and print the substring BEARS.

Correct:

```
20   A$ = "THREE BEARS"
40   L = LEN(A$)
60   FOR I = 1 TO L
80        IF MID$(A$,I,1) = "B" THEN PRINT RIGHT$(A$,L-I+1)
100  NEXT I
```

Incorrect (same program, but line 80 is changed):

```
80        IF LEFT$(A$,I) = "B" THEN . . .
```

(The letter B is included when I = 7. However, the substring LEFT$(A$,I) = "THREE B" and not just the letter B. The IF condition, therefore, will never be met.)

Key Terms and Concepts

comparisons
LEN
type mismatch error
STR$
VAL
LEFT$
MID$
RIGHT$
concatenation
sorting strings
sorting names

Exercises

1. Write a program that will produce the following output by using a LEFT$ function in a loop.

```
U
UN
UND
UNDE
UNDER
UNDERS
UNDERST
UNDERSTA
UNDERSTAN
UNDERSTAND
```

2. Using a MID$ command, write a program to produce the following output. *Hint:* Use only a single argument.

```
PROBABILITY
ROBABILITY
OBABILITY
BABILITY
ABILITY
BILITY
ILITY
LITY
ITY
TY
Y
```

3. Write a program that prints only the names of those whose surnames end with -son. The data lines contain the following names:

```
10000 DATA "JOHN A. ROBERTSON", "LINDA D. SANFORTE"
10010 DATA "CYNTHIA K. JACKSON", "JAMES D. BORDON"
10020 DATA "WILLIAM E. MORSE", "ELMER L. MORRISON"
```

4. Modify the program in Example 6.10 to produce the following output. *Hint:* Do another loop with a continuation symbol (;), using a PRINT statement outside this loop to terminate the continuation.

```
*   E * * * VALUE   *   E * * * VALUE   *
*   UE * * * ALUE   *   UE * * * ALUE   *
*   LUE * * * LUE   *   LUE * * * LUE   *
*   ALUE * * * UE   *   ALUE * * * UE   *
*   VALUE * * * E   *   VALUE * * * E   *

*   E * * * VALUE   *   E * * * VALUE   *
*   UE * * * ALUE   *   UE * * * ALUE   *
*   LUE * * * LUE   *   LUE * * * LUE   *
*   ALUE * * * UE   *   ALUE * * * UE   *
*   VALUE * * * E   *   VALUE * * * E   *
```

5. Use a MID$ function to write a program that will print only the last name when you input the first name, the middle initial, and the last name. A sample input/output follows:

```
ENTER YOUR NAME: FIRST NAME, MIDDLE INITIAL,
LAST NAME. (EXAMPLE: JANE Q. DOE) SOUPIE D. GANDER

YOUR LAST NAME IS GANDER

ENTER YOUR NAME: FIRST NAME, MIDDLE, INITIAL
LAST NAME. (EXAMPLE JANE Q. DOE) GONDOLA F. TERRIFIC

YOUR LAST NAME IS TERRIFIC
```

6. Now modify the program in Exercise 5 so that it will produce the same input/output with a RIGHT$ function.

7. Write a program to print the list of last names in alphabetical order; the data lines follow:

```
10000  DATA  "WILLIAM A. ROBBINS","899-3572"
10020  DATA  "SEMANTHA L. DORDON","723-1295"
10040  DATA  "CYNTHIA B. ARMSTRONG","897-3290"
10060  DATA  "EMERY G. GAFFE","998-2337"
10080  DATA  "JAMES P. KNOXX","734-2117"
29000  DATA  "END OF DATA","000-0000"
30000  END
```

(**Note:** Ignore the telephone numbers at this point.)
The program's output follows.

```
  ORIGINAL NAMES        SORTED LAST NAMES
--------------------    -----------------

WILLIAM A. ROBBINS      ARMSTRONG
SEMANTHA L. DORDON      DORDON
CYNTHIA B. ARMSTRONG    GAFFE
EMERY G. GAFFE          KNOXX
JAMES P. KNOXX          ROBBINS
```

8. Now modify the program you wrote in Exercise 7 to include the correct telephone number, as well. The output should look like this:

```
NAME                  TELEPHONE #
---------             -----------

ARMSTRONG              897-3290
DORDON                 723-1295
GAFFE                  998-2337
KNOXX                  734-2117
ROBBINS                899-3572
```

These names and telephone numbers are correctly matched.

9. Without using any dimensioned variables and using strings only, write a program to print address labels. Give the user an option to print 1, 2, or 3 labels across the page, using the data lines shown.

```
10000 DATA ANNE G. ROBYM,"RT. 8, BOX 164D","MURFREESBORO, TN 37130"
10020 DATA JOHN Q. DOER,"215 ORANGE LANE","CENTER CITY, OH 21228"
10040 DATA ANNELISE T. COLLINS,"624 BANYAN ST.","HONOLULU, HI 28716"
10060 DATA JEROME D. ADLER,"229 E. LAKE DR.","DETROIT, MI 31217"
10080 DATA KALIL E. ANOTTO,"131 E. MAIN","HUNTSVILLE, AL 35345"
30000 DATA EOF,EOF,EOF

HOW MANY LABELS ACROSS (1, 2, OR 3)? 3

ANNELISE T. COLLINS     JOHN Q. DOER             ANNE G. ROBYM
624 BANYAN ST.          215 ORANGE LANE          RT. 8, BOX 164D
HONOLULU, HI 28716      CENTER CITY, OH 21228    MURFREESBORO, TN 37130

KALIL E. ANOTTO         JEROME D. ADLER
131 E. MAIN             229 E. LAKE DR.
HUNTSVILLE, AL 35345    DETROIT, MI 31217
```

7

Objectives

- To use subroutines to perform specific programming tasks.
- To structure the program by letting a main routine call the various program subroutines.
- To use a menu in which any selection leads to the use of a specific subroutine.
- To use ON . . . GOSUB to branch the program to specific subroutines.

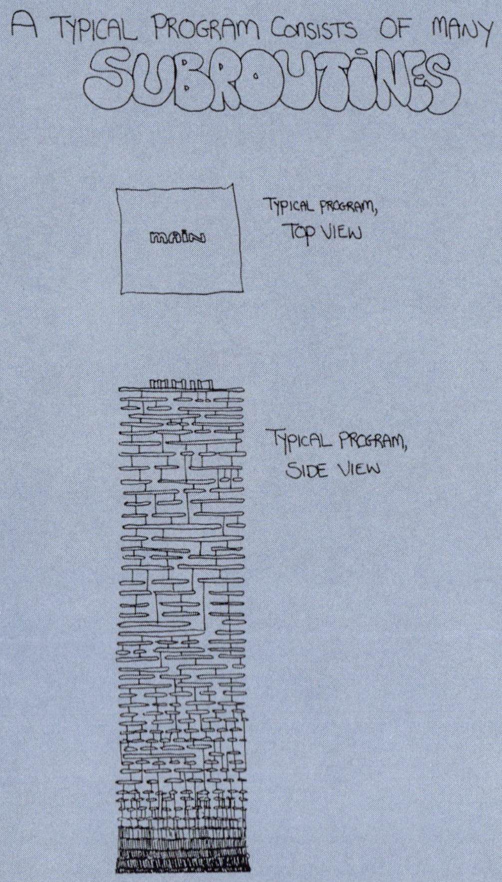

USING SUBROUTINES

We have discussed programming techniques used to perform specific tasks. Many of these tasks were performed repeatedly, and many were done on a conditional basis. Some of the more complex programs used multiple IF statements to branch to various portions of the program. Although the programs performed their intended functions, program logic and program structure were occasionally difficult to follow.

In this chapter we learn to structure programs more carefully by using modules known as *subroutines*. Subroutines help us to perform specific programming tasks, each functioning as a nearly independent program. We also discover that programs can be written to give the program user various options, which are presented in the form of a *menu* that lists a set of choices from which the user may make a selection. Such choices lead to specific subroutines.

7.1. Subroutines and Why They are Used

As programming experience is gained and more complex problems are handled, programs tend to become longer and more complicated. Longer and more complex programs become difficult to read when they contain multiple GOTO statements and/or numerous calculation and heading duplications. A program that is difficult to read is, no doubt, difficult to write and, even worse, difficult to modify. Errors, too, are hard to find and correct when multiple GOTO statements criss-cross programs. Therefore, we need to develop a way of breaking a program into manageable parts, or modules. Such modules, called **subroutines,** act as small, independent programs that perform specific tasks.

If a program contains several subroutines, it can be divided into a *main program* and a set of subroutines. More complex programs are often written so that the main program's primary function is to call the necessary subroutines. Programs of this type are easier to read and, more important, can be written by a team of programmers, with each team member programming a separate subroutine. A program coordinator may direct a team's activities and put the various subroutines together. Using such an approach, complex programs can be written in a fraction of the time that otherwise would have been needed.

GOSUB and RETURN: Calling a Subroutine and Returning to the Main Program

Control is transferred to a subroutine by using the **GOSUB** statement. Control is returned to the main program by terminating the subroutine with a **RETURN** statement. For example, let us examine the program lines in Example 7.1. The brackets show the effect of the control transfer procedure.

example 7.1

```
20   PRINT "USING A SUBROUTINE":PRINT
40   GOSUB 1000
60   PRINT:PRINT "WE HAVE RETURNED."
80   END
1000   FOR I = 1 TO 2
1020        PRINT TAB(5):"WE ARE IN THE SUBROUTINE"
1040   NEXT I
1060   RETURN
```

When the preceding program is run, the following lines are printed:

```
USING A SUBROUTINE

     WE ARE IN THE SUBROUTINE
     WE ARE IN THE SUBROUTINE

WE HAVE RETURNED
```

There are a few points worth noting in the program. First, the GOSUB statement in line 40 passes control to line 1000. Second, the RETURN statement returns control to the main program one line *after* the GOSUB statement. (If control is returned to line 40, the program will be stuck in an infinite loop.) Third, the program is terminated with an END statement. If we forget to insert line 80, the program will run into line 1060 again, this time without the benefit of a GOSUB statement. The reward for this event will be an error message:

```
RETURN WITHOUT GOSUB
```

or other words to that effect. We do not, apparently, want to run into a subroutine accidentally.

In such a simple program it is tempting (*and definitely not recommended!*) to use GOTO rather than GOSUB. For instance, the preceding program can be rewritten as follows.

example 7.2

```
20   PRINT : PRINT "USING A GOTO STATEMENT": PRINT
40   GOTO 1000
60   PRINT : PRINT "WE HAVE RETURNED."
80   GOTO 30000
1000   FOR I = 1 TO 2
1040        PRINT TAB(5);"WE ARE IN THE `GOTO' LOOP!'
1060   NEXT I
1080   GOTO 60
30000   END
```

```
RUN

USING A GOTO STATEMENT

      WE ARE IN THE 'GOTO' LOOP!
      WE ARE IN THE 'GOTO' LOOP!

WE HAVE RETURNED.
```

Apparently, the GOTO statement can perform functions similar to those performed by the GOSUB procedure. As programs become more complex, however, such multiple GOTO statements are likely to lead to increased complexity and, therefore, to an increased error probability. The use of such multiple GOTO statements is, therefore, not recommended.

Multiple Subroutines

A program may contain **multiple subroutines.** As more subroutines are used and the "modular" design of the program has to be highlighted, REM statements are often used to focus attention on the subroutine's location. A line such as:

```
REM ******** START OF SUBROUTINE ********
```

can be very useful for this purpose. The use of REM statements in conjunction with multiple subroutines is illustrated in Example 7.3.

example 7.3

```
20   PRINT : PRINT "THIS IS AN EXERCISE IN THE"
40   PRINT "USE OF A SUBROUTINE."
60   GOSUB 500
80   PRINT : PRINT "FIRST SUBROUTINE IS DONE!"
200  GOSUB 1000
220  PRINT : PRINT "SECOND SUBROUTINE IS DONE!"
240  END
490  REM  ********** START SUBROUTINE #1 ***********
500  PRINT : PRINT "FIRST SUBROUTINE IS STARTED!"
510  PRINT
520  FOR I = 1 TO 2
540      PRINT "PASS #";I;"IN SUBROUTINE #1"
550  NEXT I
560  RETURN
570  REM  **********  END SUBROUTINE #1   ***********
580  REM
990  REM  ********** START SUBROUTINE #2 ***********
```

```
1000  PRINT : PRINT "SECOND SUBROUTINE IS STARTED!"
1010  PRINT
1020  FOR I = 1 TO 3
1040      PRINT "PASS #";I;"IN SUBROUTINE #2"
1050  NEXT I
1060  RETURN
1070  REM  **********  END SUBROUTINE #2  **********


RUN

THIS IS AN EXERCISE IN THE
USE OF A SUBROUTINE.

FIRST SUBROUTINE IS STARTED!

PASS # 1 IN SUBROUTINE #1
PASS # 2 IN SUBROUTINE #1

FIRST SUBROUTINE IS DONE!

SECOND SUBROUTINE IS STARTED!

PASS # 1 IN SUBROUTINE #2
PASS # 2 IN SUBROUTINE #2
PASS # 3 IN SUBROUTINE #2

SECOND SUBROUTINE IS DONE!
```

Making Subroutines Very Visible

Since subroutines are, in effect, program modules that are capable of performing a particular activity, they must be readily identifiable. Recall the REM format shown in Example 7.3.

```
490  REM  **********  START SUBROUTINE #1  **********
```

Many programmers, however, use an alternate REM format:

```
490  REM
492  REM  ****************************************
494  REM  *           SUBROUTINE #1              *
496  REM  ****************************************
498  REM
```

and this one is preferable. Each of the activities within the subroutine is highlighted with an individual REM statement, as demonstrated in Example 7.4, below.

NOTE

Although the REM shown in Example 7.4 is preferred, it also uses up much space on the page. Therefore, we will use the less space-consuming REM procedure (shown in Example 7.3) in the remainder of this text. The more elaborate version should be used whenever you are involved with a complex programming procedure!

Application of Multiple Subroutines

Let us now take a look at an application of the GOSUB command, Example 7.4 illustrates the use of two subroutines: one for students and one for people over 65 years of age. The program consists of two parts: the main program (lines 20–460) and the subroutines. (In many complex programs the main program serves primarily to transfer control to the various subroutines.)

The program output consists of sales receipts, and each receipt has a message appropriate to one of our two age groups. The program is run twice, once for each group, to illustrate the effect of the subroutines.

example 7.4

```
20 INPUT "PLEASE ENTER THE LIST PRICE";L
40 PRINT: PRINT "PLEASE SELECT ONE OF THE FOLLOWING:": PRINT
60 PRINT TAB(10);"1. STUDENT"
80 PRINT TAB(10);"2. OVER 65": PRINT
100 INPUT "SELECTION";S
120 IF S = 1 THEN GOSUB 5000
140 IF S = 2 THEN GOSUB 6000
160 P = L - D*L: REM ** DISCOUNT PRICE                      **
180 P1 = P*T: REM ** SALES TAX AMOUNT                       **
200 P2 = P + P1: REM ** DISCOUNT PRICE PLUS TAX             **
300 PRINT: PRINT: PRINT S$: PRINT
340 PRINT "LIST PRICE ====================> $";
350 PRINT USING "###.##";L
360 PRINT D$;" DISCOUNT PRICE ========> $";
370 PRINT USING "###.##";P
380 PRINT "TAX PAID (";T*100;"%) ==============> $ ";
390 PRINT USING "###.##";P1
400 PRINT
```

```
420 PRINT "TOTAL PAID ===================> $";
430 PRINT USING "###.##";P2
440 PRINT: PRINT "THANKS FOR STOPPING AT ** K&D **"
460 END
5000 REM
5005 REM ***********************************************
5010 REM *              STUDENT SUBROUTINE              *
5015 REM ***********************************************
5020 REM
5030 T = .06: REM ** TAX RATE                          **
5040 D = .1: REM ** DISCOUNT RATE                      **
5060 D$ = "STUDENT"
5080 S$ = " GO, GO, GO BIG BLUE! BEAT THE LIONS!"
5100 RETURN
5140 REM
6000 REM
6005 REM ***********************************************
6010 REM *              OVER 65 SUBROUTINE              *
6015 REM ***********************************************
6020 REM
6030 T = .06: REM ** TAX RATE                          **
6040 D = .15: REM ** DISCOUNT RATE                     **
6060 D$ = "OVER 65"
6080 S$ = "HAVE YOU CHECKED OUR OTHER SPECIALS?"
6100 RETURN
```

```
RUN
PLEASE ENTER THE LIST PRICE? 37.97

PLEASE SELECT ONE OF THE FOLLOWING:

1. STUDENT
2. OVER 65

SELECTION? 1

GO, GO, GO BIG BLUE! BEAT THE LIONS!

LIST PRICE ===================> $ 37.97
STUDENT DISCOUNT PRICE ========> $ 34.17
TAX PAID ( 6%) ================> $  2.05

TOTAL PAID ===================> $ 36.22

THANKS FOR SHOPPING AT ** K&D **
```

```
RUN
PLEASE ENTER THE LIST PRICE? 37.97

PLEASE SELECT ONE OF THE FOLLOWING:

1. STUDENT
2. OVER 65

SELECTION? 2


HAVE YOU CHECKED OUR OTHER SPECIALS?

LIST PRICE ====================> $ 37.97
OVER 65 DISCOUNT PRICE ========> $ 32.27
TAX PAID ( 4%) ================> $  1.29

TOTAL PAID ====================> $ 33.56

THANKS FOR SHOPPING AT ** K&D **
```

7.2 The ON . . . GOSUB Command

Reviewing the program presented in Example 7.4, we note that the subroutine is selected on the basis of a menu consisting of two choices. We type either a 1 for students or a 2 for people over 65; then the program branches to the subroutine on the basis of the IF statements in lines 120 and 140. (The term "branch" indicates that control is passed to a different portion of the program.) IF statements work well when only a few choices are available; they become cumbersome when there are many possible choices. The **ON . . . GOSUB** command takes the place of the IF statements in Example 7.4 if we delete lines 120 and 140 and substitute a single line:

```
120 ON S GOSUB 5000,6000
```

Line 120 now directs the program to pass control to the subroutine starting with line 5000 if S = 1. The condition S = 2 causes the program to pass control to the subroutine that starts with line 6000. We should note that the input value in line 100 in Example 7.4 provides the value for S in the new line 120.

The efficiency of the ON ... GOSUB command becomes obvious when the menu provides many possible choices. For example, if the menu contains five choices, we can write:

```
IF S = 1 THEN GOSUB 5000
IF S = 2 THEN GOSUB 6000
```

```
IF S = 3 THEN GOSUB 7000
IF S = 4 THEN GOSUB 8000
IF S = 5 THEN GOSUB 9000
```

Or these five IF statements can be replaced by:

```
ON S GOSUB 5000,6000,7000,8000,9000
```

A subroutine can be used more than once. For example, a single subroutine may satisfy the requirements of several selections from this menu. For instance, the statement:

```
ON S GOSUB 2000,3000,2000,4000,3000
```

is quite acceptable. The only restriction is that there must be as many GOSUB selections as there are possible menu selections. If, for example, there are five possible values for S, there must be five GOSUB selections, even if some of the GOSUB selections refer to the same subroutine.

Procedure for Calling a Subroutine from a Subroutine

Subroutines are very flexible. Not only can they be called from any portion of the main program, but **calling a subroutine from a subroutine** is also possible. Let us examine the sequence of events in Example 7.5.

example 7.5

```
20 PRINT: PRINT "WE WILL NOW ILLUSTRATE THE USE OF A"
40 PRINT "SUBROUTINE CALLED FROM A SUBROUTINE."
50 PRINT
60 GOSUB 5000
80 PRINT: PRINT "THAT'S ALL, FOLKS!"
100 END
5000 REM ******** START OF THE FIRST SUBROUTINE ********
5020 PRINT "WE ARE NOW IN THE FIRST SUBROUTINE"
5040 GOSUB 6000
5060 PRINT "WE ARE NOW BACK IN THE FIRST SUBROUTINE"
5080 RETURN
5100 REM ******** END OF THE FIRST SUBROUTINE    ********
5120 REM
6000 REM ******** START THE SECOND SUBROUTINE    ********
6020 PRINT
6040 FOR I = 1 TO 3
6060      PRINT TAB(5);"PASS #";I;"IN THE 2ND. SUBROUTINE"
6080 NEXT I
6100 PRINT
```

```
6120 RETURN
6140 REM ******** END THE SECOND SUBROUTINE     ********

RUN

WE WILL NOW ILLUSTRATE THE USE OF A
SUBROUTINE CALLED FROM A SUBROUTINE.

WE ARE NOW IN THE FIRST SUBROUTINE

    PASS # 1 IN THE 2ND. SUBROUTINE
    PASS # 2 IN THE 2ND. SUBROUTINE
    PASS # 3 IN THE 2ND. SUBROUTINE

WE ARE NOW BACK IN THE FIRST SUBROUTINE

THAT'S ALL, FOLKS!
```

Remember that the RETURN command always returns the program to the statement after the GOSUB command that transferred control to the subroutine. Therefore, the RETURN command in line 5080 returns control to line 80, and the RETURN command in line 6120 returns control to line 5040 in the first subroutine. The program always "remembers" where to return. Such a feature makes the GOSUB statement far superior to a GOTO statement.

Calling a Subroutine from a Subroutine: An Application

The program in Example 7.6 illustrates how useful calling a subroutine from a subroutine can be. In this case, the output lines are printed by the subroutine that starts with line 2000. However, to prevent the output from scrolling past the screen, we have inserted an output line counter in line 2120. If the number of output lines becomes greater than 10, the output will stop until the RETURN key has been tapped. The selection of the value 10 as a line-count maximum was arbitrary . . . up to a point. The output heading takes 7 lines. We must reserve the last line on the screen to print the message in line 2180. Since the screen has a maximum of 25 lines, that leaves us 17 lines for output before the output goes past the screen limits.

Naturally, if we do not care about the scrolling and we want to use limits on the printer paper, we can use a line count to reflect those needs. Whatever limits are used, the output heading must be printed after each break. Calling the heading subroutine from the subroutine that reads the data and prints the output (starting with line 2000) is, therefore, essential.

The program in Example 7.6 also contains some other features that are worth examining:

1. Note the use of buffer number 2 in the screen/printer option. Therefore, we use PRINT #2, in the output lines. The comma after the PRINT command is essential. The elimination of the comma will produce a syntax error message. Note especially how the two output lines were skipped in line 3030: Both commas are in place.

2. The ! symbol was used to identify the numeric values in line 2100 as single precision numbers. Actually, when the program was written, the ! symbol was not used and the numeric values automatically defaulted to single precision.

3. Note that the COUNT in line 2160 must be set back to zero each time its limit is reached in line 2140. Leaving line 2160 out of the program means that the output heading would be printed for every line after the first 10 lines. Also, if the COUNT is not reset, the program cannot break out of the WHILE/WEND loop.

example 7.6

```
100 CLS : KEY OFF : REM ** CLEAR THE SCREEN                          **
120 GOSUB 1000: REM ** SCREEN/PRINTER OPTION                         **
140 GOSUB 2000: REM ** READ DATA AND PRINT OUTPUT                    **
160 CLOSE 2:  END
1000 REM ************     SCREEN/PRINTER OPTION    **************
1020 LOCATE 10,20
1040 INPUT "DO YOU WANT A PRINTED COPY (Y/N)";Y$
1060 IF LEFT$(Y$,1) = "Y" OR LEFT$(Y$,1) = "y" THEN A$ = "LPT1:"
     ELSE A$ = "SCRN:"
1080 OPEN A$ FOR OUTPUT AS 2
1100 WIDTH #2,132
1120 RETURN
2000 REM **********    READ DATA AND PRINT OUTPUT     **********
2020 GOSUB 3000: REM ** PRINT THE HEADING                            **
2040 P$ = " ###        \  \          ##.#        ##,###.##"
2060 READ PERSON$,SALES
2080 WHILE PERSON$ <> "XXX" AND SALES <> -999
2100    IF SALES > 10! THEN BONUS = (SALES*100000!-1000000!)*.01
        ELSE BONUS = 0
2120    COUNT = COUNT + 1: REM ** COUNT THE NUMBER OF LINES    **
2140    WHILE COUNT > 10
2160        COUNT = 0: LOCATE 20,10
2180        INPUT "TAP THE RETURN KEY TO CONTINUE ",R
2200        GOSUB 3000: REM ** PRINT THE HEADING AGAIN          **
2210    WEND
2220    PERIOD = PERIOD + 1
2240    PRINT #2, USING P$;PERIOD,PERSON$,SALES,BONUS
2260    READ PERSON$,SALES
2280 WEND
2300 RETURN
3000 REM **********          PRINT THE HEADING           **********
3020 CLS: REM ** CLEAR THE SCREEN                                    **
```

```
3030 PRINT #2,: PRINT #2,
3040 PRINT #2,"           TOP        SALES"
3060 PRINT #2,"SALES      SALES      AMOUNT"
3080 PRINT #2,"PERIOD     PERSON     (00,000$)     BONUS PAID"
3100 PRINT #2,"------     ------     ---------     ----------"
3120 PRINT #2,
3140 RETURN
10000 DATA AKW,12.5,BBW,11.9,AKW,11.7,PRP,12.6,AAH,11.8,WDD,14.9
10020 DATA AKW,9.3,AAH,12.4,PRP,12.5,AKW,11.8,WDD,12,JJW,12.1
10040 DATA WDD,14.9,AKW,9.6,AKW,13.8,PRP,12.7,AAH,15
29000 DATA XXX,-999
```

Running the program will yield this input/output result:

```
        DO YOU WANT A PRINTED COPY (Y/N)? N

            TOP        SALES
SALES       SALES      AMOUNT
PERIOD      PERSON     (00,000$)     BONUS PAID
------      ------     ---------     ----------

   1         AKW          12.5         2,500.00
   2         BBW          11.9         1,900.00
   3         AKW          11.7         1,700.00
   4         PRP          12.6         2,600.00
   5         AAH          11.8         1,800.00
   6         WDD          14.9         4,900.00
   7         AKW           9.3             0.00
   8         AAH          12.4         2,400.00
   9         PRP          12.5         2,500.00
  10         AKW          11.8         1,800.00

        TAP THE RETURN KEY TO CONTINUE

            TOP        SALES
SALES       SALES      AMOUNT
PERIOD      PERSON     (00,000$)     BONUS PAID
------      ------     ---------     ----------

  11         WDD          12.0         2,000.00
  12         JJW          12.1         2,100.00
  13         WDD          14.9         4,900.00
  14         AKW           9.6             0.00
  15         AKW          13.8         3,800.00
  16         PRP          12.7         2,700.00
  17         AAH          15.0         5,000.00
```

7.3 Subroutines and Structured Programming

Advantages of Using Subroutines

So far, we have managed to write fairly good programs, having outputs that fit our requirements. Why, then, are subroutines considered to be so very important to good programming? The reason is program structure. Clearly, there are many ways to produce any output. However, as programs become more complex or repetitive, it is increasingly necessary to break them into manageable modules. Following are some of the **advantages of subroutine-based programming,** in accordance with the principles of modular design:

1. Complex programs can be subdivided into easily understood parts, resulting in fewer writing problems and fewer logical errors.

2. Programming errors are easier to find and to correct.

3. Since each module can be written as a unit, several people can work on the program at the same time, thereby speeding up the programming activity.

4. Many of the subroutines can be used by different kinds of program. Therefore, a library of subroutines can be created from which we can borrow extensively.

5. Many of the most successful programs are "menu driven." Such programs often require subroutines, especially when a menu provides choices that lead to complex calculations or other manipulations.

Subroutines, then, are essential to complex programming. In fact, some **structured programming** activity is so completely geared to using subroutines that the primary function of the short "main program" is to call the various subroutines. Although we will not write the complex programs in which subroutines are indispensable—this is, after all, an introductory text—using subroutines properly is good programming practice. As we become more adept at programming, we will devote more attention to program structure, and program efficiency and "elegance" assume greater importance. The use of subroutines is an important step in the development of programming expertise.

If using subroutines is so important, why did we postpone for so long our introduction to the concept? Proverbially speaking, we learn to crawl before we learn to walk, and many of the earlier programs were too simple to warrant the use of subroutines. Having gained some programming proficiency, however, we can begin to appreciate the need for structure. We are, in short, ready to begin fine-tuning our programming.

Chapter Review

As programs become more complex, program structure becomes more important. Highly structured programs generally are composed of "modules," each of which performs a specific task. Such modules are known as *subroutines*.

Many programs are based on a design that allows the program user to make a choice from a list of options. Such programs are said to be *menu driven*. IF statements may branch the program to a specific subroutine based on menu selections, but the ON ... GOSUB procedure performs the same task more efficiently.

Using subroutines is considered to be good programming practice because:

1. Program structure makes it easier to follow programming logic.

2. If errors are made, they are more easily found and corrected.

3. Team programming is possible when subroutines for a single program may be written by different people.

4. Specific subroutines may be used by more than one program.

5. Menu-driven programs often require the use of subroutines.

Since subroutines are, in effect, single-task programs, it is possible to build "libraries" of such subroutines that may be "patched" into any program that requires their use. The availability of a library of subroutines tends to make programming much more efficient. Many computing magazines, journals, and textbooks contain subroutines that may be copied into subroutine libraries for personal use.

Common Errors

1. Failing to terminate subroutines properly.

Correct:

```
20   GOSUB 1000
40   GOSUB 2000
60   END
1000   PRINT "SUBROUTINE 1"
1020   GOSUB 3000
1040   RETURN
2000   PRINT "SUBROUTINE 3"
2020   RETURN
3000   PRINT "SUBROUTINE 2"
3020   RETURN
```

Incorrect:

```
20   GOSUB 1000
40   GOSUB 2000
60   END
1000   PRINT "SUBROUTINE 1"
1020   GOSUB 3000
2000   PRINT "SUBROUTINE 3"
3000   PRINT "SUBROUTINE 2"
3020   RETURN
```

2. Failing to include an END statement, thereby causing a subroutine to run into a RETURN statement accidentally, as in the following sequence:

```
20   GOSUB 200
40   PRINT "FINISHED."
200   PRINT "SUBROUTINE 1"
220   GOSUB 500
240   RETURN
500   PRINT "SUBROUTINE 2"
520   RETURN

RUN
SUBROUTINE 1
SUBROUTINE 2
FINISHED
SUBROUTINE 1
SUBROUTINE 2

?RETURN WITHOUT GOSUB ERROR IN 240
```

To fix the problem, insert a line:

```
60   END

RUN
SUBROUTINE 1
SUBROUTINE 2
FINISHED.
```

Key Terms and Concepts

subroutine
GOSUB and RETURN
multiple subroutines
ON ... GOSUB
calling a subroutine from a subroutine
clearing the CRT screen
advantages of subroutine-based programming
structured programming

Exercises

1. Rewrite the following program by using subroutines.

```
20   INPUT "ENTER AN INTEGER BETWEEN 1-3, INCLUSIVE";N
40   IF N = 1 THEN 1000
60   IF N = 2 THEN 2000
80   IF N = 3 THEN 3000
1000 PRINT "N = 1" : GOTO 30000
2000  PRINT "N = 2" : GOTO 30000
3000  PRINT "N = 3" : GOTO 30000
30000  END
```

2. What will be the output for the following program?

```
10   CLS : REM /// CLEAR SCREEN ///
20   PRINT "SELECT ONE OF THE FOLLOWING:" : PRINT
40   PRINT TAB(10);"1.  FIRST SUBROUTINE"
60   PRINT TAB(10);"2.  SECOND SUBROUTINE" : PRINT
80   INPUT "SELECTION";S
100  ON S GOSUB 1000, 2000
120  END
1000 PRINT "SUBROUTINE #1"
1020  GOSUB 3000
1040  RETURN
2000  PRINT "SUBROUTINE #2"
2020  GOSUB 3000
2040  RETURN
3000  PRINT "SUBROUTINE #3"
3020  RETURN
```

3. Using only the definition of the A$ in the segment shown below, finish the program by writing the appropriate subroutines.

```
RUN

WHICH GEOMETRIC FIGURE DO YOU WANT?

    1. RECTANGLE
    2. PARALLELOGRAM
```

```
ENTER YOUR SELECTION 2

              ************
             *          *
            *          *
           *          *
          *          *
         *          *
        *          *
       ************

LIST

20   A$ = "******"
60   PRINT : PRINT
80   PRINT "WHICH GEOMETRIC FIGURE DO YOU WANT?": PRINT
100   PRINT TAB(5);"1. RECTANGLE"
120   PRINT TAB(5);"2. PARALLELOGRAM": PRINT
140   INPUT "ENTER YOUR SELECTION ";S
160   ON S GOSUB 2000,3000
180   END
```

4. Add to the program the necessary subroutines that will use the following menu. The subroutines called by menu items 1–4 should each call a subroutine that will allow you to enter the two numbers. Make sure that you do not allow the program to try to divide a number by zero.

```
100 CLS: KEY OFF: REM ** CLEAR THE SCREEN                          **
110 PRINT "PLEASE SELECT ONE OF THE FOLLOWING OPTIONS:"
120 PRINT: PRINT TAB(5);"1. MULTIPLY THE NUMBERS"
140 PRINT TAB(5);"2. ADD THE NUMBERS"
160 PRINT TAB(5);"3. SUBTRACT THE NUMBERS"
180 PRINT TAB(5);"4. DIVIDE THE NUMBERS"
200 PRINT TAB(5);"5. STOP THE PROGRAM"
220 PRINT: INPUT "ENTER YOUR SELECTION NOW";S
240 CLS: REM ** CLEAR THE SCREEN                                   **
260 ON S GOSUB 1000,2000,3000,4000,5000
300 END
```

5. Write a program that uses a subroutine to calculate and print a factorial value. A factorial is a multiplication series involving a decreasing multiplication base. For example, 4 factorial, written as 4!, is equal to 4*3*2*1. Similarly, 6! = 6*5*4*3*2*1. However, both 0! and 1! are 1. Use numbers of 20 or less. The first portion of the program looks like this:

```
20 CLS: KEY OFF: REM *** CLEAR THE SCREEN                          **
40 PRINT  "THIS PROGRAM CALCULATES A FACTORIAL VALUE"
60 PRINT  "FOR INTEGERS LESS THAN OR EQUAL TO 20."
70 PRINT  "PLEASE NOTE: NUMBERS CANNOT BE LESS THAN 0."
80 PRINT
```

```
100 INPUT  "PLEASE ENTER THE VALUE";N
105 WHILE N<Ø OR N>20
110     PRINT: PRINT "YOU ENTERED THE NUMBER";N
112     PRINT "THE NUMBER MUST BE IN THE RANGE 0-20, INCLUSIVE."
114     INPUT "PLEASE ENTER THE NUMBER AGAIN ",N
116 WEND
120 GOSUB 1000
```

6. Using the factorial calculation in Exercise 5 as a subroutine, calculate a binomial coefficient that is defined as $N!/((N - X)!(X!))$, where $X <= N$. For example, the binomial coefficient for the numbers $N = 4$ an $X = 2$ is calculated by $4!/((4 - 2)!(2!))$, or $(4*3*2*1)/((2*1)*(2*1))$.

7. Using the data lines shown, write a program to produce the sales report that follows the data lines. Note that the report heading subroutine keeps track of the page count. The printer/screen option is buffer-based.

```
10000 REM ******************************************************************
10020 REM *                          DATA VALUES                                   *
10040 REM ******************************************************************
10060 DATA PENCIL,.11,15824,1827,4362,826,7818,-999
10080 DATA T-SHIRT,3.99,185,18,41,19,56,-999
10100 DATA NOTEPAD,1.29,325,43,14,108,49,-999
29999 DATA END OF FILE, -999,-999,-999,-999,-999,-999,-999

PLEASE ENTER THE CURRENT DATE, USING THE FORMAT XX/XX/XX.
(FOR EXAMPLE, JULY 8, 1985 WOULD BE ENTERED AS 07/08/85) 08/01/85

WOULD YOU LIKE A PRINTED COPY (Y/N)?N


      SALES REPORT, BY PRODUCT, 08/01/85, XYZ CORPORATION, PAGE 1
---------------------------------------------------------------------

                                                                  CUMULATIVE
          SALES   STARTING         # SOLD  REMAINING    VALUE OF    VALUE OF
PRODUCT   PRICE   INVENTORY  QTR   IN QTR  INVENTORY  GOODS SOLD  GOODS SOLD
-------   -----   ---------  ---   ------  ---------  ----------  ----------

PENCIL     0.11      15,824    1    1,827     13,997      200.97      200.97
                               2    4,362      9,635      479.82      680.79
                               3      826      8,809       90.86      771.65
                               4    7,818        991      859.98    1,631.63
---------------------------------------------------------------------

T-SHIRT    3.99         185    1       18        167       71.82       71.82
                               2       41        126      163.59      235.41
                               3       19        107       75.81      311.22
                               4       56         51      223.44      534.66
---------------------------------------------------------------------
```

```
                    TAP THE RETURN KEY TO CONTINUE

      SALES REPORT, BY PRODUCT, 08/01/85, XYZ CORPORATION, PAGE 2
------------------------------------------------------------------------

                                                            CUMULATIVE
        SALES  STARTING          # SOLD  REMAINING   VALUE OF    VALUE OF
PRODUCT PRICE  INVENTORY   QTR   IN QTR  INVENTORY  GOODS SOLD  GOODS SOLD
------- -----  ---------   --    ------  ---------  ----------  ----------

NOTEPAD  1.29        325    1       43        282       55.47       55.47
                            2       14        268       18.06       73.53
                            3      108        160      139.32      212.85
                            4       49        111       63.21      276.06
------------------------------------------------------------------------

        THE TOTAL VALUE OF ALL GOODS SOLD IS ==========>       $2,442.37
```

8. Write a program to produce the monthly payment schedule shown. Use a counter to limit the output to twelve months per screen or page. The equation that produces the monthly payment values was first used in Chapter 5, problem 21. The printer/screen option, the report heading, the calculations and the printing of the monthly payment schedule, and the final totals are all produced by different subroutines.

```
WHAT IS THE PRINCIPAL? 5000
WHAT IS THE NUMBER OF YEARS? 2

WHAT IS THE INTEREST RATE (DECIMAL FORM: FOR EXAMPLE,
AN INTEREST RATE OF 12.8% WOULD BE ENTERED AS .128) .125

DO YOU WANT A PRINTED COPY (Y/N)? N


         MONTHLY PAYMENT SCHEDULE
(MONTHLY PAYMENT IS ========>      $236.54)

MONTH   INTEREST   PRINCIPAL   BALANCE DUE
-----   --------   ---------   -----------

  1       52.08      184.45      4,815.55
  2       50.16      186.38      4,629.17
  3       48.22      188.32      4,440.85
  4       46.26      190.28      4,250.57
  5       44.28      192.26      4,058.31
  6       42.27      194.26      3,864.05
  7       40.25      196.29      3,667.76
  8       38.21      198.33      3,469.43
  9       36.14      200.40      3,269.03
 10       34.05      202.49      3,066.55
 11       31.94      204.59      2,861.95
 12       29.81      206.73      2,655.23
```

```
          TAP THE RETURN KEY TO CONTINUE

             MONTHLY PAYMENT SCHEDULE
    (MONTHLY PAYMENT IS ========>     $236.54)

    MONTH    INTEREST    PRINCIPAL    BALANCE DUE
    -----    --------    ---------    -----------

     13         27.66       208.88       2,446.35
     14         25.48       211.05       2,235.29
     15         23.28       213.25       2,022.04
     16         21.06       215.47       1,806.56
     17         18.82       217.72       1,588.84
     18         16.55       219.99       1,368.85
     19         14.26       222.28       1,146.58
     20         11.94       224.59         921.98
     21          9.60       226.93         695.05
     22          7.24       229.30         465.75
     23          4.85       231.69         234.07
     24          2.44       234.07           0.00

          TAP THE RETURN KEY TO CONTINUE


               TOTAL AMOUNTS PAID
    ---------------------------------------

    TOTAL INTEREST PAID ====>        $676.87
    TOTAL AMOUNT PAID ======>      $5,676.87
    LAST PAYMENT IS ========>         236.50
```

9. You have been asked to write a program that will produce the grade report shown below, based on the following data lines. The final percent grade is determined by dropping the lowest test grade, adding the three remaining test grades, the lab grade, and the final examination and using this total as a percentage of the total possible points. The total possible points are determined this way:

```
Three remaining tests @ 100 points per test ==> 300
Lab grade ===================================>  30
Final examination grade =====================> 150
                                               ---
                         Total possible points 480
```

The letter grade is determined on the basis of this scale.

```
 A = 90% or better
 B = 80-89%
 C = 70-79%
 D = 60-69%
 F = less than 60%
```

```
10000 REM ******************************************************************
10020 REM *                          DATA SECTION                          *
10040 REM ******************************************************************
10060 DATA 3,480: REM ** CLASS SECTION, POINTS POSSIBLE                   **
10080 DATA F-341AA,73,48,81,71,28,123
10100 DATA T-122CA,68,73,83,75,21,109
10120 DATA T-326DD,97,86,92,94,27,146
10140 DATA A-439AK,83,89,75,84,30,132
10160 DATA B-248AA,49,33,51,40,11,102
10180 DATA B-155BD,73,58,83,88,21,121
10200 DATA C-149BA,72,71,76,75,23,123
10220 DATA A-340KL,79,84,81,91,25,128
10240 DATA T-220DE,63,73,81,88,27,131
10260 DATA F-831EE,78,43,35,41,12,109
10280 DATA Q-379QM,70,71,63,62,19,110
10300 DATA D-199KD,89,73,71,49,22,114
10320 DATA D-245DP,73,71,73,68,20,118
10340 DATA A-182FS,61,79,89,88,27,148
29999 DATA END OF FILE,-999,-999,-999,-999,-999,-999
```

```
PLEASE ENTER THE CURRENT DATE, USING THE FORMAT XX/XX/XX.
(FOR EXAMPLE, JULY 8, 1985 WOULD BE ENTERED AT 07/08/85) 08/05/85

WOULD YOU LIKE A PRINTED COPY (Y/N)? N


                              PAGE 1

                 INFS 320 GRADES, 08/05/85, SECTION 3
-----------------------------------------------------------------------

                     TEST SCORES
STUDENT  CLASS   ------------------  LOW        FINAL  PERCENT  FINAL
NUMBER   NUMBER  #1   #2   #3   #4   TEST  LAB  EXAM    GRADE   GRADE
-------  ------  --   --   --   --   ----  ---  -----  -------  -----

F-341AA     1    73   48   81   71    48    28   123    78.33     C
T-122CA     2    68   73   83   75    68    21   109    75.21     C
T-326DD     3    97   86   92   94    86    27   146    95.00     A
A-439AK     4    83   89   75   84    75    30   132    87.08     B
B-248AA     5    49   33   51   40    33    11   102    52.71     F
B-155BD     6    73   58   83   88    58    21   121    80.42     B
C-149BA     7    72   71   76   75    71    23   123    76.88     C
A-340KL     8    79   84   81   91    79    25   128    85.21     B
T-220DE     9    63   73   81   88    63    27   131    83.33     B
F-831EE    10    78   43   35   41    35    12   109    58.96     F
Q-379QM    11    70   71   63   62    62    19   110    69.38     D

                   TAP THE RETURN KEY TO CONTINUE
```

```
                          PAGE 2

             INFS 320 GRADES, 08/05/85, SECTION 3
-----------------------------------------------------------------------

                    TEST SCORES
STUDENT  CLASS     -----------------   LOW        FINAL  PERCENT  FINAL
NUMBER   NUMBER    #1   #2   #3   #4   TEST  LAB  EXAM    GRADE   GRADE
-------  ------    --   --   --   --   ----  ---  -----  -------  -----

D-199KD    12      89   73   71   49    49    22   114    76.88     C
D-245DP    13      73   71   73   68    68    20   118    73.96     C
A-182FS    14      61   79   89   88    61    27   148    89.79     B
```

10. Using the quarterly sales data shown in the following data lines, write a program that produces the sales report shown. The number of lines per screen or per page is limited by both the counter value and the quarter value in order to make sure that the year's quarter values are never split between succeeding screens or pages.

```
10000 REM ***************************************************************
10020 REM *                        DATA SECTION                         *
10040 REM ***************************************************************
10060 DATA 1981,2: REM ** STARTING YEAR AND QUARTER                     **
10080 DATA 12.8,13.2,11.9,12.3,14.1,15.3,12.9,14.0,14.5,16.2,14.8
10100 DATA 14.3,15.1,18.3,18.1,18.4
29999 DATA -999
```

```
PLEASE ENTER THE CURRENT DATE, USING THE FORMAT XX/XX/XX.
(FOR EXAMPLE, JULY 8, 1985 WOULD BE ENTERED AS 07/08/85) 08/06/85

WOULD YOU LIKE A PRINTED COPY (Y/N)? N


                     PAGE 1

   SALES REPORT, XYZ CORPORATION, 08/06/85

                    SALES
YEAR   QUARTER    (000 TONS)   CHANGE   % CHANGE
----   -------    ----------   ------   --------

1981      2          12.8       ----      -----
          3          13.2        0.4       3.12
          4          11.9       -1.3      -9.85

END-OF-YEAR TOTAL    37.9
```

```
1982        1          12.3      0.4        3.36
            2          14.1      1.8       14.63
            3          15.3      1.2        8.51
            4          12.9     -2.4      -15.69

END-OF-YEAR TOTAL      54.6

          TAP THE RETURN KEY TO CONTINUE ?

                       PAGE 2

   SALES REPORT, XYZ CORPORATION, 08/06/85

                      SALES
YEAR    QUARTER    (000 TONS)    CHANGE    % CHANGE
----    -------    ----------    ------    --------

1983        1          14.0      1.1        8.53
            2          14.5      0.5        3.57
            3          16.2      1.7       11.72
            4          14.8     -1.4       -8.64

END-OF-YEAR TOTAL      59.5

1984        1          14.3     -0.5       -3.38
            2          15.1      0.8        5.59
            3          18.3      3.2       21.19
            4          18.1     -0.2       -1.09

END-OF-YEAR TOTAL      65.8

          TAP THE RETURN KEY TO CONTINUE ?


                       PAGE 3

   SALES REPORT, XYZ CORPORATION, 08/06/85

                      SALES
YEAR    QUARTER    (000 TONS)    CHANGE    % CHANGE
----    -------    ----------    ------    --------

1985        1          18.4      0.3        1.66
```

8

Objectives

- To use file terminology.
- To explain the basic structure of sequential files.
- To write a program that creates a sequential file.
- To write a program that prints the sequential file contents.
- To write a program that will add records to a sequential file.
- To write a program that will correct records in a sequential file.
- To write a program that will delete records from a sequential file.

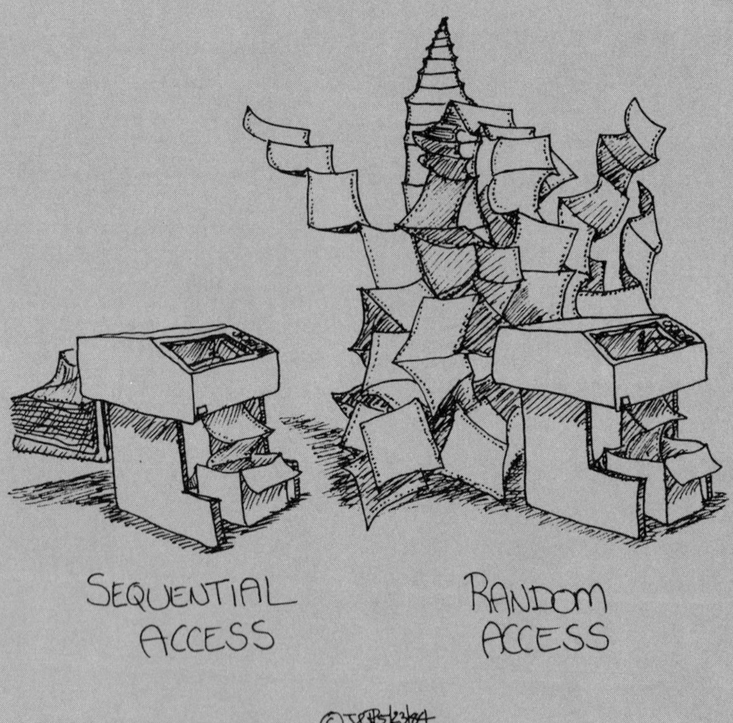

SEQUENTIAL FILES

In the preceding chapters we entered data into the computer by using INPUT or READ (DATA). Programs perform their assigned tasks using either format, but neither data entry procedure is satisfactory. The INPUT format is "volatile"; that is, the data are lost when the computer is turned off, when another program is loaded, or even when the same program is run again. The READ (DATA) format is clumsy, since the data lines become part of the program itself.

In this chapter we learn to use *sequential files* to store data. Programs requiring the data can access such files, retrieving the data as necessary. The file options discussed include creating files, printing file contents, correcting files, adding to or deleting from files, and gaining access to files by other programs.

8.1 Defining FILE Terminology

Before the computer, certain kinds of information were kept in a filing cabinet: Each drawer was filled with file folders, and each file folder contained specific information. Imagine, for example, a set of file folders containing information on a group of students, one file folder per student. Each folder contains the following information: student name, major, grade point average (GPA), age, sex, and classification (freshman, sophomore, junior, or senior). This information may be kept on a computer disk as well as in a filing cabinet. To define precisely what information is stored on the disk we use the following **rules for naming files:**

1. The smallest complete unit of information is called a **field,** composed of one or more bytes. Therefore, the student name is one field, the major is another field, the GPA is yet another field, and so on.

2. The collection of all fields pertaining to a particular student is called a **record.** Thus the fields in the record are related, and a computer file record is very similar to an individual file folder.

3. A computer *file* is a collection of records; functionally, it resembles the collection of file folders in a file drawer.

Let us now take a look at how a file is created. To keep the data file as simple as possible, we will use the information presented in Table 8.1, which presents only two fields per record, for a total of three records.

To we create a data file for these three records, the following procedures must be performed by the computer:

1. The data are typed on the keyboard.

table 8.1
THE FIRST DATA FILE: A LIST OF CONTRIBUTORS

Name	Contribution
John B. Armsdell	\$ 12.75
Jane L. Whiteside	\$ 25.00
Susan B. Notecaf	\$ 11.50

2. The keyboard information goes to a portion of the memory known as the **buffer.** (To send the data to the buffer, we use a special procedure that lets the computer know that it is going to be working with a file.)

3. The data in the buffer are written onto the disk.

4. Each file has a buffer assigned to it, one file per buffer. Up to 15 buffers are generally available for file work.

The sequence of events we have just described can be traced through Figure 8.1. *Writing* the data on the diskette is equivalent to *printing* the information on the CRT screen; the data are deposited on the diskette, of course, rather than being displayed on the screen.

8.2 Sequential Files

A **sequential file** works exactly as the name implies: The data are retrieved from the file in the same order (sequence) as they were written into the file. We cannot retrieve a specific field from the file without first reading all the preceding fields. Thus if the item to be retrieved from a sequential file happens to

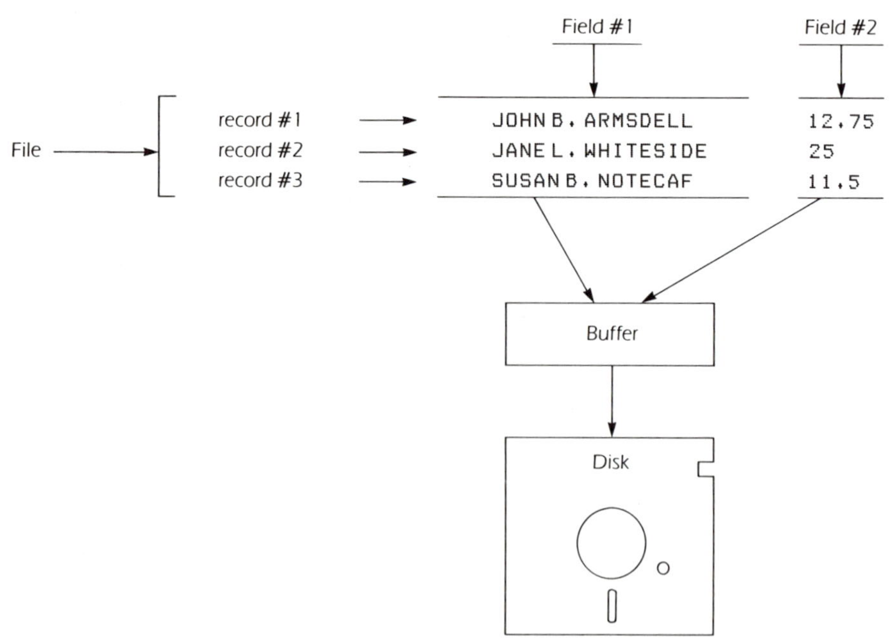

figure 8.1
HOW DATA ARE WRITTEN ON A DISK

be the last item in it, all the file records must be read before retrieval can be accomplished. If we must be able to retrieve individual records in random order efficiently, the sequential file is not for us. However, if we usually retrieve the records in sequence anyway, the sequential file is perfect. Activities such as monthly billing and generating mailing labels are well suited to the sequential file. Although sequential filing has its limitations, the virtue of the system lies in its simplicity.

Some Basic Housekeeping

The sequential file makes very few programming demands on us. The first procedure used with sequential files is naming the file. Data file names carry the same restrictions as those carried by the processing programs. Specifically, we must meet the following requirements:

1. Use a maximum of eight characters, or eight characters plus a three-character extension.

2. The first character in the file name must be a letter. The remaining characters may be letters, numerals, or a variety of symbols. Do not, however, use a point (decimal) as part of the name. (Anything after the point is seen as an extension.)

3. Names may *not* contain blank spaces.

The following examples illustrate the rules just enumerated.

File Name	Correct?	Comment
RECEIPTS	Yes	Follows rules 1, 2, and 3.
RECEIPTS.TXT	Yes	Follows rules 1, 2, and 3.
*B-5D	No	First character must be a letter.
WAREHOUSE	No	Exceeds 8-place limitation.
ACC.22.DTA	No	Anything following a point is seen as an extension. The extension 22.DTA following ACC is not legal, since only a 3-place extension is allowed.
ACC 22.DTA	No	No blanks allowed. Exceeds 3-place extension limit.
ACCT22.DTA	Yes	Good extension label. Reminds user that the stored program is a data file.
A-2875@@.DTA	Yes	Better use a name that reminds user of file contents.

Having named a file properly—*make sure that there is no other BASIC program with the same name*—we can now define the general sequential file programming procedure.

1. Open the file. The basic sequential file opening statements could be written like this:

```
OPEN "ACCESS MODE", BUFFER NUMBER, "FILENAME"
```

2. The two *access mode* designations are INPUT and OUTPUT. When we examine a program that creates a file, we note that the file is opened for OUTPUT even though we are entering data into the file. This apparent contradiction can be eliminated by thinking of data entry into a file as data going *from* (OUTPUT) the buffer to the disk. Therefore, to enter data into the file we use the command **OPEN "O"**:

```
OPEN "O", BUFFER NUMBER, "FILENAME"
```

   To use the data in the file we must pull the data from the disk *into* (INPUT) the buffer. Therefore, to pull data from the file we use the command **OPEN "I"**:

```
OPEN "I", BUFFER NUMBER, "FILENAME"
```

3. The **buffer number** must be specified (review Section 8.1). Up to 15 buffers may be available. If we manipulate more than one file at a time, we must make sure that the files have different buffer numbers. Naturally, if we only have one file open at a time, we may use the same buffer number.

```
OPEN "I",1,"FILENAME"
OPEN "O",3,"FILENAME"
```

   The file name must be entered in quotes, or a string variable may be used.

If we place the data on the disk, we can think of *writing* the data from the memory to the disk. Therefore, we can use the command **WRITE #:**

```
WRITE #BUFFER NUMBER, VARIABLE NAME(S)
```

Variable names are separated by commas. The buffer number is preceded by the "#" symbol. We must use the same buffer number that was specified in our opening statements. For example, if we specified buffer number 1 in the opening statement and we are saving two variables (N$ and C) to disk, we would . . .

```
WRITE #1, N$,C
```

Similarly, if we were saving five variables (A$, B, Q, D, and C1$) to disk, using buffer number 3, we would . . .

```
WRITE #3, A$, B, D, C1$
```

Finally, if we were asking the computer to print the contents of a file currently saved on disk, we would have to INPUT the data from the disk to the buffer before the PRINT command could be issued successfully. If we had saved variables N$ and C on the disk, we would prepare the data for printing by using the command **INPUT #:**

```
INPUT #1, N$, C
```

The preceding command would place variables N$ and C in buffer number 1. *CAUTION: Always write into the same buffer that you used in the "OPEN" statement.* Trying to write into buffer number 1 after you have prepared buffer number 3 will not be very productive.

Creating a Sequential File

Having reviewed the general sequential file program commands, we are ready to see these commands applied. To keep the program simple and to make program comparisons easier, we will load the data shown in Table 8.1, which lists three names of contributors and their contributions. If we define the variable "name" to be N$ and the variable "contribution" to be C, while naming the file "CONTRIB.DTA", we can follow the file development in Example 8.1. (The program will be saved as X8-1.BAS. Remember to give the file and the program that creates the file *different* names.)

Program Example 8.1 demonstrates the following points:

1. Writing a program that creates a file requires that we open the file for OUTPUT ("O") because we are moving the data from the buffer to the disk in line 1040.

2. Screen prompts are not changed: The standard INPUT statements are used in lines 1080 and 1100.

3. We must write from the same buffer number that we used in our opening statement. Since we opened buffer number 1 we must write to buffer number 1 in line 1120. If we had used buffer number 3 in line 1040 we would have had to use WRITE #3 in line 1120.

4. When we are finished with our file work we must CLOSE the file. Since buffer number 1 was specified in lines 1040 and 1120, we must write CLOSE 1 in line 1200. If buffer number 3 had been used, we would have written CLOSE 3 in line 1200.

example 8.1

```
1000 CLS: KEY OFF: REM ** CLEAR THE SCREEN                          **
1020 REM ****** START ROUTINE TO CREATE A SEQUENTIAL FILE *****
1040 OPEN "O",1,"CONTRIB.DTA"
1060 WHILE Y$ <> "Y"
1080     PRINT: INPUT "NAME";N$
1100     INPUT "CONTRIBUTION AMOUNT";C
1120     WRITE #1,N$,C
1140     PRINT: INPUT "LAST RECORD (Y/N)";Y$
1160     IF LEFT$(Y$,1) = "Y" OR LEFT$(Y$,1) = "y" THEN Y$ = "Y"
1180 WEND
1200 CLOSE 1
```

Running the program in Example 8.1 yields the following results. Note the simplicity of the input prompting.

```
NAME? JOHN B. ARMSDELL
CONTRIBUTION AMOUNT? 12.75

LAST RECORD (Y/N)? N

NAME? JANE L. WHITESIDE
CONTRIBUTION AMOUNT? 25.00

LAST RECORD (Y/N)? N

NAME? SUSAN B. NOTECAF
CONTRIBUTION AMOUNT? 11.50

LAST RECORD (Y/N)? Y
```

Since we will use the program in Example 8.1 as part of a larger file system later in the chapter, we must be able to merge it with other program segments. Therefore, using the program name X8-1.BAS, we will save it in ASCII format by:

```
SAVE "X8-1.BAS",A
```

One other point is worth noting. Some programmers prefer to allow the program's user to input the file name. For this approach, we must modify the program in Example 8.1 by adding:

```
1010 PRINT: INPUT "ENTER THE FILE NAME";F$
```

and rewriting line 1040 to read:

```
1040 OPEN "O",1,F$
```

Allowing the program's user to input the file name may create problems later: if, for example, the next user does not know the file name and cannot access the file easily. Since our file is designed for a particular data set (i.e., is user-specific), it is advisable to make the file name part of the program.

Printing the File Contents

Since the data have been deposited on disk rather than on the screen, we cannot be sure that we have been successful in creating the file. The data are deposited on the diskette where we cannot "see" the results of our activities. Therefore, we need to write a program that can "pull" the data from the disk to the screen and, if needed, to the printer. If we think in terms of getting the data from the disk *into* the memory, we realize that the file should be opened for INPUT. Therefore, program line 2100 (Example 8.2) uses "I" in the opening statement:

```
OPEN "I",1,"CONTRIB.DTA"
```

The opening statement specifies the use of buffer number 1. We could have used buffer number 2 or 3 just as easily. As long as the buffer is free, it may be specified in the opening statement. We do need to remember, of course, that only a limited number of buffers are available at any one time.

Special note: The program must have an "END-OF-FILE" marker. If such a marker is not specified, the program tries to read past the last record in the file, thereby generating an "Input past end" error. The resulting error message is shown immediately below the output. The error must be deleted because such errors, when encountered in processing programs, cause these programs to prematurely terminate their activities.

The error is easily prevented through the use of an "end-of-file check," specifying EOF (buffer number). Since we are using buffer number 1, we would write EOF(1). The use of buffer number 3 would have required EOF(3), and so on. Note particularly line 2140 in which we specify that the output should be printed as long as the EOF condition has not been encountered.

example 8.2

```
2000 CLS: KEY OFF: REM ** CLEAR THE SCREEN                                **
2020 REM ********* START ROUTINE TO PRINT FILE CONTENTS   *********
2040 PRINT:PRINT
2060 PRINT "NAME";TAB(25);"CONTRIBUTION"
2080 PRINT "--------------------";TAB(25);"------------": PRINT
2100 OPEN "I",1,"CONTRIB.DTA"
2120 REM ** PRINT CONTENTS UNTIL THE END OF THE FILE IS REACHED **
2140 WHILE NOT EOF(1)
2160     INPUT #1,N$,C
2180     PRINT N$;TAB(27);"$";C
2200 WEND
2220 CLOSE 1
```

Remember to save the program in Example 8.2 (and all the other programs in this chapter) in the ASCII format to permit merging with other program segments later.

Creating an Elementary File System

Earlier we had to use one program (Example 8.1) to create a file and another program (Example 8.2) to print the file contents. Putting the creating and printing options into a single program, as in Example 8.3, is much more convenient, especially for menu-driven programs.

Rather than typing up the various program sections, we can use the MERGE command to combine the programs in Examples 8.1 and 8.2. The following procedure may be used. (Disk drive A is assumed.)

1. Load program Example 8.2, named X8-2.BAS:

   ```
   LOAD "X8-2.BAS"
   ```

2. Use the MERGE command to merge the program we loaded into memory (X8-2.BAS) with the program on the diskette (X8-1.BAS):

   ```
   MERGE "X8-1.BAS"
   ```

   Note that the program on disk follows the MERGE command.

3. Use the LIST procedure to verify that the two programs have, in fact, been merged.

4. The programs are merged in memory only, so we need to save the program—which will be the program in Example 8.3—by using:

   ```
   SAVE "X8-3.BAS",A
   ```

5. Then add lines 100–440 and lines 2240–2260 to the program, as well as the RETURN statements in lines 1220 and 2280. Also rewrite the REM statements to reflect the fact that these are subroutines. Save the results.

   ```
   SAVE "X8-3.BAS",A
   ```

6. Note the construction of the menu. Since CHOICE has not yet been defined in line 120, its value is initially equal to zero. Since 0 is less than 3, the program enters into the loop and the menu is printed. If the selection is outside the range, the loop in lines 280–400 is executed. Note that the CHOICE value must be reset to some value within the limits in line 380. Failure to include line 380 means that the program cannot break out of the loop.

7. Finally, note that lines 2240–2260 allow you to view the output at leisure. Tapping the RETURN key will return you to the menu. If we had left lines 2240–2260 out of the program, we would not have enough time to read the output!

The result is the menu-driven program shown in Example 8.3, followed by its run. Since the file CONTRIB.DTA was created by the program in Example 8.1, we select only options 2 and 3 to show that the program works as intended.

example 8.3

```
100 CLS: KEY OFF: REM ** CLEAR THE SCREEN                              **
120 WHILE CHOICE < 3
140     CLS
160     PRINT "PLEASE SELECT ONE OF THE FOLLOWING OPTIONS:": PRINT
180     PRINT TAB(5);"1. CREATE THE SEQUENTIAL FILE"
200     PRINT TAB(5);"2. PRINT THE SEQUENTIAL FILE CONTENTS"
220     PRINT TAB(5);"3. STOP THIS PROGRAM"
240     PRINT: INPUT "ENTER YOUR SELECTION NOW ",CHOICE
260     ON CHOICE GOSUB 1000,2000
280     WHILE CHOICE < 1 OR CHOICE > 3
300         PRINT: PRINT
320         PRINT "YOU SELECTED CHOICE NUMBER";CHOICE
340         PRINT "THE MENU ONLY ALLOWS CHOICES 1-3.":PRINT
360         INPUT "TAP THE RETURN KEY TO CONTINUE ",C
380         CHOICE = 2
400     WEND
420 WEND
440 END
1000 CLS: REM ** CLEAR THE SCREEN                                      **
1020 REM ****** START THE SUBROUTINE TO CREATE THE SEQUENTIAL FILE *****
1040 OPEN "O",1,"CONTRIB.DTA"
1060 WHILE Y$ <> "Y"
1080     PRINT: INPUT "NAME";N$
1100     INPUT "CONTRIBUTION AMOUNT";C
1120     WRITE #1,N$,C
1140     PRINT: INPUT "LAST RECORD (Y/N)";Y$
1160     IF LEFT$(Y$,1) = "Y" OR LEFT$(Y$,1) = "y" THEN Y$ = "Y"
1180 WEND
1200 CLOSE 1
1220 RETURN
2000 CLS: REM ** CLEAR THE SCREEN                                      **
2020 REM ********* START ROUTINE TO PRINT FILE CONTENTS ***************
2040 PRINT: PRINT
```

```
2060 PRINT "NAME"; TAB(25);"CONTRIBUTION"
2080 PRINT "--------------------";TAB(25);"-----------": PRINT
2100 OPEN "I",1,"CONTRIB.DTA"
2120 REM ** PRINT CONTENTS UNTIL THE END OF THE FILE IS REACHED **
2140 WHILE NOT EOF(1)
2160     INPUT #1,N$,C
2180     PRINT N$;TAB(27);"$";C
2200 WEND
2220 CLOSE 1
2240 PRINT: PRINT
2260 INPUT "TAP THE RETURN KEY TO RETURN TO THE MENU ",R
2280 RETURN
```

Although the program in Example 8.3 limits you to listing file's records on the screen, a few program modifications will let you select either the screen or the printer. The required modifications are included in the program shown in Example 8.4. Note especially these two points:

1. The program's users select a printer option to print the file's contents, using lines 2025–2035.

2. Buffer number 2 is used for printing purposes because buffer number 1 is reserved for the sequential file. Therefore, lines 2040–2080 and line 2180 use PRINT #2.

example 8.4

```
100 CLS: KEY OFF: REM ** CLEAR THE SCREEN                          **
120 WHILE CHOICE < 3
140     CLS
160     PRINT "PLEASE SELECT ONE OF THE FOLLOWING OPTIONS:": PRINT
180     PRINT TAB(5);"1. CREATE THE SEQUENTIAL FILE"
200     PRINT TAB(5);"2. PRINT THE SEQUENTIAL FILE CONTENTS"
220     PRINT TAB(5);"3. STOP THIS PROGRAM"
240     PRINT: INPUT "ENTER YOUR SELECTION NOW ",CHOICE
260     ON CHOICE GOSUB 1000,2000
280     WHILE CHOICE < 1 OR CHOICE > 3
300         PRINT: PRINT
320         PRINT "YOU SELECTED CHOICE NUMBER";CHOICE
340         PRINT "THE MENU ONLY ALLOWS CHOICES 1-3.": PRINT
360         INPUT "TAP THE RETURN KEY TO CONTINUE ",C
380         CHOICE = 2
400     WEND
420 WEND
440 END
```

```
1000 CLS: REM ** CLEAR THE SCREEN                                        **
1020 REM ****** START SUBROUTINE TO CREATE THE SEQUENTIAL FILE  *****
1040 OPEN "O",1,"CONTRIB.DTA"
1060 WHILE Y$ <> "Y"
1080    PRINT: INPUT "NAME";N$
1100    INPUT "CONTRIBUTION AMOUNT";C
1120    WRITE #1,N$,C
1140    PRINT: INPUT "LAST RECORD (Y/N)";Y$
1160    IF LEFT$(Y$,1) = "Y" OR LEFT$(Y$,1) = "y" THEN Y$ = "Y"
1180 WEND
1200 CLOSE 1
1220 RETURN
2000 CLS: REM ** CLEAR THE SCREEN                                        **
2020 REM ********* START ROUTINE TO PRINT FILE CONTENTS *************
2025 PRINT: INPUT "WOULD YOU LIKE A PRINTED COPY? (Y/N) ",Y$
2030 IF LEFT$(Y$,1) = "Y" OR LEFT$(Y$,1) = "y" THEN A1$ = "LPT1:"
     ELSE A1$ = "SCRN:"
2035 OPEN A1$ FOR OUTPUT AS 2
2040 PRINT #2,: PRINT #2,
2060 PRINT #2,"NAME";TAB(25);"CONTRIBUTION"
2080 PRINT #2,"--------------------";TAB(25);"------------":PRINT   2
2100 OPEN "I",1,"CONTRIB.DTA"
2120 REM ** PRINT CONTENTS UNTIL THE END OF THE FILE IS REACHED     **
2140 WHILE NOT EOF(1)
2160    INPUT #1,N$,C
2180    PRINT #2,N$;TAB(27);"$";C
2200 WEND
2220 CLOSE 1: CLOSE 2
2240 PRINT: PRINT
2260 INPUT "TAP THE RETURN KEY TO RETURN TO THE MENU ",R
2280 RETURN
```

Searching the File for Specific Information

Any program may be written to access any file. Program Example 8.5 selects values from a file only to produce a requested listing, but programs may use the same file access techniques to process the information at will. As long as a processing program contains the sequence of lines 200–260, the program can process the data contained in the file exactly as we processed such data with the INPUT or READ (DATA) formats shown in earlier chapters. Note also that we are using buffer number 3 in lines 200, 220, and 280.

example 8.5

```
20 CLS: KEY OFF: REM ** CLEAR THE SCREEN                              **
40 REM **** THIS ROUTINE SELECTS (A) VALUE(S) FROM A FILE *****
80 PRINT: INPUT "WHAT IS THE CONTRIBUTION LIMIT";C1
```

```
100 PRINT: PRINT
120 PRINT "CONTRIBUTORS WHO GAVE $";C1;" OR MORE": PRINT: PRINT
140 PRINT "CONTRIBUTORS NAME";TAB(25);"AMOUNT"
160 PRINT "-----------------";TAB(25);"------": PRINT
200 OPEN "I",3,"CONTRIB.DTA"
210 WHILE NOT EOF(3)
220     INPUT #3,N$,C
240     IF C >= C1 THEN PRINT N$;TAB(25);"$";C
260 WEND
280 CLOSE 3

RUN

WHAT IS THE CONTRIBUTION LIMIT? 12.00


CONTRIBUTORS WHO GAVE $ 12 OR MORE


CONTRIBUTOR'S NAME        AMOUNT
------------------        ------

JOHN B. ARMSDELL          $ 12.75
JANE L. WHITESIDE         $ 25
```

Processing Data in the File

Data coming from the file may be processed exactly as they were before: All the procedures learned in the preceding chapters work the same way. Note, for example, the processing that takes place in Example 8.6, lines 230–248. Recall that a low value is initialized as a very large number to make sure that the first value read will be smaller than the initialized value. Therefore, line 180 uses a very large number. The high value is initialized by using the value zero, to make sure that the first value read will be larger than zero.

example 8.6

```
20 CLS: KEY OFF: REM ** CLEAR THE SCREEN                              **
40 REM **** THIS ROUTINE SELECTS THE HIGH AND LOW VALUES          *****
50 REM **** IN A FILE AND CALCULATES AN AVERAGE VALUE             *****
100 PRINT: PRINT
140 PRINT "CONTRIBUTOR'S NAME";TAB(25);"AMOUNT"
160 PRINT "------------------";TAB(25);"------": PRINT
180 L = 9.99E+11: REM ** INITIALIZE THE LOW VALUE                     **
190 H = 0: REM ** INITIALIZE THE HIGH VALUE                           **
200 OPEN "I",3,"CONTRIB.DTA"
```

```
210 WHILE NOT EOF(3)
220     INPUT #3,N$,C
230     IF C > H THEN H = C: REM ** FIND THE HIGH VALUE          **
240     IF C < L THEN L = C: REM ** FIND THE LOW VALUE           **
245     T = T + C: REM ** TOTAL CONTRIBUTIONS                    **
248     N = N + 1: REM ** NUMBER OF CONTRIBUTIONS                **
250     PRINT N$; TAB (24);" ";
255     PRINT USING "$##.##";C
260 WEND
280 CLOSE 3
290 A = T/N: REM ** AVERAGE CONTRIBUTION                         **
300 PRINT:PRINT "HIGH CONTRIBUTION"; TAB(24);" ";
320 PRINT USING "$##.##";H
340 PRINT "LOW CONTRIBUTION"; TAB(24);" ";
360 PRINT USING "$##.##";L
380 PRINT:PRINT "AVERAGE CONTRIBUTION"; TAB(24);" ";
400 PRINT USING "$##.##";A
```

Running the program in Example 8.6 yields this output:

```
CONTRIBUTOR'S NAME        AMOUNT
------------------        ------

JOHN B. ARMSDELL          $12.75
JANE L. WHITESIDE         $25.00
SUSAN B. NOTECAF          $11.50

HIGH CONTRIBUTION         $25.00
LOW CONTRIBUTION          $11.50

AVERAGE CONTRIBUTION      $16.42
```

Adding Data to a Sequential File

We have used OPEN "I" and OPEN "O" to indicate the input and output phases of the files, using INPUT to move the data from the disk to the memory and OUTPUT to move the data from memory to disk. The latter procedure created the file, whereas the former procedure accessed it. Adding data to the sequential file is done by using **OPEN "A"**. (See line 3040 of the following program.) The "A" stands for *append,* indicating that the new records are to go at the end of the current file. The remainder of the programming procedure is identical to that used in Example 8.1. We need to edit line 1040 in Example 8.1 and renumber the lines by using RENUM. Also, we edit the remark in line 3020 to reflect the program's new function. We have elected, in the following program run, to add two records to the file CONTRIB.DTA, which already contained three records.

example 8.7

```
3000 CLS: KEY OFF: REM ** CLEAR THE SCREEN                      **
3020 REM *** START ROUTINE TO ADD DATA TO AN EXISTING FILE ****
3040 OPEN "A",1,"CONTRIB.DTA"
3060 WHILE Y$ <> "Y"
3080     PRINT: INPUT "NAME";N$
3100     INPUT "CONTRIBUTION AMOUNT";C
3120     WRITE #1,N$,C
3140     PRINT: INPUT "LAST RECORD (Y/N)";Y$
3160     IF LEFT$(Y$,1) = "Y" OR LEFT$(Y$,1) = "y" THEN Y$ = "Y"
3180 WEND
3200 CLOSE 1

NAME? JAMES F. DOLLORENTS
CONTRIBUTION AMOUNT? 14.45

LAST RECORD (Y/N)? N

NAME? WILLIAM K. TARR
CONTRIBUTION AMOUNT? 17.95

LAST RECORD (Y/N)? Y
```

To see if the program worked as expected, we can now load the program shown in Example 8.2, to print the file's contents. As the following program output demonstrates, the "appending" program shown in Example 8.7 performed as intended.

```
NAME                      CONTRIBUTION
---------------------     ------------

JOHN B. ARMSDELL          $ 12.75
JANE L. WHITESIDE         $ 25
SUSAN B. NOTECAF          $ 11.5
JAMES F. DOLLORENTS       $ 14.95
WILLIAM K. TARR           $ 17.95
```

Although the procedure worked well to append new data to an existing file, we cannot use it to directly insert data between existing records. With just a little deviousness, however, we can accomplish an insertion task. Let us suppose we want to insert a record between SUSAN B. NOTECAF and JAMES F. DOLLORENTS. We can get the job done by doing the following:

1. Read all the records up to and including SUSAN B. NOTECAF and write these records into a new file.

2. Now add the record that is to be inserted into the new file.

3. Read the remaining records from the old file and write them into the new file. Presto: The insertion has been made.

To avoid the proliferation of files on our disk, we follow these procedures:

1. Delete the old file. In this case, the old file was named CONTRIB.DTA, so we can accomplish this deletion by writing:

```
KILL "CONTRIB.DTA"
```

2. We can now rename the new file to carry the original file's label. For example, if we named the new file CONTRIB.COR we can write:

```
NAME "CONTRIB.COR" AS "CONTRIB.DTA"
```

The last two steps can even be written into the program that produced the insertion, as shown in Example 8.8, line 4260. The program that allows us to make the insertions is shown in Example 8.8.

example 8.8

```
4000 CLS: KEY OFF: REM ** CLEAR THE SCREEN                          **
4020 REM *** START ROUTINE TO INSERT DATA IN A SEQ. FILE        ****
4040 OPEN "I",1,"CONTRIB.DTA": REM ** OPEN FILE FOR READING       **
4060 OPEN "O",2,"TEMP.DTA": REM ** OPEN TEMP FILE FOR WRITING *
4080 PRINT: PRINT "AFTER WHOSE RECORD DO YOU WANT TO MAKE AN"
4100 PRINT "INSERTION? PLEASE ENTER THE PERSON'S NAME:"
4120 INPUT N1$
4140 WHILE NOT EOF(1)
4160    INPUT #1,N$,C
4180    WRITE #2,N$,C
4200    IF N1$ = N$ THEN GOSUB 4500
4220 WEND
4240 CLOSE 1: CLOSE 2
4260 KILL "CONTRIB.DTA": NAME "TEMP.DTA" AS "CONTRIB.DTA"
4280 PRINT: PRINT "THE RECORD FOR ";N2$;" HAS BEEN INSERTED."
4300 END
4500 REM *** SUBROUTINE TO WRITE THE NEW RECORD TO THE FILE    **
4520 PRINT: INPUT "NAME TO BE ADDED =======> ";N2$
4540 INPUT "CONTRIBUTION ===========> ";C
4560 WRITE #2,N2$,C
4580 RETURN
```

Running the program in Example 8.8 yields the following results:

```
AFTER WHOSE RECORD DO YOU WANT TO MAKE AN
INSERTION? PLEASE ENTER THE PERSON'S NAME:
? SUSAN B. NOTECAF
```

```
NAME TO BE ADDED =======> ? DOLORES D. KOBACH
CONTRIBUTION ===========> ? 25.00

THE RECORD FOR DOLORES D. KOBACH HAS BEEN INSERTED.
```

To find out if the program in Example 8.8 did, in fact, make the insertion, we can run the program in Example 8.2 again. The program run yields the following output, showing that the insertion was made by the program in Example 8.8.

```
NAME                      CONTRIBUTION
--------------------      ------------

JOHN B. ARMSDELL            $ 12.75
JANE L. WHITESIDE           $ 25
SUSAN B. NOTECAF            $ 11.5
DOLORES D. KOBACH           $ 25
JAMES F. DOLLORENTS         $ 14.45
WILLIAM K. TARR             $ 17.95
```

This procedure may also be used to correct any records in a sequential file. This application is shown in the next section.

Correcting Data in a Sequential File

The procedure used to insert data can be adapted readily to the task of correcting records in the file. The program in Example 8.9 uses the same logic as the insertion procedure just discussed. (But the order in lines 5140–5180 is different.)

example 8.9

```
5000 CLS: KEY OFF: REM ** CLEAR THE SCREEN                          **
5020 REM *** START ROUTINE TO CORRECT DATA IN A SEQ. FILE        ****
5040 OPEN "I",1,"CONTRIB.DTA": REM ** OPEN FILE FOR READING       **
5060 OPEN "O",2,"TEMP.DTA": REM ** OPEN TEMP FILE FOR WRITING *
5080 PRINT: PRINT "WHOSE RECORD DO YOU WANT TO CORRECT? PLEASE"
5100 INPUT "ENTER THE PERSON'S NAME: ",N1$
5120 WHILE NOT EOF(1)
5140    INPUT #1,N$,C
5160    IF N1$ = N$ THEN GOSUB 5500
5180    WRITE #2,N$,C
5200 WEND
5220 CLOSE 1: CLOSE 2
5240 KILL "CONTRIB.DTA": NAME "TEMP.DTA" AS "CONTRIB.DTA"
5260 PRINT: PRINT "THE RECORD FOR ";N2$;" HAS BEEN CORRECTED."
5280 END
```

```
5500 REM *** SUBROUTINE TO MAKE A CORRECTION IN THE FILE     ***
5520 PRINT: INPUT "TYPE THE CORRECT NAME ======> ",N2$
5540 INPUT "TYPE THE CORRECT AMOUNT ====> ",C
5550 N$ = N2$
5560 RETURN
```

If this program is run, we will see the following sequence of events. We have elected, in this example, to correct the record for JANE L. WHITESIDE, whose current contribution is (incorrectly) listed as $25. The amount should be $28.93. While reading through the sequence, try to match the events with the program lines in Example 8.9. (*Note:* Since the names were originally entered into the file in capital letters, make sure you type the name in caps. The computer will "see" JANE L. WHITESIDE and Jane L. Whiteside as different strings.)

```
WHOSE RECORD DO YOU WANT TO CORRECT? PLEASE
ENTER THE PERSON'S NAME: JANE L. WHITESIDE

TYPE THE CORRECT NAME ======> JANE L. WHITESIDE
TYPE THE CORRECT AMOUNT ====> 28.93

THE RECORD FOR JANE L. WHITESIDE HAS BEEN CORRECTED.
```

Having run the program, we need to ensure that the file really has been corrected. We perform this check by loading and running the "file printing" program shown in Example 8.2. The program yields the following results:

```
NAME                     CONTRIBUTION
--------------------     ------------

JOHN B. ARMSDELL           $ 12.75
JANE L. WHITESIDE          $ 28.93
SUSAN B. NOTECAF           $ 11.5
DOLORES D.  KOBACH         $ 25
JAMES F. DOLLORENTS        $ 14.45
WILLIAM K. TARR            $ 17.95
```

The record for JANE L. WHITESIDE was, in fact, corrected to reflect the appropriate contribution.

Let us check to see what happened in the program (Example 8.9) when the preceding run was made.

1. Two files were opened, *each using a different buffer.* The first file was opened to read the existing records (line 5040). The second file was opened to write all the records (including the corrected one) into a new file (line 5060).

2. The program checked the requested name JANE L. WHITESIDE against the records in the first (original) file. Since the first name in the file (JOHN B. ARMSDELL) did not match the requested name, JOHN B. ARMSDELL was written into the new file as its first entry (line 5180).

3. Since JANE L. WHITESIDE matched the second name in the original file (line 5160), the program branched to line 5500 to allow the correction to be made.

If JAMES B. DOE had been requested during the first pass through the program, an exact duplicate file would be created, since JAMES B. DOE is not found in the file.

Deleting Data from a Sequential File

The procedure shown in the preceding section also allows us to delete records from a file. The following variation should be used:

1. Read all records up to the record to be deleted and write those records into a new file.

2. Read the record to be deleted, but do *not* write this record into the new file.

3. Read the remaining records in the file and write them into the new file.

We can, apparently, manipulate data in a sequential file if we observe the structural limitations of this file type.

The deletion sequence is demonstrated in Example 8.10. Note especially line 5160 and observe that the record is written into the new file only if the condition in line 5160 is satisfied.

example 8.10

```
5000 CLS: KEY OFF: REM ** CLEAR THE SCREEN                     **
5020 REM *** START ROUTINE TO DELETE DATA IN A SEQ. FILE    ****
5040 OPEN "I",1,"CONTRIB.DTA": REM ** OPEN FILE FOR READING   **
5060 OPEN "O",2,"TEMP.DTA": REM ** OPEN TEMP FILE FOR WRITING *
5080 PRINT: PRINT "WHOSE RECORD DO YOU WANT TO DELETE? PLEASE"
5100 INPUT "ENTER THE PERSON'S NAME: ",N1$
5120 WHILE NOT EOF(1)
5140     INPUT #1,N$,C
5160     IF N1$ <> N$ THEN WRITE #2,N$,C
5200 WEND
5220 CLOSE 1: CLOSE 2
5240 KILL "CONTRIB.DTA": NAME "TEMP.DTA" AS "CONTRIB.DTA"
5260 PRINT: PRINT "THE RECORD FOR ";N1$;" HAS BEEN DELETED."
5280 END
```

To see if the program in Example 8.10 works, check the following runs.

```
RUN

WHOSE RECORD DO YOU WANT TO DELETE? PLEASE
ENTER THE PERSON'S NAME: DOLORES D. KOBACH

THE RECORD FOR DOLORES D. KOBACH HAS BEEN DELETED.
```

Now run the program in Example 8.2 again to see if the deletion was actually made.

```
NAME                   CONTRIBUTION
--------------------   ------------

JOHN B. ARMSDELL         $ 12.75
JANE L. WHITESIDE        $ 28.93
SUSAN B. NOTECAF         $ 11.5
JAMES F. DOLLORENTS      $ 14.45
WILLIAM K. TARR          $ 17.95
```

The listing demonstrates that the program in Example 8.10 performed its intended function.

To make sequential file handling as simple as possible for the user of our programs, it is desirable to include all the options in a menu-driven file system. (*Note:* A file system is a combination of file programs that allows the user to create a file, make corrections in a file, add to a file, and delete from a file.) We started a file system in Example 8.3, so all we need to do is add the features of CORRECT, ADD, and DELETE to the program.

Chapter Review

A computer file is a collection of records, each containing one or more fields. In a way, the computer file resembles a file drawer in an office cabinet. The records are the equivalent of file folders, while the fields are the equivalent of the folder contents.

A sequential file is one in which we can access records only in a specific order. To get to a particular record, we must read through all the preceding records. Therefore, the sequential file represents a rather "slow" system. However, since the sequential file records are automatically "packed," sequential files take up less disk space than other files. In addition, sequential file programs are easy to write because we do not need to define record and/or field size.

To put records into a file, the information is usually typed in at a keyboard. From the keyboard, the information goes into a part of the memory known as the buffer. The record is then transferred from the buffer to the disk. Putting the information on disk, therefore, involves getting the buffer's output ("O"). The file statement would read:

```
OPEN "O",buffer number,"filename"
```

Having opened the file, we can write records into the file, using the format:

```
WRITE # buffer number,variable names separated by commas
```

To read information from a sequential file, we must first place the file records into a buffer. Therefore, getting records from a diskette involves buffer input ("I"). The statement looks like this:

```
OPEN "I",buffer number,"filename"
```

The actual record transfer takes place when we write:

```
INPUT # buffer number, variable names separated by commas
```

Trying to read past the last record in the file will cause an "out-of-data" error condition. Therefore, we use an end-of-file (EOF) designator, using:

```
EOF(buffer number)
```

in conjunction with an IF statement or a WHILE statement to close the file, as follows:

```
CLOSE buffer number
```

Up to 15 buffers are available for microcomputer file work.

The complete file sequences are as follows:

To put records on disk:	To read records from disk:
OPEN "O",buffer number,"filename" (input variables from keyboard)	OPEN "I",buffer number,"filename" IF EOF(buffer number)THEN (use line number of closing statement)
WRITE # buffer number,variables, separated by commas	INPUT # buffer number,variables, separated by commas
CLOSE buffer number	CLOSE buffer number

Common Errors

1. Not closing the same file that was opened.

Correct:

```
20   OPEN "O",3,"SAMPLE.DAT"
.
.
.
40   CLOSE 3
```

Incorrect:

```
20   OPEN "O",3,"SAMPLE.DAT"
.
.
.
40   CLOSE 1
```

2. Forgetting that a buffer is being used by one file when a second file is opened.

Correct:

```
20   OPEN "O",1,"EX-1.DAT"
.
.
.
200   OPEN "O",2,"EX-2.DAT"
.
.
.
500   CLOSE 1: CLOSE 2
```

Incorrect:

```
20   OPEN "O",1,"EX-1.DAT"
.
.
.
200   OPEN "O",1,"EX-2.DAT"
.
.
.
500 CLOSE 1
```

3. Trying to read a record you have already passed. If you are currently using the fifth record, you cannot go back and read the fourth record. You must go to the end of the file and start over again. This limitation of sequential files is particularly bothersome if you must do much file updating or if the file must be corrected.

4. Nonstandard entry of file records. For example, if you sometimes enter names in "all caps" and sometimes in mixed caps and lowercase letters, you may have trouble finding the records.

   Example: Suppose you put the name J. D. DOE into the file, but you search the file for J. D. Doe. The record will not be found because DOE and Doe are not "seen" as identical strings.

Key Terms and Concepts

rules for naming files
field
record
buffer
sequential file
OPEN "O"
OPEN "I"
buffer number
WRITE #
INPUT #
CLOSE
EOF(buffer number)
MERGE
OPEN "A"

Exercises

1. Store the following five coded items and their prices in a sequential file; then write a menu-driven program to provide the following options.

   Items to be stored in the file are:

```
                                NUMBER IN
ITEM CODE        PRICE          INVENTORY
---------        -----          ---------

11-AB/ACE      $ 12.85            106
143AK-433      $ 74.18            227
125/35/DD      $ 20.89            83
B9B-3D/BE      $ 11.97            14
K55A-99KA      $ 92.44            392
```

   The program runs that follow show the use of all options:

```
RUN

PLEASE SELECT ONE OF THE FOLLOWING:

     1. CREATE THE FILE
     2. PRINT THE FILE'S CONTENTS
     3. SEARCH FOR AN ITEM CODE
     4. STOP THIS PROGRAM

ENTER THE SELECTED OPTION: 1

ENTER THE FILE NAME: INVENTOR.Y

ITEM CODE: 11-AB/ACE
PRICE: 12.85
NUMBER IN INVENTORY: 106

LAST ENTRY (Y/N)? N
```

```
ITEM CODE: 143AK-433
PRICE: 74.18
NUMBER IN INVENTORY: 227

LAST ENTRY (Y/N)? N

ITEM CODE: 125/35/DD
PRICE: 20.89
NUMBER IN INVENTORY: 83

LAST ENTRY (Y/N)? N

ITEM CODE: B9B-3D/BE
PRICE: 11.97
NUMBER IN INVENTORY: 14

LAST ENTRY (Y/N)? N

ITEM CODE: K55A-99KA
PRICE: 92.44
NUMBER IN INVENTORY: 392

LAST ENTRY (Y/N)? Y

PRESS/RELEASE THE 'ENTER' KEY TO CONTINUE?

PLEASE SELECT ONE OF THE FOLLOWING:

     1. CREATE THE FILE
     2. PRINT THE FILE'S CONTENTS
     3. SEARCH FOR AN ITEM CODE
     4. STOP THIS PROGRAM

ENTER THE SELECTED OPTION: 2

ENTER THE FILE NAME: INVENTOR.Y


                        NUMBER IN
ITEM CODE    PRICE     INVENTORY
---------    -----     ---------


11-AB/ACE    $12.85       106
143AK-433    $74.18       227
125/35/DD    $20.89       83
B9B-3D/BE    $11.97       14
K55A-99KA    $92.44       392
```

```
PRESS/RELEASE THE 'ENTER' KEY TO CONTINUE?

PLEASE SELECT ONE OF THE FOLLOWING:

     1. CREATE THE FILE
     2. PRINT THE FILE'S CONTENTS
     3. SEARCH FOR AN ITEM CODE
     4. STOP THIS PROGRAM

ENTER THE SELECTED OPTION: 3

ENTER THE FILE NAME: INVENTOR.Y

ENTER THE ITEM CODE: B9B-3D/BE

ITEM CODE: B9B-3D/BE
ITEM PRICE: $11.97
ITEM INVENTORY: 14

PRESS/RELEASE THE 'ENTER' KEY TO CONTINUE?

PLEASE SELECT ONE OF THE FOLLOWING:

     1. CREATE THE FILE
     2. PRINT THE FILE'S CONTENTS
     3. SEARCH FOR AN ITEM CODE
     4. STOP THIS PROGRAM

ENTER THE SELECTED OPTION: 3

ENTER THE FILE NAME: INVENTOR.Y

ENTER THE ITEM CODE: B5R/G67R

ITEM B54/G67R IS NOT IN THE FILE.

PRESS/RELEASE THE 'ENTER' KEY TO CONTINUE?

PLEASE SELECT ONE OF THE FOLLOWING:

     1. CREATE THE FILE
     2. PRINT THE FILE'S CONTENTS
     3. SEARCH FOR AN ITEM CODE
     4. STOP THIS PROGRAM

ENTER THE SELECTED OPTION: 4
```

2. Write a sequential program that will access the data in the file created in Exercise 1. The program should calculate the total inventory value for each item by multiplying price and inventory. The output should look like this:

ITEM CODE	PRICE	NUMBER IN INVENTORY	INVENTORY TOTAL VALUE
---------	------	---------	-----------
11-AB/ACE	$12.85	106	$ 1,362.10
143AK-433	$74.18	227	$16,838.86
125/35/DD	$20.89	83	$ 1,733.87
B9B-3D/BE	$11.97	14	$ 167.58
K55A-99KA	$92.44	392	$36,236.48

3. Write a sequential file program to store the following data in a file named STUDENT. Then write a program to read the data in the STUDENT file and store the male and female data into separate files named MALE and FEMALE, respectively. Make sure that each program allows you to print the contents of each file.

STUDENT NUMBER	SEX	GPA
--------------	---	----
AA-4591	M	2.12
AA-7298	M	2.78
BD-5721	F	2.57
BB-1225	M	3.02
AA-3284	F	3.45

4. Using the data in the file named STUDENT, (see Exercise 3), write a program to produce the following output. The averages are calculated for each category by adding the GPA scores and dividing by the number of scores that were added. For example, the male GPA mean score would be calculated by $(2.12 + 2.78 + 3.02)/3$.

	ALL MALES	ALL FEMALES	OVERALL
	---------	-----------	-------
MEAN GPA	2.64	3.01	2.78
LOW GPA	2.12	2.57	2.12
HIGH GPA	3.02	3.45	3.45

5. Let us suppose you have two sequential data files named CLASS-1 and CLASS-2, respectively. (The data to be entered into the files are shown below.) Write a program to combine these two files into a third file, named CLASS-3. *Hint:* First copy the records from CLASS-1 into CLASS-3, then use the APPEND function to copy the records from CLASS-2 into CLASS-3. Make the program flexible enough to handle the building and printing of any of the first two files without further modification. Then modify this program to combine CLASS-1 and CLASS-2 into CLASS-3.

CLASS-1 DATA	CLASS-2 DATA
------------	------------
1.73	2.99
3.59	3.02
2.28	

The result of combining the two files should be printed as shown:

```
CLASS-3 DATA
------------

   1.73
   3.59
   2.28
   2.99
   3.02
```

9

Objectives

- To learn the PC BASIC random access file structure.
- To learn the random access file commands.
- To write random access file programs that create files, print file contents, add to files, delete from files, and correct files.

RANDOM ACCESS FILES

Chapter 8 introduced sequential files. You learned to write programs that created sequential files, printed sequential file contents, added records to sequential files, deleted records from sequential files, and corrected records in sequential files. Menu-driven sequential file systems were also introduced.

This chapter tells you how to create random access files using all the options discussed in Chapter 8. To make the random access/sequential files comparable for discussion purposes, we use the data set presented in Chapter 8.

9.1 Random Access Files

General Structure

Random access files are also called *direct access* files. The names are indicative of file structure and use. The records in a random access file may be accessed in any (random) order. Any record in the file may be accessed directly, without having to read the preceding records. Therefore, the random access file is more efficient than the sequential file if individual records must be accessed frequently. For example, if we update inventory records based on current sales, random access records are superior. (Sales of inventory items would not be expected to take place in the order in which these items are stored in the inventory file!) Similarly, airline reservations programs are best based on random access files so that any passenger or seat can be accessed directly.

The access speed of the random access file makes it the generally preferred file type. However, we will discover that we must pay a price for such speed: Writing random access file programs requires more planning than is necessary for sequential files. Also, a random access file requires more disk space than a sequential file. Fortunately, random access file procedures become second nature once the general random access file structure is understood.

To facilitate comparisons between random access and sequential files, we make use of the same data used in Chapter 8. The information in Table 9.1 should look familiar.

table 9.1
DATA FOR THE FIRST RANDOM ACCESS FILE: A LIST OF CONTRIBUTORS AND THEIR CONTRIBUTIONS

Name	Contribution
JOHN B. ARMSDELL	$12.75
JANE L. WHITESIDE	$25.00
SUSAN B. NOTECAF	$11.50

Space Requirement

The first major difference between random access and sequential files is that the former require the reservation of space for fields and records. This is because to find a record directly, the computer must be able to use the record number to go to a specific spot on the disk. If all the records are known to be of a given length, the computer can use the record length and the record number to wind up at the required disk location. If the records are of different lengths, as they are in a sequential file, knowing the record number is not much help. Therefore, the first requirement is to determine the space required for the fields and to make sure that the sum of the field lengths in a record is equal to a record length.

To ensure sufficient space for storing the field values, we must anticipate the largest number of bytes required. For example, we may want to reserve 25 bytes of space to handle each contributor's name. Although none of the three names in Table 9.1 is 25 bytes long, we may expect to encounter longer names as the list grows. Thus far, however, the unused spaces are clearly "wasted." Therefore, a random access file takes more room on disk than a sequential file would, since the sequential file records are simply laid end to end.

Figure 9.1 compares the space requirements of sequential and random access files.

If we fail to reserve a specific number of bytes per record, the computer will automatically assign 128 bytes to each record, resulting in much wasted disk space in this case. It pays to make reservations!

We will also discover that we cannot directly store numerical information in the random access file: Before being inserted, the values must be converted to strings. As the next few sections show, we may make a distinction between integers, single-precision numbers, and double-precision numbers. Failure to de-

figure 9.1
A COMPARISON OF SPACE REQUIREMENTS FOR SEQUENTIAL AND RANDOM ACCESS FILES: TWO RECORDS

Sequential File

JOHN B. ARMSDELL	12.75	JANE L. WHITESIDE	25

Random Access File

JOHN B. ARMSDELL	12.75	JANE L. WHITESIDE	25

clare the number type will cause the computer to assume single precision, which is usually adequate anyway. Regardless of the number of digits used, single-precision numbers require only 4 bytes of storage in the random access file. Therefore, using the data in Table 9.1 and reserving 25 bytes for the names and 4 bytes for the contributions, the reserved record length must be 29 bytes. The following examples show variables N1$ (contributor name) and C (contribution amount) requiring a record length of 29 bytes.

9.2 Writing a Random Access File Program

Opening the Random Access File

We must begin by opening the file, showing that the file will be of the random access ("R") variety, and defining the record length. For our file named "CONTRIBR.DTA" we write the following line:

```
OPEN "R",1,"CONTRIBR.DTA",29
```

File name — Record length

Buffer number

Random access file designator

If we previously had defined the file name by:

```
F$ = "CONTRIBR.DTA"
```

we could have written our file opening statement as follows:

```
OPEN "R",1,F$,29
```

If the record length is *not* specified, the IBM PC will assume a maximum record length of 128 characters.

Organizing the Buffer Space: The FIELD Statement

Buffer number assignment takes place as soon as the **OPEN** statement has assigned a buffer to the file—in this case, buffer number 1. Then we need a **FIELD**

statement to organize the buffer space, making it ready to receive our data. The field statement uses the same buffer number as the one we reserved in the OPEN statement.

```
FIELD 1,25 AS N1$,4 AS C$
```

Space reserved for variable C$

Space reserved for variable N1$

Buffer number

The variable N1$ is used to define the buffer portion for the contributor's name. But how does the variable C$ come into the picture? We define C$ as the string equivalent of the contribution amount because the IBM PC operating system is designed so that *the random access file can store only strings.* Therefore, we must convert any numeric variable into a string variable. The conversion is done as shown in Table 9.2.

In the preceding example, 25 spaces are reserved for variable N1$ and 4 spaces (bytes) are reserved for variable C$. Note that the sum of the spaces reserved for each field is equal to the record length. In this case, 25 + 4 = 29, the record length shown in the file opening statement. Why did we reserve only 4 bytes for the variable C, even though the contribution values could consist of 5 or even more digits? The reason is found in the way the IBM PC distinguishes between the following numeric value types:

1. *Integer value.* Integers are whole numbers. Therefore, if certain variables occur only as integers, they may be identified by the "%" symbol. For example, C%, A9%, and X% all represent integers. So do the subscripted variables C%(I), A9%(J), and X%(Q).

2. *Single-precision values.* These values are accurate up to six digits. Single-precision variables are identified by the "!" symbol. Therefore, Z8!, X!, and D5! all represent single-precision variables, as do the subscripted variables Z8!(I), X!(Q), and D5!(J). If no symbol is used to declare precision, the IBM PC assumes single precision. Therefore, Z8, X, and D5 are all assumed to be single-precision variables, as are the subscripted variables Z8(I), X(N), and D5(Q).

3. *Double-precision values.* These are values that are accurate up to 16 digits. Double-precision values are identified by the "#" symbol. Variables Y#,

K3#, and T5# are all double-precision variables. Similarly, the subscripted variables Y#(I), K3#(Q), and T5#(J) represent double-precision variables.

table 9.2
CONVERTING NUMBERS INTO STRINGS BEFORE STORING THEM IN A RANDOM ACCESS FILE

Statement	Effect
`C$ = MKI$(C%)`	Changes the integer value (C%) into a 2-character string named C$.
`C$ = MKS$(C!)`	Changes a single-precision number (C!) into a 4-character string named C$.
`C$ = MKD$(C#)`	Changes a double-precision value (C#) into an 8-character string named C$.

Armed with this information let us examine the summary of procedures for the **numeric conversion to strings** presented in Table 9.2.

Remember, since the lack of a precision symbol causes the computer to assume the single-precision condition, the contribution amount (C) is converted by:

```
C$ = MKS$(C)
```

without declaring the variable 'C' to be single precision. We now see why we reserved only 4 spaces for the variable C$ in the FIELD definition shown earlier. With numbers like dollar values (accurate to only two decimal places), we usually do not bother to declare precision, letting the computer assume single precision.

Transferring the Strings to the Buffer: LSET and RSET

The FIELD statement only reserves spaces for the strings; it does *not* actually put the strings in the buffer. To accomplish this task, we need to use either an:

```
LSET
```

or an:

```
RSET
```

statement. Not only do the **LSET** and **RSET** commands transfer the strings to the buffer, they also format the strings so that they will fit into the space that was reserved in the FIELD definition. LSET provides a *left*-justified format, while

RSET creates a *right*-justified format. Remember, we reserved 25 spaces for the name variable N1$ in our FIELD statement, writing FIELD 1, 25 AS N1$, 4 AS C$. If N1$ contains more than 25 spaces (characters), the LSET (or RSET) command will *truncate* the variable to fit the assigned space. If N1$ contains fewer than 25 spaces, the LSET (or RSET) command will add blanks to fill up the remaining space. Using LSET N1$ = N$, the data we are using would be put into the buffer as follows:

```
                    SPACE NUMBER

                  1 1 1 1 1 1 1 1 1 1 2 2 2 2 2 2
1 2 3 4 5 6 7 8 9 0 1 2 3 4 5 6 7 8 9 0 1 2 3 4 5

J O H N   B .   A R M S D E L L
J A N E   L .   W H I T E S I D E
S U S A N   B .   N O T E C A F
```

On the other hand, defining:

```
RSET N1$ = N$
```

would have formatted the field as follows:

```
                    SPACE NUMBER

                  1 1 1 1 1 1 1 1 1 1 2 2 2 2 2 2
1 2 3 4 5 6 7 8 9 0 1 2 3 4 5 6 7 8 9 0 1 2 3 4 5

                  J O H N   B .   A R M S D E L L
                J A N E   L .   W H I T E S I D E
                  S U S A N   B .   N O T E C A F
```

Either format is acceptable. In this chapter, however, we normally use LSET to format the strings in the buffer.

One last note about LSET and RSET. Apparently, we introduced yet another variable when we used our LSET statement, writing LSET N1$ = N$. The N$ string is the one that was INPUT, whereas the N1$ string defines the LSET condition. The IBM PC allows us to use larger variable names, and we could, of course, write ourselves a reminder by defining the LSET string to be PERSON$, since N$ represents a person. Similarly, we might define the contribution variable to be CONTRIB$. Therefore, we could write:

```
LSET PERSON$ = N$
LSET CONTRIB$ = MKS$(C)
```

We do need to remember not to use reserved words in LSET or RSET strings, however.

So far, we have prepared our random access file by writing:

```
OPEN "R",1,F$,29
FIELD 1, 25 as PERSON$,4 AS CONTRIB$
    .
    .
    .
LSET PERSON$ =N$
LSET CONTRIB$ = MKS$(C)
```

We now have the variables PERSON$ and CONTRIB$ in the buffer, but we have not yet put the buffer contents on the disk.

Transferring the Buffer Contents to the Disk: PUT

To transfer the buffer contents to the disk, that is, to **PUT** the data on the disk, we use:

```
PUT buffer number, record number
```

For example, PUT 1,4 tells the computer to put the contents of buffer number 1 into the fourth record in the file. We may use the PUT statement without a record number, writing:

```
PUT buffer number
```

If we do not use a record number, the computer will automatically assign a record number to the record. For example, the first record will be given a record number of 1, the next one will be record number 2, the next one will be record number 3, and so on. Thus far, our random access file is prepared by:

```
OPEN "R",1,F$,29
FIELD 1,25 AS PERSON$,4 AS CONTRIB$
    .
    .
    .
LSET PERSON$ = N$
LSET CONTRIB$ = MKS$(C)
PUT 1
```

Closing the File

The last act of creating a random access file is to **CLOSE** the file. We must make sure to close the same file that we opened. For example, if we started the file by writing OPEN "R", 1, F$, 29 we must use CLOSE 1. If we had opened a file in buffer number 3, we would have used CLOSE 3.

Writing the First Random Access File Program

Let us now take a look at the program in Example 9.1, which contains all the required random access file statements (lines 1060, 1080, 1220, and 1240). In this case, however, it was decided to incorporate the file name CONTRIBR.DTA in the opening statement. We also could have added a line:

```
1030 PRINT: INPUT "ENTER THE FILE NAME";F$
```

We would then have rewritten line 1060 as follows:

```
1060 OPEN "R",1,F$,29
```

The approach that is used is largely a matter of the writer's choice between flexibility and convenience.

Note also the following special features in Example 9.1:

1. Record number one is reserved to store the number of records, written into the file in line 1360.

2. The first "real" record is written into the file as record position number 2. Therefore, we initialize N = 1 in line 1040 and we use N = N + 1 in line 1120, before we write the record.

3. Since the first record is not a "real" record—no contributor data is stored in it—we let N$ be a dummy variable XXXX. The number of records is stored in the field CONTRIB$.

The reason for this procedure becomes apparent when we realize that the random access file does not have an EOF function as the sequential file did. Although there are many different ways of preventing the problem of reading past the last record, the procedure shown here turns out to be the most convenient when additional file features are introduced.

example 9.1

```
1000 CLS: KEY OFF: REM ** CLEAR THE SCREEN                              **
1020 REM ****** ROUTINE TO CREATE A RANDOM ACCESS FILE            ******
1040 N = 1: REM ** INITIALIZE THE RECORD COUNTER                        **
1060 OPEN "R",1,"CONTRIBR.DTA",29
1080 FIELD 1, 25 AS PERSON$, 4 AS CONTRIB$
1100 WHILE Y$ <> "Y"
1120     N = N + 1: REM ** ADD 1 TO THE RECORD COUNTER                  **
1140     CLS:LOCATE 10,15:PRINT "RECORD 1 STORES THE # OF RECORDS."
1160     LOCATE 12,15: PRINT "YOU ARE ENTERING RECORD";N
1180     LOCATE 14,15: INPUT "NAME ==============> ",N$
1200     LOCATE 15,15: INPUT "CONTRIBUTION ======> ",C
```

```
1220    LSET PERSON$ = N$: LSET CONTRIB$ = MKS$(C)
1240    PUT 1,N
1260    LOCATE 17,15: INPUT "LAST RECORD";Y$
1280    IF LEFT$(Y$,1) = "Y" OR LEFT$(Y$,1) = "y" THEN Y$ = "Y"
1300 WEND
1320 N$ = "XXXX": REM ** STORE A DUMMY STRING                      **
1340 LSET PERSON$ = N$: LSET CONTRIB$ = MKS$(N)
1360 PUT 1,1: REM ** STORE THE NUMBER OF RECORDS IN RECORD 1      **
1380 CLOSE 1
1400 LOCATE 19,15
1420 PRINT "YOU ENTERED";N;"RECORDS INTO THE FILE NAMED"
1440 LOCATE 20,15
1460 PRINT "CONTRIB.DTA. RECORD #1 WAS USED TO STORE THE"
1480 LOCATE 21,15
1500 PRINT "# OF RECORDS SAVED IN THIS RANDOM ACCESS FILE."
1520 END
```

When we run this program, we enter the data as follows:

```
RECORD 1 STORES THE # OF RECORDS.

YOU ARE ENTERING RECORD 2

NAME ==============> JOHN B. ARMSDELL
CONTRIBUTION ======> 12.75

LAST RECORD? N

RECORD 1 STORES THE # OF RECORDS.

YOU ARE ENTERING RECORD 3

NAME ==============> JANE L. WHITESIDE
CONTRIBUTION ======> 25.00

LAST RECORD? N

RECORD 1 STORES THE # OF RECORDS.

YOU ARE ENTERING RECORD 4

NAME ==============> SUSAN B. NOTECAF
CONTRIBUTION ======> 11.50

LAST RECORD? Y
```

```
YOU ENTERED 4 RECORDS INTO THE FILE NAMED
CONTRIBR.DTA. RECORD #1 WAS USED TO STORE THE
# OF RECORDS SAVED IN THIS RANDOM ACCESS FILE.
```

Having written the program shown in Example 9.1 and having entered the three records as shown, we probably want "proof" that the data really are on the disk. Therefore, we must write a program that will transfer (print) the data from the disk to the screen.

Getting a Copy of the Random Access File: The GET Command

To **GET** data from the disk to the screen, we need, not surprisingly, a statement such as the following:

```
GET buffer number, record number
```

For example, GET 1,3 would get record number 3 from buffer number 1.

Remember that we transformed numerical data into strings before putting them on the disk. Therefore, we need to change the strings back into numbers before trying to process them. Table 9.3 shows the procedure for **string conversion to numbers.**

table 9.3
CONVERTING STRINGS INTO NUMBERS

Statement	Effect
C% = CVI(C$)	Changes a 2-character string into an integer (C%).
C! = CVS(C$)	Changes a 4-character string into a single-precision number (C!).
C# = CVD(C$)	Changes an 8-character string into a double-precision number (C#).

We do not need to assign %, !, or # to the numeric variable if we elect not to. For example, our single-precision contribution amount can be created by writing C = CVS(C$), since *undeclared variables are assumed to be composed of single-precision numbers.* Both the conversion and the GET statement are demonstrated in Example 9.2.

Note that we start the FOR/NEXT loop in line 2200 at the value 2 because the first record stores the number of records.

example 9.2

```
2000 CLS: KEY OFF: REM ** CLEAR THE SCREEN                            **
2020 REM ******* ROUTINE TO PRINT FILE CONTENTS ***************
2040 PRINT:      PRINT
```

```
2060 PRINT "RECORD #          NAME";TAB(36);"CONTRIBUTION"
2080 PRINT "--------  ---------------------";
2100 PRINT TAB(36);"------------": PRINT
2120 OPEN "R",2,"CONTRIBR.DTA",29
2140 FIELD 2, 25 AS PERSON$, 4 AS CONTRIB$
2160 GET 2,1: REM ** GET THE NUMBER OF RECORDS IN RECORD #1   **
2180 N = CVS(CONTRIB$): I = 2
2200 WHILE I < =N
2220      GET 2,I
2240      C = CVS(CONTRIB$)
2260      PRINT TAB(4);I;TAB(13);PERSON$;TAB(39);"$";C
2270      I = I + 1
2280 WEND
2300 CLOSE 2
2320 END
```

Running the program in Example 9.2 will yield the following output:

```
RECORD #           NAME             CONTRIBUTION
--------  ---------------------     ------------

    2        JOHN B. ARMSDELL         $ 12.75
    3        JANE L. WHITESIDE        $ 25
    4        SUSAN B. NOTECAF         $ 11.5
```

9.3 Creating a Simple Random Access File System

We can easily combine the file creation and file printing options into a simple menu-driven file system, just as we did in the sequential file chapter. (Remember to patch the programs in Examples 9.1 and 9.2 together with the MERGE command!) After the programs have been merged, add lines 100–440 and lines 2320–2360 shown in Example 9.3 and add the RETURN statements in lines 1560 and 2340. The RETURN statements will cause the program to return to the menu.

example 9.3

```
100 CLS: KEY OFF: REM ** CLEAR THE SCREEN                           **
120 WHILE CHOICE < 3
140      CLS
160      PRINT "PLEASE SELECT ONE OF THE FOLLOWING OPTIONS:": PRINT
180      PRINT TAB(5);"1. CREATE THE RANDOM ACCESS FILE"
200      PRINT TAB(5);"2. PRINT THE RANDOM ACCESS FILE CONTENTS"
220      PRINT TAB(5);"3. STOP THIS PROGRAM"
```

```
240     PRINT: INPUT "ENTER YOUR SELECTION NOW ",CHOICE
260     ON CHOICE GOSUB 1000,2000
280     WHILE CHOICE < 1 OR CHOICE > 3
300         PRINT: PRINT
320         PRINT "YOU SELECTED CHOICE NUMBER",CHOICE
340         PRINT "THE MENU ONLY ALLOWS CHOICES 1-3.": PRINT
360         INPUT "TAP THE RETURN KEY TO CONTINUE ",C
380         CHOICE = 2
400     WEND
420 WEND
440 END
1000 REM ***********************************************************
1010 REM                 CREATE A RANDOM ACCESS FILE               *
1020 REM ***********************************************************
1030 CLS: REM ** CLEAR THE SCREEN                                 **
1040 N = 1: REM ** INITIALIZE THE RECORD COUNTER                  **
1060 OPEN "R",1,"CONTRIBR.DTA",29
1080 FIELD 1, 25 AS PERSON$, 4 AS CONTRIB$
1100 WHILE Y$ <> "Y"
1120    N = N + 1: REM ** ADD 1 TO THE RECORD COUNTER             **
1140    CLS:LOCATE 10,15:PRINT "RECORD 1 STORES THE # OF RECORDS."
1160    LOCATE 12,15: PRINT "YOU ARE ENTERING RECORD";N
1180    LOCATE 14,15: INPUT "NAME =============> ",N$
1200    LOCATE 15,15: INPUT "CONTRIBUTION ======> ",C
1220    LSET PERSON$ = N$: LSET CONTRIB$ = MKS$(C)
1240    PUT 1,N
1260    LOCATE 17,15: INPUT "LAST RECORD(Y/N)";Y$
1280    IF LEFT$(Y$,1) = "Y" OR LEFT$(Y$,1) = "y" THEN Y$ = "Y"
1300 WEND
1320 N$ = "XXXX": REM ** STORE A DUMMY STRING                     **
1340 LSET PERSON$ = N$: LSET CONTRIB$ = MKS$(N)
1360 PUT 1,1: REM ** STORE THE NUMBER OF RECORDS IN RECORD 1      **
1380 CLOSE 1
1400 LOCATE 19,15
1420 PRINT "YOU ENTERED";N;"RECORDS INTO THE FILE NAMED"
1440 LOCATE 20,15
1460 PRINT "CONTRIBR.DTA. RECORD #1 WAS USED TO STORE THE"
1480 LOCATE 21,15
1500 PRINT "# OF RECORDS SAVED IN THIS RANDOM ACCESS FILE."
1520 LOCATE 23,15
1540 INPUT "TAP THE RETURN KEY TO RETURN TO THE MENU. ",C
1560 RETURN
2000 REM ***********************************************************
2010 REM *                  PRINT THE FILE CONTENTS                *
2020 REM ***********************************************************
2030 CLS: REM ** CLEAR THE SCREEN                                 **
2040 PRINT: INPUT "WOULD YOU LIKE A PRINTED COPY? (Y/N) ",Y$
```

```
2050 IF LEFT$(Y$,1) = "Y" OR LEFT$(Y$,1) = "y" THEN A1$ = "LPT1:"
     ELSE A1$ = "SCRN:"
2055 OPEN A1$ FOR OUTPUT AS 1: WIDTH 1, 132
2057 PRINT #1,: PRINT #1,
2060 PRINT #1, "RECORD #           NAME";TAB(36);"CONTRIBUTION"
2080 PRINT #1, "--------  --------------------";
2100 PRINT #1, TAB(36);"------------": PRINT #1,
2120 OPEN "R",2,"CONTRIBR.DTA",29
2140 FIELD 2, 25 AS PERSON$, 4 AS CONTRIB$
2160 GET 2,1: REM ** GET THE NUMBER OF RECORDS IN RECORD #1    **
2180 N = CVS(CONTRIB$): I = 2
2200 WHILE I <= N
2220      GET 2,I
2240      C = CVS(CONTRIB$)
2260      PRINT #1, TAB(4);I;TAB(13);PERSON$;TAB(39);"$";C
2270     I = I + 1
2280 WEND
2300 CLOSE 2: CLOSE 1: PRINT: PRINT
2320 INPUT "TAP THE RETURN KEY TO RETURN TO THE MENU. ",C
2340 RETURN
```

Running the program with option number 2 yields the following output. Remember, the file CONTRIBR.DTA was created by program Example 9.1.

```
PLEASE SELECT ONE OF THE FOLLOWING OPTIONS:

    1. CREATE THE RANDOM ACCESS FILE
    2. PRINT THE RANDOM ACCESS FILE CONTENTS
    3. STOP THIS PROGRAM

ENTER YOUR SELECTION NOW 2


WOULD YOU LIKE A PRINTED COPY? (Y/N) N

RECORD #           NAME           CONTRIBUTION
--------  --------------------  ------------

    2      JOHN B. ARMSDELL       $ 12.75
    3      JANE L. WHITESIDE      $ 25
    4      SUSAN B. NOTECAF       $ 11.5

TAP THE RETURN KEY TO RETURN TO THE MENU
```

```
PLEASE SELECT ONE OF THE FOLLOWING OPTIONS:

     1. CREATE THE RANDOM ACCESS FILE
     2. PRINT THE RANDOM ACCESS FILE CONTENTS
     3. STOP THIS PROGRAM

ENTER YOUR SELECTION NOW 3
```

Finding a Record in a Random Access File

Since the specific location of any record in a random access file can be accessed directly, finding a specific record is very easy. Unlike the case of sequential files, we can "jump" back and forth in a random access file, retrieving information at will. For example, we can specify:

```
GET 1,3
```

which will find record number 3 in buffer number 1.

Program Example 9.4 demonstrates that we can access any record in any order from the file we have named CONTRIB.DTA.

example 9.4

```
3000 CLS: KEY OFF: REM ** CLEAR THE SCREEN                            **
3020 Y$ = "Y"
3040 OPEN "R",2,"CONTRIBR.DTA",29
3060 FIELD 2, 25 AS PERSON$, 4 AS CONTRIB$
3080 GET 2,1: N = CVS(CONTRIB$)
3100 WHILE Y$ = "Y"
3120    CLS: REM ** CLEAR THE SCREEN                                  **
3140    LOCATE 3,15: PRINT "THERE ARE";N;"RECORDS IN THIS FILE."
3145    LOCATE 4,15
3150    PRINT "(RECORD 1 IS USED TO STORE THE # OF RECORDS.)"
3160    LOCATE 6,15: PRINT "WHICH RECORD DO YOU WANT TO SEE?"
3180    LOCATE 7,15: INPUT "ENTER THE RECORD NUMBER: ",R1
3200    GET 2,R1
3220    C = CVS(CONTRIB$)
3240    LOCATE 9,15: PRINT "CURRENT DATA IN RECORD NUMBER";R1
3260    LOCATE 11,15: PRINT "CONTRIBUTOR ===============> ";PERSON$
3280    LOCATE 12,15: PRINT "AMOUNT OF CONTRIBUTION ====> $";C
3300    LOCATE 14,15: INPUT "WANT TO SEE ANOTHER RECORD? (Y/N) ",Y$
3320    IF LEFT$(Y$,1) = "Y" OR LEFT$(Y$,1) = "y" THEN Y$ = "Y"
3340 WEND
3360 CLOSE 2
```

```
THERE ARE 4 RECORDS IN THIS FILE.
(RECORD 1 IS USED TO STORE THE # OF RECORDS.)

WHICH RECORD DO YOU WANT TO SEE?
ENTER THE RECORD NUMBER: 2

CURRENT DATA IN RECORD NUMBER 2

CONTRIBUTOR ===============> JOHN B. ARMSDELL
AMOUNT OF CONTRIBUTION ====> $ 12.75

WANT TO SEE ANOTHER RECORD? (Y/N) Y


THERE ARE 4 RECORDS IN THIS FILE.
(RECORD 1 IS USED TO STORE THE # OF RECORDS.)

WHICH RECORD DO YOU WANT TO SEE?
ENTER THE RECORD NUMBER: 3

CURRENT DATA IN RECORD NUMBER 3

CONTRIBUTOR ===============> JANE L. WHITESIDE
AMOUNT OF CONTRIBUTION ====> $ 25

WANT TO SEE ANOTHER RECORD? (Y/N) N
```

Correcting Data in a Random Access File

Since we can go directly to any record in a random access file, correcting records turns out to be much simpler than it was for the sequential files. Program Example 9.5 asks the user to designate the file record number for the record to be changed (see line 4180). If another record is to be corrected, the program loops back when line 4420 is executed.

example 9.5

```
4000 CLS: KEY OFF: REM ** CLEAR THE SCREEN                              **
4020 Y$ = "Y"
4040 OPEN "R",2,"CONTRIBR.DTA",29
4060 FIELD 2, 25 AS PERSON$, 4 AS CONTRIB$
4080 GET 2,1: N = CVS(CONTRIB$)
4100 WHILE Y$ = "Y"
4120     CLS: REM ** CLEAR THE SCREEN                                   **
```

```
4140      LOCATE 3,15: PRINT "THERE ARE";N;"RECORDS IN THIS FILE." **
4145      LOCATE 4,15
4150      PRINT "(RECORD 1 IS USED TO STORE THE # OF RECORDS.)"
4160      LOCATE 6,15: PRINT "WHICH RECORD TO YOU WANT TO CORRECT?"
4180      LOCATE 7,15: INPUT "ENTER THE RECORD NUMBER: ",R1
4200      GET 2,R1
4220      C = CVS(CONTRIB$)
4240      LOCATE 9,15: PRINT "CURRENT DATA IN RECORD NUMBER";R1
4260      LOCATE 11,15: PRINT "CONTRIBUTOR ===============> ";PERSON$
4280      LOCATE 12,15: PRINT "AMOUNT OF CONTRIBUTION ====> $";C
4300      LOCATE 14,15: INPUT "TYPE THE CORRECT NAME =====> ",N$
4320      LOCATE 15,15: INPUT "TYPE THE CORRECT AMOUNT ===> ",C
4340      LSET PERSON$ = N$: LSET CONTRIB$ = MKS$(C)
4360      PUT 2,R1
4380      LOCATE 17,15
4400      INPUT "WANT TO CORRECT ANOTHER RECORD (Y/N) ",Y$
4420      IF LEFT$(Y$,1) = "Y" OR LEFT$(Y$,1) = "y" THEN Y$ = "Y"
4440 WEND
4460 CLOSE 2
```

```
THERE ARE 4 RECORDS IN THIS FILE.
(RECORD 1 IS USED TO STORE THE # OF RECORDS.)

WHICH RECORD DO YOU WANT TO CORRECT?
ENTER THE RECORD NUMBER: 3

CURRENT DATA IN RECORD NUMBER 3

CONTRIBUTOR ===============> JANE L. WHITESIDE
AMOUNT OF CONTRIBUTION ====> $ 25

TYPE THE CORRECT NAME =====> JANE L. WHITESIDE
TYPE THE CORRECT AMOUNT ===> $ 27.95

WANT TO CORRECT ANOTHER RECORD? (Y/N) N
```

To determine that the record has, in fact, been changed, we can run program Example 9.2 (which prints the file contents) or we can use the sample file system shown in Example 9.3, using option number 2. The program run demonstrates that we have been successful. JANE L. WHITESIDE's contribution was changed from $25 to $27.95.

```
RECORD #           NAME                 CONTRIBUTION
--------   ---------------------   ------------

   2          JOHN B. ARMSDELL         $ 12.75
```

```
3        JANE L. WHITESIDE        $ 27.95
4        SUSAN B. NOTECAF         $ 11.5
```

Adding Records to a Random Access File

A simple way to add records to a file is demonstrated in Example 9.6. The program demonstrates several interesting procedures.

1. The program reads the number of records in line 5100.

2. Since the CONTRIBR.DTA file currently contains four records, we must begin with the fifth record. Line 5220 makes sure that we do.

3. The updated number of records is written back into the file in lines 5440–5460.

example 9.6

```
5000 REM ***** ADD DATA TO THE RANDOM ACCESS FILE                    *****
5020 CLS: KEY OFF: REM ** CLEAR THE SCREEN                              **
5040 Y$ = "Y"
5060 OPEN "R",2,"CONTRIBR.DTA",29
5080 FIELD 2, 25 AS PERSON$, 4 AS CONTRIB$
5100 GET 2,1: N = CVS(CONTRIB$): N1 = N
5120 WHILE Y$ = "Y"
5140    CLS: REM ** CLEAR THE SCREEN                                    **
5160    LOCATE 3,15: PRINT "THERE ARE";N1;"RECORDS IN THIS FILE."
5180    LOCATE 5,15: PRINT "THE FOLLOWING RECORD WILL BE ADDED TO"
5200    LOCATE 6,15: PRINT "THE RANDOM ACCESS FILE CONTRIBR.DTA"
5220    N1 = N1 + 1
5240    R = R + 1: REM ** KEEP TRACK OF THE # OF RECORDS ADDED          **
5260    LOCATE 8,15: PRINT "THE NEXT RECORD WILL BE #";N1
5280    LOCATE 10,15: INPUT "NAME ===========> ",N$
5300    LOCATE 11,15: INPUT "CONTRIBUTION ===> ",C
5320    LSET PERSON$ = N$: LSET CONTRIB$ = MKS$(C)
5340    PUT 2,N1
5360    LOCATE 14,15
5380    INPUT "WANT TO ADD ANOTHER RECORD? (Y/N) ",Y$
5400    IF LEFT$(Y$,1) = "Y" OR LEFT$(Y$,1) = "y" THEN Y$ = "Y"
5420 WEND
5440 N$ = "XXXX": LSET PERSON$=N$: LSET CONTRIB$=MKS$(N1)
5460 PUT 2,1: CLOSE 2
5480 IF R = 1 THEN L$ = "RECORD" ELSE L$ = "RECORDS"
5500 LOCATE 17,15: PRINT "YOU HAVE ADDED";R;L$;" TO THE FILE."
5520 LOCATE 18,15
```

```
5540 PRINT "THE FILE NAMED CONTRIBR.DTA NOW CONTAINS";N1;"RECORDS."
5545 LOCATE 19,15
5550 PRINT "(THE 1st RECORD WAS USED TO STORE THE # OF RECORDS.)
5560 END
```

Running the program in Example 9.6 will yield the following input/output sequence:

```
THERE ARE 4 RECORDS IN THIS FILE.

THE FOLLOWING RECORD WILL BE ADDED TO
THE RANDOM ACCESS FILE CONTRIBR.DTA

THE NEXT RECORD WILL BE # 5

NAME ===========> ALICE G. DONNER
CONTRIBUTION ===> 35.75


WANT TO ADD ANOTHER RECORD? (Y/N) Y

THERE ARE 5 RECORDS IN THIS FILE.

THE FOLLOWING RECORD WILL BE ADDED TO
THE RANDOM ACCESS FILE CONTRIBR.DTA

THE NEXT RECORD WILL BE # 6

NAME ===========> HENRY E. BRABBLETT
CONTRIBUTION ===> 13.65


WANT TO ADD ANOTHER RECORD? (Y/N) N

YOU HAVE ADDED 2 RECORDS TO THE FILE.
THE FILE NAMED CONTRIBR.DTA NOW CONTAINS 6 RECORDS.
(THE 1st RECORD WAS USED TO STORE THE # OF RECORDS.)
```

To check whether the addition to the file CONTRIBR.DTA was successful, we can run the program shown in Example 9.2 again. We will see the following results, confirming that the addition program functioned properly.

```
RECORD #            NAME               CONTRIBUTION
--------   ---------------------   ------------

   2        JOHN B. ARMSDELL          $ 12.75
   3        JANE L. WHITESIDE         $ 27.95
```

```
4         SUSAN B. NOTECAF          $ 11.5
5         ALICE G. DONNER           $ 35.75
6         HENRY E. BRABBLETT        $ 13.65
```

Deleting Records from a File

Suppose we want to delete record number 4 from the file. We may write the last current record and write it over the fourth record, thereby eliminating it. Now subtract 1 from the number of records in the file and rewrite this value into record number 1. Presto, the deed is done. Of course, the original last record is still in the file, but you will never know it is there because it will never be read. When you add new records to the file, you will write over the remaining "old" record, anyway. The procedure is demonstrated in Example 9.7. Note particularly lines 6380–6400.

example 9.7

```
6000 REM ***  DELETE DATA FROM A RANDOM ACCESS FILE                    ****
6020 CLS: KEY OFF: REM ** CLEAR THE SCREEN                               **
6040 Y$ = "Y"
6060 OPEN "R",2,"CONTRIBR.DTA",29
6080 FIELD 2, 25 AS PERSON$, 4 AS CONTRIB$
6100 GET 2,1: N = CVS(CONTRIB$)
6120 WHILE Y$ = "Y"
6140    CLS: REM ** CLEAR THE SCREEN                                     **
6160    LOCATE 3,15: PRINT "THERE ARE";N;"RECORDS IN THIS FILE."
6180    LOCATE 5,15: PRINT "WHICH RECORD DO YOU WANT TO DELETE?"
6200    LOCATE 6,15: INPUT "ENTER THE RECORD NUMBER: ",R1
6220    GET 2,R1
6240    C = CVS(CONTRIB$)
6260    LOCATE 8,15: PRINT "CURRENT DATA IN RECORD NUMBER";R1
6280    LOCATE 10,15: PRINT "CONTRIBUTOR ===============> ";PERSON$
6300    LOCATE 11,15: PRINT "AMOUNT OF CONTRIBUTION ====> $";C
6320    LOCATE 13,15: PRINT "THIS RECORD IS NOW DELETED."
6340    REM ** WRITE THE LAST RECORD TO REPLACE THE DELETED              **
6360    REM ** RECORD, THEN REDUCE THE RECORD COUNT BY 1.                **
6380    GET 2,N: N = N-1
6400    PUT 2,R1
6420    R = R + 1: REM ** KEEP TRACK OF THE # OF DELETED RECORDS **
6440    LOCATE 15,15
6460    INPUT "WANT TO DELETE ANOTHER RECORD? (Y/N) ",Y$
6480    IF LEFT$(Y$,1) = "Y" OR LEFT$(Y$,1) = "y" THEN Y$ = "Y"
6500 WEND
6520 PERSON$ = "XXXX": LSET PERSON$ = N$: LSET CONTRIB$ = MKS$(N)
6540 PUT 2,1: CLOSE 2
```

```
6560 IF R = 1 THEN L$ = "RECORD" ELSE L$ = "RECORDS"
6580 LOCATE 17,15: PRINT "YOU HAVE DELETED";R;L$;" FROM THE FILE."
6600 LOCATE 18,15
6620 PRINT "THE FILE NAMED CONTRIBR.DTA NOW CONTAINS";N;"RECORDS."
6640 LOCATE 19,15
6660 PRINT "(THE 1st RECORD WAS USED TO STORE THE # OF RECORDS.)"
6680 END
```

Running the program in Example 9.7 yields the following input/output sequence:

```
THERE ARE 6 RECORDS IN THIS FILE.

WHICH RECORD DO YOU WANT TO DELETE?
ENTER THE RECORD NUMBER: 4

CURRENT DATA IN RECORD NUMBER 4

CONTRIBUTOR ===============> SUSAN B. NOTECAF
AMOUNT OF CONTRIBUTION ====> $ 11.5

THIS RECORD IS NOW DELETED.

WANT TO DELETE ANOTHER RECORD? (Y/N) N

YOU HAVE DELETED 1 RECORD FROM THE FILE.
THE FILE NAMED CONTRIBR.DTA NOW CONTAINS 5 RECORDS.
(THE 1st RECORD WAS USED TO STORE THE # OF RECORDS.)
```

To see if the record has actually been deleted, run the program in Example 9.2 again. The output demonstrates that the record for SUSAN B. NOTECAF has been eliminated.

```
RECORD #           NAME             CONTRIBUTION
--------   --------------------   ------------

    2        JOHN B. ARMSDELL        $ 12.75
    3        JANE L. WHITESIDE       $ 27.95
    4        HENRY E. BRABBLETT      $ 13.65
    5        ALICE G. DONNER         $ 35.75
```

Chapter Review

Random access files, also called direct access files, are so named because we may access any record in the file in any (random) order, without having to read all the preceding file records. To gain such flexibility, the random access file needs more structuring than the sequential file. The increased structuring requires that we declare field and record lengths. The record length is equal to the sum of the field lengths. Failure to declare record length causes the computer to assume a record length of 128 bytes.

To open the file we use the format:

```
OPEN "R",buffer number,"filename",record length
```

Before we can put records on disk, we must use a FIELD statement to organize the buffer space. Generally, the FIELD statement assumes the following format:

```
FIELD buffer number,number of bytes reserved for variable(s)
```

Using variables K5$, D, and X#, using buffer number 3, we would write the following statement. (Since the random access file can store only strings, D$ is used to represent the string equivalent of numeric variable D, and X$ is used to represent the string equivalent of numeric variable X#.)

```
FIELD 3, 10 AS K5$, 4 AS D$, 8 AS X$
```

Undeclared variables (such as D) are assumed to be single precision, requiring the reservation of four bytes. Double-precision variables (such as X#) require a reservation of eight bytes.

Numbers may be converted to strings for use in the random access file by using MKI$(variable name) for integers, MKS$(variable name) for single-precision numbers, and MKD$(variable name) for double-precision numbers.

Variable Type	Variable	Conversion	Bytes
Integer	A%	A$ = MKI$(A%)	2
Single precision	A!	A$ = MKS$(A!)	4
Double precision	A#	A$ = MKD$(A#)	8

Strings must be transferred to the buffer by LSET or RSET, conforming to left- and right-justification, respectively. Strings longer than those specified by the field statement will be truncated to fit the reserved space. The format for a sample variable B$ would be:

```
LSET B1$ = B$
```

or:

```
RSET B1$ = B$
```

The buffer contents are transferred to disk by the command PUT, using:

```
PUT buffer number,record number
```

Failure to declare a record number causes the computer to assume consecutive record numbers. Therefore, PUT 3 and PUT 3,I would give identical results in a loop FOR I = 1 TO N . . . NEXT I.

Retrieving data from disk requires the use of GET, as follows:

```
GET buffer number,record number
```

Failure to declare a record number causes the computer to assume consecutive record numbers just as it did in the case of the PUT statement.

Remembering that the random access file stores only strings, we must convert string variables representing numeric variables by using the following conversion:

Variable Type	Variable Conversion
Integer	`A% = CVI(A$)`
Single precision	`A! = CVS(A$)`
Double precision	`A# = CVD(A$)`

When you are finished using the file, don't forget to close it. The closing statement must use the same buffer number used by the OPEN, GET, or WRITE sequences. If buffer number 2 was used, close the file by CLOSE 2.

Although random access files tend to use more disk space than comparable sequential files, random access files are much "faster" because records may be accessed directly, without taking the time to read preceding records.

Key Terms and Concepts

- buffer number assignment
- OPEN
- FIELD
- numeric conversion to strings
- LSET
- RSET
- PUT
- CLOSE
- GET
- string conversion to numbers

Common Errors

1. Not making sure that the sum of the field lengths is equal to the declared record length.

Correct:

```
20   OPEN "R",1,"SAMPLE.DAT",15
40   FIELD 1,6 AS A$,4 AS C$,5 AS D$
```

Incorrect:

```
20   OPEN "R",1,"SAMPLE.DAT",15
40   FIELD 1,10 AS A$,4 AS C$,5 AS D$
```

2. Improper number–string or string–number conversion. Suppose you want to change a double-precision number into a string.

Correct:

```
100   INPUT C#
120   LSET C$ = MKD$(C#)
```

Incorrect:

```
100   INPUT C#
120   LSET C$ = MKD$(C)
```

In the incorrect version the computer will see C and C# as different numbers. Therefore, if you input C#, the variable C will be equal to zero because C is not defined. Similar problems occur when you do the following:

Correct:

```
400   C# = CVD(C$)
420   PRINT C#
```

Incorrect:

```
400   C = CVD(C$)
420   PRINT C
```

Also incorrect:

```
400   C# = CVD(C$)
420   PRINT C
```

3. Looking for the wrong character string in the file. Suppose you used LSET K$ = "***" in a field that was defined by FIELD 2,10 AS K$. Looking for the string *** would be done as follows:

Correct:

```
500   IF LEFT$(K$,3) = "***" THEN 800
```

Incorrect:

```
500   IF K$ = "***" THEN 800
```

The incorrect statement will never be executed because K$ = "***   ". In other words, given the field definition, K$ is composed of three asterisks and seven blanks! We could correct the situation by:

a. Using the LEFT$ format shown first.
b. Writing:

```
500   IF K$ = "***       " THEN ...
```

c. Defining K$ to be "**********" and using:

```
500   IF K$ = "**********" THEN ...
```

4. Not declaring record numbers if the first record is to be used to store the record number. Such an oversight will cause the number of records to be written over the first data record.

Correct:

```
PUT 1,C
```

Incorrect:

```
PUT 1
```

There is no problem if the first record is not used to store the record number.

5. Failing to use LSET or RSET.

Correct:

```
FIELD 1, 4 AS A$
LSET A$ = MKS$(A)
```

Incorrect:

```
FIELD 1, 4 AS A$
A$ = MKS$(A)
```

Exercises

1. The following program was written to put 25 sets of three variable values on a disk. The first two variables are numerical; the third is a string variable. Unfortunately, the program contains some errors. Make the necessary corrections and then run the program.

```
20 CLS
40 OPEN R,2,"SAMPLE",35
60 FIELD 1, 10 AS VALUE1$, 5 AS VALUE2$, 20 AS NAME$
70 I = 1
80 WHILE I <= 35
100     PRINT: INPUT "VALUE 1";V1
120     INPUT "VALUE 2";V2
140     INPUT "NAME";N$
160     LSET NAME$ = N$
180     LSET VALUE1$ = MKI$(V1)
200     LSET VALUE2$ = V2
220     PUT 3,V1,V2,N$
240 WEND
30000 END
```

2. Having written the program in Exercise 1, you decide to retrieve the data from the disk. You write the following program, but when you try to run it you wind up with error messages. Correct the errors; then run the program.

```
10 CLS
20 PRINT: PRINT "VALUE 1";TAB(15);"VALUE 2";
40 PRINT TAB(30);"NAME": PRINT
50 I = 1
60 WHILE I <= 35
80      OPEN "R",3,"SAMPLE",35
100     FIELD 1, 4 AS VALUE1$, 4 AS VALUE2$, 15 AS NAME$
120     GET 1,I
140 WEND
160 CLOSE 1
30000 END
```

3. Modify Problem 8.1 (Chapter 8) so that it will build an inventory in a random access file. The inventory product code is never more than eight characters long. After you have created the file named INVENTOR.Y, the program input/output sequence should look like this:

```
PLEASE SELECT ONE OF THE FOLLOWING:

    1. CREATE THE RANDOM ACCESS FILE
    2. PRINT THE FILE'S CONTENTS
    3. STOP THIS PROGRAM

ENTER THE SELECTED OPTION? 2

ENTER THE FILE NAME? INVENTOR.Y

DO YOU WANT A PRINTED COPY (Y/N)? N

RECORD #     PRODUCT CODE     CURRENT INVENTORY
--------     ------------     -----------------

   2            AA-35-3B              22
   3            AB-21-3A              38
   4            BC-10-5C              35

TAP THE 'ENTER' KEY TO CONTINUE?

PLEASE SELECT ONE OF THE FOLLOWING:

    1. CREATE THE RANDOM ACCESS FILE
    2. PRINT THE FILE'S CONTENTS
    3. STOP THIS PROGRAM

ENTER THE SELECTED OPTION? 3
```

4. Add a subroutine to the program in Problem 3 to update the inventory in the file named INVENTOR.Y. The revised program should yield these input/output results:

```
PLEASE SELECT ONE OF THE FOLLOWING:

    1. CREATE THE RANDOM ACCESS FILE
    2. PRINT THE FILE'S CONTENTS
    3. UPDATE THE FILE RECORDS
    4. STOP THIS PROGRAM

ENTER THE SELECTED OPTION? 3

ENTER THE FILE NAME? INVENTOR.Y


RECORD NUMBER TO BE UPDATED? 3
CODE OF PURCHASED ITEM AB-21-3A
NUMBER PURCHASED? 14


ITEM CODE AB-21-3A
ORIGINAL INVENTORY 38
CURRENT INVENTORY 24

TAP THE 'ENTER' KEY TO CONTINUE?


PLEASE SELECT ONE OF THE FOLLOWING:

    1. CREATE THE RANDOM ACCESS FILE
    2. PRINT THE FILE'S CONTENTS
    3. UPDATE THIS PROGRAM
    4. STOP THIS PROGRAM

ENTER THE SELECTED OPTION?
```

To see if the revision in the INVENTOR.Y file has, in fact, been made, run the program again, using menu number two. (Compare the file results with those of Exercise 3 and note that the file has been updated!)

```
PLEASE SELECT ONE OF THE FOLLOWING:

    1. CREATE THE RANDOM ACCESS FILE
    2. PRINT THE FILE'S CONTENTS
    3. UPDATE THE FILE RECORDS
    4. STOP THIS PROGRAM

ENTER THE SELECTED OPTION? 2

ENTER THE FILE NAME? INVENTOR.Y


DO YOU WANT A PRINTED COPY (Y/N)? N
```

```
RECORD #     PRODUCT CODE     CURRENT INVENTORY
--------     ------------     -----------------

   2           AA-35-3B               22
   3           AB-21-3A               24
   4           BC-10-5C               35

TAP THE 'ENTER' KEY TO CONTINUE
```

5. Write a program to create a random access file for pilots flying for a charter company. The input variables are pilot name, number, date, destination, customer, number of multiengine aircraft hours flown, number of single-engine aircraft hours flown, and waiting time. The destination code consists of the airport's three-letter identifier. For example, Los Angeles is LAX, Nashville is BNA, and so on. All time values are entered to the nearest tenth of an hour.
   Also stored in the file: gross pay. Pilots are paid $20 per hour for multiengine hours, $15 for single-engine hours, and $10 per waiting hour. Two sample entries are shown. Note that the program updates files.

```
PLEASE SELECT ONE OF THE FOLLOWING:

    1. CREATE THE RANDOM ACCESS FILE
    2. UPDATE THE FILE
    3. STOP THIS PROGRAM

PLEASE ENTER YOUR SELECTION? 1



PILOT'S NAME ===============> ? PETER ROB
PILOT NUMBER ===============> ? 1

DATE (USE FORMAT mm/dd/yy) ==========> ? 08/22/85
DESTINATION (3-LETTER IDENTIFIER) ===> ? BNA
CUSTOMER ============================> ? H&G ENTERPRISES
MULTI-ENGINE HOURS FLOWN ============> ? 1.6
SINGLE-ENGINE HOURS FLOWN ===========> ? 0
HOURS WAITING TIME ==================> ? 0

LAST ENTRY (Y/N)? Y


YOU ENTERED 2 RECORDS INTO THE FILE NAMED
PILOT- 1. RECORD #1 WAS USED TO STORE THE
# OF RECORDS STORED IN THE RANDOM ACCESS FILE.


PLEASE TAP THE RETURN KEY TO CONTINUE?
```

```
PLEASE SELECT ONE OF THE FOLLOWING:

    1. CREATE THE RANDOM ACCESS FILE
    2. UPDATE THE FILE
    3. STOP THIS PROGRAM

PLEASE ENTER YOUR SELECTION? 2


PILOT'S NAME ===============> ? PETER ROB
PILOT NUMBER ===============> ? 1

DATE (USE FORMAT mm/dd/yy) ==========> ? 08/25/85
DESTINATIUN (3-LETTER IDENTIFIER) ===> ? STL
CUSTOMER ============================> ? MKD INDUSTRIES
MULTI-ENGINE HOURS FLOWN ============> ? 0
SINGLE-ENGINE HOURS FLOWN ===========> ? 2.3
HOURS WAITING TIME ==================> ? 5.6

LAST ENTRY (Y/N)? Y


YOU HAVE ADDED 1 RECORD TO THE FILE NAMED PILOT- 1

THE FILE NOW CONTAINS 3 RECORDS.
(THE 1st RECORD WAS USED TO STORE THE # OF RECORDS.)


PLEASE TAP THE RETURN KEY TO CONTINUE?
```

6. Modify the program in Problem 5 to add a menu item that will allow you to print the results shown next. Make sure that the report has a hard copy option.

```
PLEASE SELECT ONE OF THE FOLLOWING:

    1. CREATE THE RANDOM ACCESS FILE
    2. UPDATE THE FILE
    3. PRINT THE REPORT
    4. STOP THIS PROGRAM

PLEASE ENTER YOUR SELECTION? 3



ENTER THE FILE NAME? PILOT- 1
DO YOU WANT A PRINTED COPY (Y/N)? N
```

```
                          PILOT- 1 RECORDS
-----------------------------------------------------------------------

 DATE     DEST.  CUSTOMER           ME.   SE.   WAIT   GROSS PAY   RECORD
--------  -----  --------           ---   ---   ----   ---------   ------

08/22/85   BNA   H&G ENTERPRISES    1.6   0.0   0.0       $32.00      2
08/25/85   STL   MKD INDUSTRIES     0.0   2.3   5.6       $90.50      3

                    TOTALS TO DATE  1.6   2.3   5.6    $122.50

PLEASE TAP THE RETURN KEY TO CONTINUE?


PLEASE SELECT ONE OF THE FOLLOWING:

    1. CREATE THE RANDOM ACCESS FILE
    2. UPDATE THE FILE
    3. PRINT THE REPORT
    4. STOP THIS PROGRAM

PLEASE ENTER YOUR SELECTION? 4
```

INDEX/GLOSSARY

036791 A033951

2. Reading data from the file and printing the file contents:
Five records. (Note that the file is closed in line 220.)

```
100 F$ = "CONTRIBS.DTA"
120 OPEN "I",1,F$
140 FOR I = 1 TO 5
160      INPUT #1,N$,C
180      PRINT N$,C
200 NEXT I
220 CLOSE 1
```

D. Checking for the end-of-file marker when the loop limit has not been defined. The program reads and prints records as long as the EOF marker has not been reached. (Note that the buffer is specified in line 140.)

```
100 F$ = "CONTRIBS.DTA"
120 OPEN "I",1,F$
140 WHILE NOT EOF(1)
160      INPUT #1,N$,C
180      PRINT N$,C
200 WEND
220 CLOSE 1
```

III. GENERAL RANDOM ACCESS FILE PROCEDURES

File name "MEMBERS.DTA", buffer number 1, variable names N$,C, field names PERSON$,CONTRIB$, with field lengths 20 and 4, respectively.

A. General preparations: Naming the file

```
100 F$ = "MEMBERS.DTA"
```

B. Opening the file and defining the file structure

```
120 OPEN "R",1,F$,24
140 FIELD 1, 20 AS PERSON$, 4 AS CONTRIB$
```

C. Working with the file contents

The IBM PC requires that numeric values be converted into strings before file storage. Undeclared numeric precision causes the computer to assume single precision.

C1$=MKI$(C%) changes an integer C% into a 2 character string C1$.

C1$=MKS$(C!) changes a single precision number C! into a 4 character string C1$. Using the undeclared precision variable C rather than C! yields the same results.

C1$=MKD$(C#) changes a double precision number C# into an 8 character string C1$.

To retrieve numbers from the random access file, these numbers must be converted from the stored strings back into numbers. Undeclared number precision causes the computer to assume single precision.

C%=CVI(C1$) changes a 2 character string C1$ into an integer value C%.

C!=CVS(C1$) changes a 4 character string C1$ into a single precision number C! Using the variable name C rather than C! yields the same result.

C#=CVD(C1$) changes an 8 character string C1$ into a double precision number C#.

1. Entering five records into the file, using variables N$ and C

```
100 F$ = "MEMBERS.DTA"
120 OPEN "R",1,F$,24
140 FIELD 1, 20 AS PERSON$, 4 AS CONTRIB$
160. FOR R = 1 TO 5
180      INPUT "ENTER NAME, CONTRIBUTION";N$,C
200      LSET PERSON$ = N$
220      LSET CONTRIB$ = MKS$(C)
240      PUT 1,R
260 NEXT R
280 CLOSE 1
```